LITERATURE AND THEOLOGY AT CENTURY'S END

AAR

American Academy of Religion
Studies in Religion

Editor
David E. Klemm

Number 72
LITERATURE AND THEOLOGY AT
CENTURY'S END

edited by
Gregory Salyer
Robert Detweiler

LITERATURE AND THEOLOGY AT CENTURY'S END

edited by

Gregory Salyer
Robert Detweiler

Scholars Press
Atlanta, Georgia

LITERATURE AND THEOLOGY AT CENTURY'S END

edited by
Gregory Salyer
Robert Detweiler

© 1995
The American Academy of Religion

Library of Congress Cataloging in Publication Data

Literature and theology at century's end / edited by Gregory Salyer,
 Robert Detweiler.
        p.   cm. — (Studies in religion / American Academy of Religion;
 no. 72)
      Includes bibliographical references.
      ISBN 0-7885-0070-8 (cloth : alk. paper). — ISBN 0-7885-0071-6
 (paper : alk paper)
      1. Religion and literature. 2. Literature, Modern—History and
 criticism. I. Salyer, Gregory. II. Detweiler, Robert.
 III. Series: AAR studies in religion ; no. 72.
 PN49.L5195 1995
 809'.93382—dc20   94–40612
                                                         CIP

Printed in the United States of America
on acid-free paper

For David Jasper

ACKNOWLEDGMENTS

The editors wish to thank Vicki Salyer, Mark Ledbetter, Greta Boers, and Susan Rook for their assistance in preparing this volume for publication via camera-ready copy.

CONTENTS

Contents

PREFACE

Robert Detweiler

The title we have given this volume of essays, *Literature and Theology at Century's End,* brings three concepts to mind: apocalypse, new beginnings, and celebration. The end of the millennium just a few years away has already inspired many visions and predictions of the demise of humankind, the planet, and even the galaxy and the universe. The end of the world has been a part of global mythologies since humans emerged as worshiping and storytelling creatures; what is new amidst the myths of cataclysm these days, during the final decade of the twentieth century, is imaginative (and no so imaginative) speculation on how the end will come: global warming and a resultant massive flooding; global freezing; overpopulation, famine, and great struggles for dwindling resources, especially water; new strains of viruses that resist drugs and cause worldwide pestilence; a new kind of perpetual crime waged against the privileged by Third World "have-nots" who have nothing to lose; lethal poisoning of the earth by waste and chemical pollution; and nuclear energy out of control. According to some the Four Horsemen ride again, though now they also guide oil-laden supertankers, helicopters spreading defoliant, logging vehicles, and the bulldozers on huge landfills.[1]

Not that the religious prophecies and actions of the chiliasts have lessened. We can reckon with the accelerating lunacy of sects old and new that expect the Second Coming before 1999 rings—or burns—out, and even among the more sober the belief in Armageddon at hand is rife.[2] Against this background the essays of this volume are remarkably sanguine. Although the conference at which they were presented was called "Toward the Year 2000," they do not display an apocalyptic strain. Rather, a number of them are more soberly concerned with history and time, with how to understand historical thinking and the nature of temporality against the background or with the help of philosophers and theologians (Hegel, Nietzsche, Emerson, Heidegger, Levinas, Marion, et al.) who contemplate such matters.

Eschatology and teleology, in other words, become the broader context for the "prophetic" and enthusiastic preoccupations of the apocalypticists. In this regard one thinks of Vassilis Lambropoulos's aggressive book *The Rise of Eurocentrism.*[3] Lambropoulos traces our obsession with interpretation to the Protestant ideal of the independent reading of scripture and argues that the marriage of Athens and Jerusalem never really happened, that Hebraic interpretation has triumphed over Hellenistic "aestheticism," even though in the era of Derrida the rabbinic complexity of interpretive strategies has developed a playfulness that reflects the otherwise disregarded Greek spirit.

Apocalypticism comes into the picture insofar as Derrida, according the Lambropoulos, "interprets Levinas as an apocalyptic thinker, whose eschatology envisions a triumph against the powers of evil. . . . The failure of Levinas's virulent attack on Christianity proves that rejections of the Protestant Logos as the sin of Greek language are always already expressed in Hellenic terms. Derrida criticizes the acceptance of revelation (*apokalypsis*) as unveiling of truth by Heidegger and Levinas. True Jewish faith, he counters, is Messianic (that is, grounded in deferral), not apocalyptic (based on epiphany)."[4]

This is not the place to carry through or challenge Lambropoulos's argument. I only want to remind how, late in the century, a hermeneutical awareness of apocalypticism flourishes that is an extension of the reflective tradition, which tradition the essays in this volume elucidate.

The turn of the millennium ahead of us also suggests new beginnings. The very idea of one time unit ending and another commencing is of course wholly arbitrary. There is no sound reason why the numerological fact of the year 2000 should signify a new start anymore than, say, 1997 or 2013. It is simply that in our tenacious mythology of chronologizing we are charmed by the temporal units of 100 and 1000 years, or centuries and millennia, just as the concept of one thousand pounds or one million dollars exerts a particular magic. One might conjecture that we in the West, at least, are wedded to a base-ten plot of time. Yet the concept of a new decade, a new century, a new millennium, however artificially conceived and implemented, has come to stand for a fresh start, a starting over, in ways that apocalyptic linearity, with its *final* new beginning beyond time, does not. One even sees the sentiment in the annual newspaper cartoons that appear in late December: the old year is personified as a scarred and weary old man, to be replaced by the new year as a lively infant.

Certainly the 1990s thus far have experienced a plethora of endings and beginnings: the fall of the Soviet Union and the rise of independent nations out of that collapse; the merging of east and west Germany, the arrival at last of an inclusive government in South Africa are ready examples. In academic humanities and social science circles, the past three decades have seen the rise and fall of structuralism, the exercising (and exorcising) of deconstruction and other poststructuralisms, and the current attraction of political criticism. All of these have left their mark on the literature and theology enterprise, and the essays of this volume witness to their influence. They manifest a critical awareness and finesse that characterize the best contemporary writing in literary interpretation, biblical studies, and theological hermeneutics. They also show forth the advances made in feminist criticism and in what we might call "postimperialist" approaches. Since most feminist critics remain oblivious to the potential of theological and religious readings, preferring to follow the ideologies of, say, psychoanalysis or Marxism, the essays here on sex roles and gender are especially welcome contributions to the feminist invigoration of scholarship.[5]

For some scholars the controlling patriarchy of Western culture is part of the imperialist mode that forcefully Christianized much of the world and that today in secularized form continues, through various First-World strategies, to dominate and exploit weaker nations. However facile this judgment may be, particularly in such a simplified version, it would demand our attention if for no other reason than that liberation theologians are asserting it. Edward Said's very provocative (and for some inflammatory) *Culture and Imperialism* ought to be required reading for persons concerned with the future of literature and theology.[6] Said's argument that Western expansionism, reinforced by chauvinist readings of the Christian gospel, functions today in secular variations, invites us to scrutinize our complicitness in perpetuating that hegemony, just as his recognition of writers from "victim" cultures who challenge the hegemony suggests that we should, at the very least, learn to be alert to their voices. John Strugnell's essay on Australia in our volume can stand as an example of what a new beginning aligned to a complex and multicultural consciousness may look and sound like.

Said's recognition of Third World writers such as Chinua Achebe, Aimé Césaire, and V. S. Naipaul amounts to a celebration of them and reminds us of how celebration itself attends the end of century and millennium transitions. Elaborate festivities are being planned for New Year's Eve of 1999, for example, celebrating—what? Probably few of the revellers will have thought it through, although the more reflective ones will mark the occasion, perhaps, as a leave-taking of one of history's bloodiest centuries or a ritual passage into a more responsible, electronically-connected world community. Our volume celebrates a variety of good and great writers, some of them familiar and some virtually unknown. That we accord their texts theological interpretation is an indication of our esteem for them and an acknowledgment of the central role that the religious imagination plays in our lives.

These pages are also the place to celebrate another occasion: a decade, from 1982-92, during which six literature and theology conferences were organized and held in the United Kingdom under the guidance of David Jasper and the auspices of the Centre for the Study of Literature and Theology. As is well known (but perhaps not well enough), David founded the Centre in Durham, moved it to Glasgow in 1991, and used it at both locations as the site for the highly successful conferences. At these gatherings established scholars as well as younger academicians from the United Kingdom and Commonwealth nations, the European continent, the United States, Africa, and the Far East have presented their work to each other and formed an international community practicing vigorous scholarship. A good deal of this research has been published in previous volumes, edited by David, of papers from earlier conferences. We owe a great debt to David for his vision and initiative as well as to his colleagues Stephen Prickett and Robert Carroll at the University of Glasgow, and to the administration of that distinguished institution for their generous support of the Centre and its work. It is our pleasure to recognize David's leadership by dedicating this volume to him.

NOTES

1. For an "apocalyptic" report on the state of the world and its approaching demise, see Robert D. Kaplan, "The Coming Anarchy," *The Atlantic Monthly* (February, 1994): 44-76.

2. See Charles B. Strozier, *Apocalypse: On the Psychology of Fundamentalism in America* (Boston: Beacon Press, 1994).

3. Vassilis Lambropoulos, *The Rise of Eurocentrism: Anatomy of Interpretation* (Princeton: Princeton University Press, 1993).

4. Lambropoulos, *The Rise of Eurocentrism*, p. 266.

5. For an example of excellent feminist scholarship, aligned to democratic socialism, that would profit greatly from attention to a theological perspective, see Iris Marion Young, *Throwing Like a Girl and Other Essays in Feminist Philosophy and Social Theory* (Bloomington and Indianapolis: Indiana University Press, 1990).

6. Edward W. Said, *Culture and Imperialism* (New York: Alfred A. Knopf, 1993).

INTRODUCTION

Gregory Salyer

Scholars working within the field of "Literature and Theology" or "Religion and Literature" have learned to live with the ambiguity and tension that is occasioned by this particular interdisciplinary endeavor. At times we seem to be preaching to the converted, to an audience for whom the connections between literature and theology seem as "obvious" as they are to us. More often, however, we are challenged to justify what we do as if it were one of the stranger adventures in scholarship. Literature specialists sometimes doubt our ability to willingly suspend our disbelief, while some theologians question why we look to products and processes of the imagination to inspire and interrogate truth, and philosophers do not know what we are up to, except perhaps no good. Despite (or perhaps because of) this perceived groundlessness, the field itself has somehow managed to do much more than survive since T. S. Eliot first called for something like it in his foundational essay "Religion and Literature" in 1935.[1] Nearly sixty years later, we find ourselves "thinking to 2000" and speculating on what changes we should expect and even encourage in our religious interpretations of the world, the text, and the critic and in our literary interpretations of traditional religious literature. As Robert Detweiler notes in his preface, our romance with round, even numbers—the larger the better—occasions Janus-like observations and speculations on our past and our future, speculations that are of course "merely" fictions.

Preparing this volume with Detweiler offered an occasion for such speculations and led me back to a 1978 essay that is one of the most important chronicles of the field (or perhaps movement) of literature and theology. David Hesla's "Religion and Literature: The Second Stage" records the genealogy of the movement as well as his confusion as to what lies ahead.[2] He begins the essay with the suggestion that a crisis is at hand: "For perhaps as long as five years now I have had the sense, vague and unfocused at first but increasingly sharpened, that the field of study known

1

variously at 'Literature and Theology' or 'Religion and Literature' (or by still other titles) was in some serious trouble." Hesla goes on to show how nascent interests in literature and theology mediated between a theology that was becoming increasingly existential (Bultmann and Tillich) and a literary criticism that was just beginning to be recognized as an alternative to literary history and biography (New Criticism). Having done its work in incorporating existential relevance and reminding New Criticism that authors and readers were in fact participants in literary enterprises, the new movement, according to Hesla, found itself written out of a job by its own success. Literature and theology, with a foot in both worlds, was destined to continue to live this academically marginalized existence with an always uncertain future, even to the edge of the twenty-first century it would appear. No wonder, then, that Robert Detweiler titled his 1983 collection of essays *Art/Literature/Religion: Life on the Borders*.3

While literature and theology continues to thrive, it is not in terms of college and university professorships. The number of jobs advertised in the United States under this rubric in the past decade could probably be counted on one hand, and apparently, the situation is as bad or worse in Europe despite David Jasper's enormous success with the Centre for the Study of Literature and Theology in Glasgow. Graduate school professors worry aloud about the future of their doctoral candidates and with good reason. And yet we continue to hear a lively conversation, a literary-theological-religious dialogue, taking place in the scholarly world in a variety of contexts: scholarly conferences such as the one that produced this volume, even conferences on the teaching of literature and theology; journals that claim the title and those that do not who publish articles falling within the purview of this discourse; and a steady flow of engaging books and essay collections. In many ways the most important conversations are taking place in the classroom where students from a variety of cultures (including local campus cultures) and with a diverse array of intellectual interests are engaged with issues that cut across disciplinary lines and arise from what can best be termed as teaching religion and literature. As Carolyn Jones remarked at a recent conference in the United States, "Religion and Literature may be absent from the academic marketplace, but it is thriving in the classroom."4 In planning my own seminars and advanced topics courses, I must sometimes remind myself that a course in Religion and Literature is an option. Religion and Literature is not only a field or a movement, it is also a pedagogical strategy, one so wedded to my overall philosophy of education that I sometimes forget that it can be studied on its own.

I began by saying that scholars who see themselves doing literature and theology opt to live with ambiguity and tension, and I have briefly given some examples of that uncertain existence. That precarious posture, I maintain, is one source for the apparent success of the movement. Perhaps our willingness to live in tension and in the anxiety that accompanies it reflects our existential heritage. Whatever its provenance, a certain risk pervades our discussions. Tension goes with the territory. Terry Wright calls it a "creative tension."[5] The contributors to this volume describe it in a variety of ways: sacramental and prophetic interpretation, Trinitarian rhetoric, self-transcendence and new interiority, theological thinking and Christian praxis, and conflicting ideologies of gender. The reader will note, however, that none of the contributors to this volume consider themselves to have resolved that tension; rather, they want to explore it, celebrate it, even supplement it and intensify it. Literature and theology remains a viable hermeneutical avenue because it values the inherently self-critical dimensions of life on the borders. It consistently shows itself open to otherness and refuses to brandish the sword of certainty wielded by so many other philosophies, theologies, and literary theories.

Whether or not its practitioners subscribe to the tenets of neo-pragmatism (I suspect that a good many do not), literature and theology may be the best example to date of what Richard Rorty envisions for a post-Philosophical culture. In describing the program for a future philosophy, Rorty evokes principles that lie at the heart of the literature and theology enterprise:

> It looks, in short, much like what is sometimes called "culture criticism". . . . The modern Western "culture critic" . . . is a prefiguration of the all-purpose intellectual of a post-Philosophical culture, the philosopher who has abandoned pretensions to Philosophy. He passes rapidly from Hemingway to Proust to Hitler to Marx, to Foucault to Mary Douglas to the present situation in Southeast Asia to Ghandi to Sophocles. He is a name-dropper, who uses

> names such as these to refer to sets of descriptions,
> symbol-systems, ways of seeing. His specialty is seeing
> similarities and differences between great big pictures,
> between attempts to see how things hang together. He is
> the person who tells you how all the ways of making
> things hang together hang together.[6]

Those familiar with this passage will know that Rorty goes on to say that by refusing to articulate *all* the possible ways of how everything *must* hang together, the philosopher in a post-Philosophical culture is doomed to be outdated; she is the one who has redescribed all the old descriptions which no one wants to hear about anymore. But Rorty wrongly assumes that we become wedded to our redescribed realities to the point where we sacrifice our role in the conversation in order to maintain a reality that we should know is fleeting. Rorty's problematic assumptions notwithstanding, he does provide an interesting proposal, to my mind, for just why the literature and theology enterprise will continue to 2000, namely, its refusal to proclaim itself in its various incarnations as the final word.

Our commitments vary, but we find commonality and community in our belief that the conversation itself has been and will continue to be edifying in both an academic and a personal sense. To be sure, there are agendas and projects within the field that exceed the number of scholars constituting the field. But what is common to all in the field is that dialogue, whether in a conference setting, a classroom, or in print, is the source of that creative tension that draws us in and keeps us searching for new ways to describe, to argue, and to interpret. David Hesla's essay ends on just this note when he remarks with a subtle warning: "'Die Sprache' does in fact speak, and in describing the second stage of our work as I have done I should like to think that I am simply reporting on what I have heard it saying. But we had better not suppose that what we are hearing is the last word."[7] This collection of essays is offered in that spirit. In the remaining pages of this introduction, I describe the particulars of the conversation taking place in this volume.

The essays are divided in a somewhat arbitrary way into two sections. The first primarily concerns issues of theory and theology but includes essay dealing with history and philosophy as well. The second section contains essays that explore particular writers and texts. Here one finds detailed discussions of poets, novelists, and biographers as well as biblical texts, devotional writing, and contemporary fiction. This is not to say that the reader will not find textual analyses in the first section or theoretical discussions in the second. Rather, the division simply marks the type of analysis that prevails in the essays.

James Champion explores Western intellectual history in terms of two complementary and contradictory impulses—the sacramental and the prophetic. The prophetic correlates to what Ricoeur terms, in a formulation that continues to help us see the forest instead of so many theoretical and theological trees, the hermeneutics of suspicion. Here all texts are approached via a profound distrust, a distrust that always is confirmed in interpretive praxis. The sacramental, on the other hand, is a positivist approach understanding that something has been given and that language can bear at least some of the weight of that thing. But Champion wants to draw out these observations further. He sees the ancient struggle between Hebraism and Hellenism being played out in these terms and in several important figures in recent hermeneutical thought. Freud, Adorno, and Derrida fuel their hermeneutical philosophy with suspicion manifested in deep cultural criticism. Parallel to these figures but representing a sacramental predisposition are Jung, Heidegger, and Gadamer, who are interesting in restoring and maintaining meaning rather than subverting it. To be sure, Champion says, none of these thinkers fit the descriptions of sacramental and prophetic without a sense of the other being present as well. He notes that the sacramental figures all descend from secularized Christian traditions while the prophetic figures operate from a secularized Jewish tradition. As Champion observes: "when intellectuals and thinkers of various stripes come from a tradition . . . which says the decisive event in history has *already* occurred, they are likely to trust culture and to view the presence of meaning in ways that are profoundly different from those who . . . [believe] the decisive event in history has *not yet* occurred." He goes on to speak of Nietzsche's unique role in the drama of these two tendencies in hermeneutical theory

From the broad sweep of Hebraism's prophetic and Hellenism's sacramental historical consciousness, we turn to another set of voices that celebrates both impulses in a different milieu. Judith Lee explores salvific expressions in recent feminist theology and women's writing. Lee begins by noting that feminist critiques of traditional ideas about salvation center on masculine imagery for God and Christ, body/spirit dualism, and the paradigm of solitary atonement. Arguing that feminist theology has not only viable alternatives to these concepts but perhaps better metaphors for understanding salvation in a world that is running out of time and space, Lee presents us with an overturned notion of traditional salvation theories that centers on embodiment, individuality of the non-rugged variety, and social justice and responsibility. She notes: "These feminist redefinitions of sin do not generate theories of salvation that merely celebrate the body and the sexuality that are devalued in traditional theology. Rather . . . many feminist theologians argue that we must replace self-transcendence with healing as the metaphor for salvation." Such a shift promises to offer "a new interiority" that can guide not only feminist but all theological reflection on salvation and conversion. Lee finds a framework for such a transition already in place in certain Native American traditions. Her careful interpretation of Anne Cameron's *Daughters of Copper Woman* approaches this text with appropriate respect and shows how the ideas of the sacred embodied in this text can inform and assist the program of redefining salvation and conversion in traditional theology. Even within Western culture Lee sees women's writing (inasmuch as women's writing is "within" Western culture) already exploring these issues and offering challenging and promising opportunities for readers to envision and experience this "new interiority." Mary Catherine Bateson, May Sarton, Madeleine L'Engle, Virginia Woolf, Doris Lessing, Margaret Atwood, Alice Walker and others are shown to be reinventing the idea of salvation in terms that recent feminist theology can appreciate. Lee takes a longer look at Isak Dinesen's theological interests in her various writings and shows that Dinesen was engaging theological concepts of salvation in ways that are complementary to the theologians she surveys at the beginning of her essay. Lee's "religious reading" of Dinesen is especially helpful.

Werner Jeanrond continues to interrogate theology in terms of immanence by orchestrating a discussion of theological praxis and literary imagination. For Jeanrond the future of theology may well depend on its ability (or inability) to offer a program for Christian praxis. "Theology," he argues, "is a theory for a better praxis." Jeanrond wants to distinguish between a theology that seeks to understand the Christian faith and a theology that seeks to transform our present relationships. He does not seek to privilege one kind of theology over the other but rather to bring into balance both understandings of the work of theology. The way to bring theological praxis back into the conversation is via the literary imagination, and one way to employ the literary imagination is through narrative theology. Jeanrond then offers a critique of Johann Baptist Metz's so-called narrative theology and an assessment of its usefulness for remedying theology's lack of attention to praxis. In his final section Jeanrond discusses how the literary imagination can challenge theology by presenting a variety of possible worlds that exceed theology's hermeneutical abilities.

From the interrogation of theology we then turn to the interrogation of history in essays by Irena Makarushka and Bernard Zelechow. Makarushka reassesses Emerson's and Nietzsche's interpretations of history and examines the connection each thinker makes to individual creativity. She notes: "In each case, history represented the process of coming to terms with the past by appropriating it into one's present in order to create a more just and harmonious future. As individuals engage in 'doing' history, they transcend the particularity of the moment as well as the discreteness of their own experience and create the possibilities promised in time." For both Emerson and Nietzsche, historians' disclosure of unity in the diversity of history is directly relevant to understanding the complexities of human nature. Makarushka weaves historical insights from Emerson and Nietzsche into an understanding of history that has ethical as well as aesthetic meaning.

Bernard Zelechow begins his essay by asking "Who's afraid of history?" His answer is "apparently everyone." From this provocative beginning Zelechow charts historical self-consciousness and its simultaneous rejection and acceptance in various historians, from Thucydides to Augustine, Kierkegaard, Nietzsche, and ultimately to the historical ruminations of Benjamin and Habermas. Zelechow's helpful survey ends by noting that the problems and possibilities of history already exist in biblical historical consciousness. He observes: "Every insight in the postmodernist worldview is already present in the framework of the Hebrew biblical texts. This fact is not coincidental. Modernism and postmodernism are grounded in an unacknowledged suppressed biblical structure." Zelechow goes on to propose that we attempt to understand the complexities of biblical historical consciousness rather than privileging postmodern views of history that offer ungrounded dialectics that lead to nihilism. For Zelechow the historical consciousness displayed in the Hebrew Bible presents us with an understanding of history where "the dialectics of truth and error can be authentically expressed" and where there is an implicit guard against totalitarianism in any form "at the warranted price of anxiety."

Our first section ends with two essays that employ theology to investigate time and representation. Robert Scharlemann asks whether there is a textual ordering of time that is different from the self's ordering of time. Scharlemann is, however, interested in more than sketching out two schemas for understanding time; he also suggests that the idea of God may be a function of textual time rather than the self's time. Scharlemann uses four points of reference to understand the nature of time: Augustine's meditation on time in his *Confessions*, Heidegger's analysis of *Dasein*, the phenomenon of monuments, and kerygma. This last concept is where theological and textual timing unite. As Scharlemann observes: "The kerygma is, in other words, both the vestige of an event which antedates everything hearers can remember as their own activity or passivity and also the coming of a possibility of being lying beyond the extreme can-be of their own." For Scharlemann, "When text is kerygma, it is timed theologically."

Graham Ward analyzes the cultural parallels between the theology arising from post World War I Germany and the theology issuing from the contemporary postmodern condition. Ward argues that the connections take three forms: that in each case the crisis that is described is a crisis of representation, that theology stands in intimate relation to that crisis by both promoting it and interpreting it, and that the theology evidenced in both crises has a similar dialectical character. Ward goes on to argue that theology can be understood as that which thematizes crises of representation. Engaging thinkers such as Marion, Barth, Lacoue Labarthe, and Derrida, Ward argues that the only coherent theological response to postmodernism is dialectical theology. In fact for Ward "dialectical theology *is* the postmodern debate." He notes: "[Dialectical theology] presents theological discourse as a palimpsest upon which the nature of discourse and representation itself is inscribed. . . . It pursues the thoughts of the the wholly other . . . by plunging into the agonistics of representation itself."

The next group of essays deals with particular writers, texts, and readers. Avril Horner begins this section of the volume with an adept analysis of the work of Geoffrey Hill and his unique views on the role of language in poetry and culture. For Hill the poem is an act of resistance through moral intelligence, an act which a computer is incapable of performing. The paradigm of the computer seems to guide the editors of the *Oxford English Dictionary,* says Hill, in that they slough off archaic meanings of words in favor of current usage. In losing those words we lose our history and with it some sense of "that aboriginal calamity" that marks the beginning of history. This observation prompts Hill to ask whether the computer is acquainted with original sin. Horner describes Hill's own intellectual and literary history by showing his similarities and differences from the likes of Pound and Eliot. She then provides a careful analysis of how Hill's ideas of tradition, resistance, ethics, and language are accomplished in his poetry. Once again postmodernism enters the picture as Horner comments: "Hill might . . . be regarded as a religious poet whose concept of 'meta-poetry' not only restores the notion of moral intelligence to the act of writing, but also revives, Lazarus-like, the author from the state of 'death' and unaccountability created by the rhetoric of postmodernism."

Toni Morrison's writings appear several times—and appropriately so—in our volume. Mark Ledbetter's essay deals exclusively with *The Bluest Eye* and examines the characteristics of victims and readers' responses to the victims who appear in this novel. Ledbetter begins with a series of observations: "Desperation characterizes the victim. . . . 'Otherness' characterizes desperation. . . . Violence characterizes otherness." The reader of a literary text, argues Ledbetter, is a special kind—the most persistent kind—of voyeur. And when victims enter our perception in literature, an ethical and religious event occurs. Ledbetter remarks: "This voyeur . . . experiences an ethical moment when she is blinded . . . when the object of her sight, the text, looks back at her. With this 'returned gaze' comes the moment of implication. Narrative's victim(s) is discovered when the text 'looks back,' and the reader (voyeur), in turn, blinks." This interpretation of *The Bluest Eye* shows how Morrison's works profit from—even invite—a religious reading.

David Cunningham offers a Trinitarian reading of Morrison's *Beloved* in concert with Iris Murdoch's *The Time of the Angels* and Dostoevsky's *The Brother's Karamozov*. Cunningham is interested in Trinitarian rhetoric, specifically *pathos* in Aristotle's terminology, and how that rhetoric can provide insight into the wider social relationships operative in literary interpretation. He notes: "My claim in this paper is that Trinitarian assumptions help to structure the 'space of subjectivity' within which each of these three writers writes." The absence of such a perspective explains "the apparent resistance of some texts to a theological reading, and also . . . the apparent incompatibility . . . of theology and literature." Cunningham shows how these barriers may be breached reading from a Trinitarian rhetorical, as opposed to doctrinal, perspective. For example, *Beloved* is seen to have Trinitarian implications not primarily because of some material manifestation (although the street number of the house is 124; the three is missing), but through the familial relationships which shift and redesign themselves at every turn. Such relationships are Trinitarian in their exploration of multiplicity and interruptions and in their preventing us from taking sides.

Margaret Atwood's *The Handmaid's Tale*, a text that continues to invite religious readings, is analyzed by Dorota Filipczak by way of its intertextual relationship to biblical understandings of women living under patriarchy. While many critics have taken note of Atwood's use of the Bible in this novel, Filipczak offers a much deeper exploration of the biblical intertext. She begins by noting two interpretations of the novel that have incorporated religious understandings. One reading sees Atwood detailing a literalizing misreading of the biblical text which serves to bind the text to the ideological functions of the fictional Republic of Gilead. Another argues that Atwood is seeking to overturn the traditional quest narrative so that what the narrator attempts to flee is Eden in hopes of finding some other ambiguous paradise. Filipczak uses biblical ideas of Gilead question these two readings in light of the intertextual nature of the novel. She concludes: "Atwood's vision of the Bible-centered society addresses the patriarchal abuse embedded in the biblical texts. At the same time it sees the patriarchal abuse as prevalent in response to the text that may be void of patriarchal intention, and yet it is violated into complicity with the governing interpretation."

John Strugnell offers a helpful survey of Australian literature and history that incorporates the unique religious expressions and problems manifested there. Strugnell points out the confluence and conflict of several ideas of what Australia was and is in terms of landscape, language, literature, and religion. As to the latter, he notes that the imported Anglican religion hopelessly attempts to recreate England on a landscape that insists on writing its own story. Australian language, too, seems to resist liturgical usage by being too ironic. Remarking on religion in Australia after the year 2000, Strugnell notes: ". . . The actual experience of living on the continent . . . raises major questions about the forms Australian religion may take in the next century. . . . We might expect Australian religion in the future . . . to be related more closely to the experiences of the Australian community and to the experience of the continent itself." The Australian landscape seems to live a life of its own and resist interpretive closure; as such it seems to generate both literary and religious imaginative responses.

Numbered among scholars of literature and theology are those who wish to bring new insights to the reading of traditional religious literature, namely, sacred texts and literary responses to those texts. Helen Wilcox shows how feminist criticism can open up devotional literature to renewed meanings. She begins her analysis by exploring a sentence from St. John's Gospel: "Greater love hath no man than this, that a man lay down his life for his friends." Love and friendship, active male expression and feminine passivity, and gendered and ungendered words combine to make this seemly simple sentence rife with issues that feminist criticism seeks to engage. Poems from George Herbert and the author of *Eliza's Babes* are equally laced with tensions and similarities that can be exposed from a perspective sensitive to gender relations in love and language. In fact her detailed readings of these poems lead Wilcox to suggest that devotional writing may be the ultimate writing of the body or *ecriture feminine*. She concludes: "Feminist critical strategies can surprise . . . but they will, importantly, take us by new routes to the central questions, such as those concerning our understanding of the nature of God and the limitations, and the possibilities, of human language."

The last two essays in the volume turn to the biblical text. Douglas A. Templeton questions the nature of the Gospels via Spinoza, Aristotle, Farrer, and others . He argues that history may try to make use of the Gospels for its own ends, but they are not primarily historical documents. While they certainly intersect with history, the Gospels are primarily literature; and while they are literature, they are not necessarily good literature, more Barbara Cartland than Proust as Templeton puts it. He finds that the best model for understanding the Gospels is the historical novel. Templeton remarks: "The critics agree that the historical novel begins with Scott, with *Waverley*. But need we agree with the critics? May we not, with pleasure and instruction, antedate the emergence of the genre to the Gospels, and antedate, in turn, that antedating to the Court Narrative of King David . . . ?" For Templeton the Gospels have yet to be fully appreciated as literature and thus can continue to be a part of our conversations, literary and otherwise, into the next century.

Finally, Jan Tarlin argues that calls to extricate ourselves from biblical texts in order to dismantle Western concepts of gender are perhaps impossible to accomplish and at the very least premature. Tarlin shows just how deeply biblical myths, such as the Eden tale, penetrate Western culture by way of the semiotics of advertising, literary criticism, and philosophical reflection. But Tarlin believes that patriarchal formulations of gender can be undone from within the system that expresses them. To show how this deconstruction can be achieved, he turns to Kaja Silverman's reflections on gender, ideology, and psychoanalysis. After exploring the possibilities of restructuring gender perceptions along these lines, Tarlin analyzes a biblical passage (I Kings 19: 9-18) to demonstrate how such a restructuring can take place. Employing the insights of Silverman and Lacan, he concludes: "Rather than presenting a seamless communion of the divine ground of patriarchy with its human representative, [I Kings 19: 9-18] embodies a struggle between Elijah's unbendingly 'male' discourse and Yahweh's ambiguous mix of conflicting 'male' and 'female' discourses. . . . God has a gender identity conflict." Such interpretations can, Tarlin suggests, guide us into the next century by undoing our patriarchal images of God.

The editors wish to thank the contributors for keeping the conversation going and invite the reader to enter the discussion that takes place in these pages and will continue to take place in a variety of ways "to 2000."

NOTES

1. T. S. Eliot, *Selected Essays* (London: Faber and Faber, 1935).

2. David H. Hesla, "Religion and Literature: The Second Stage," *Journal of the American Academy of Religion*, 46/2 (Summer 1978): 181-92.

3. Ed. Robert Detweiler, *Art/Literature/Religion: Life on the Borders* (Chico, CA: Scholars Press, 1983).

4. This conference was the Southeastern Commission on the Study of Religion (the Southeastern regional meeting of the American Academy of Religion) held in Atlanta in March, 1994. Jones was a presenter in a roundtable discussion of "Teaching Kafka's Metamorphosis."

5. T. R. Wright, *Theology and Literature* (Oxford: Blackwell, 1988).

6. Richard Rorty, "Pragmatism and Philosophy," in ed. Paul Moser and Dwayne Mulder, *Contemporary Approaches to Philosophy* (New York: Macmillan, 1994), p. 427.

7. Hesla, "Religion and Literature": 192.

SACRAMENTAL AND PROPHETIC INTERPRETATION

James Champion

Between delight in emptiness and the lie of fullness, the prevailing intellectual situation allows no third way.
Adorno, *Minima Moralia*

In our time we have not finished doing away with idols and we have barely begun to listen to symbols.
Ricoeur, *Freud and Philosophy*

Doubts of all things earthly, and intuitions of some things heavenly; this combination makes neither believer nor infidel, but makes a man who regards them both with equal eye.
Melville, *Moby-Dick*[1]

In the passage from *Moby-Dick* quoted above, Ishmael contemplates the need to regard all things with equilibrium. His reflection provides a clue to understanding some of the narrative turns which structure Melville's great novel. Key episodes in the work, such as "the first lowering" and "the spirit spout," take the reader into the realm of "intuitions," awe-awakening discoveries that seem to rise out of a profoundly sacramental understanding of our wide, watery planet. But there are many moments in *Moby-Dick* when this understanding is displaced by a contrary impulse towards prophetic criticism. In "The Try-Works," for instance, Ishmael depicts his ship, the *Pequod*, as a floating factory carrying an economic obsession out onto the seas where Ahab's despotic rampage simulates an entire society's dream of power and dominant self-assertion.

The prophetic doubt and sacramental insight combined in the fictional world of *Moby-Dick* have much in common with the two impulses Paul Ricoeur has characterized in the theory of interpretation as distinctive "hermeneutical styles": the hermeneutics of suspicion and the hermeneutics of restoration (or trust).[2] Melville, a nineteenth-century

15

novelist, and Ricoeur, a twentieth-century philosopher, speak from different angles and in different ways of the same dual vision to be found in the deeper regions of the inquiring human spirit.

To talk of "deeper regions," however, is to speak figuratively, and that is something to be suspicious about. For such language is not neutral. Our use of tropes, metaphors in particular, binds us to conceptual, rhetorical, and political agendas that come in their wake. Yet it is impossible to avoid figural expressions. The very effort to think critically and communicate one's suspicions must trust in the shared meanings of language to some degree. That language is inescapably fraught with metaphor does not, of itself, mean that all understanding is illusory.[3]

The point of these remarks is to suggest that we cannot conveniently step outside the two "hermeneutical styles" that are themselves the topic under investigation. The requirement to suspect and the need to trust in the value of communicative action cannot be observed from a purely neutral standpoint, for such needs and requirements reflect fundamental orientations with roots in nothing less than human being and consciousness. That, at least, one could argue from a philosophical standpoint. Here I turn to the sphere of religion to provide sea-room for a discussion of two parallel orientations, the sacramental and the prophetic. I hope to follow Ishmael's example here and view both with "equal eye."

Theological Specters

Properly speaking, the prophetic and the sacramental are polar elements in living religion. We live in a highly secularized culture, however, and that makes allusion to such terms problematic. Key theological polarities—such as the divine and the demonic—seem remote when, for many, the symbols of religion are dormant, if not dead. But such polarities may be interwoven with the historical fabric of our lives even though, on the surface, their meanings have been effaced. It is possible, in other words, that such terms point to submerged factors impinging upon modern and postmodern life despite the collapsed state of a traditional world of belief. These polarities may pertain despite, as well, the extensive debasements and the reductiveness of literalism—the reduction, especially, of religion to belief in a supernatural deity, of the prophetic to magical prediction, and of the sacramental to the spiritualization of matter.

In living religion, as distinct from a culture of kitsch, the prophetic and the sacramental are in tension. The prophetic has the character of profound critique; it is evident in every attack upon present conditions in the name of future justice. The sacramental, by contrast, is defined by an experience of the presence of the divine, especially in the consecration of certain objects or actions. In each of these basic dispositions, something unconditional is at issue: on the one hand, the holy that is *demanded*, on the other hand the holy that is *given*. In one direction we find a radical questioning of symbols beyond the biases of priests, in the other direction, an awareness mediated through symbols and the priestly function. The sacramental and priestly are so entwined that the notions are sometimes used interchangeably. Robert Scharlemann uses the latter term in his concise summary of the two fundamental orientations that concern us here: "the priestly represents the unconditional givenness of symbols; the prophetic judges them as culturally bound."[4]

If we understand the relation between the prophetic and sacramental dispositions in the religious sphere, we can better grasp the implications of the secularization of those dispositions. We can understand the hidden theological dimension underlying the attitudes of interpretive suspicion and interpretive trust. Ricoeur touches upon this issue when he finds himself "bluntly" inclined to call the contrary of hermeneutical suspicion "faith."[5] Hermeneutical trust is like faith, and it is allied with the sacramental, an outlook which must remain fundamentally restorative as it celebrates sacred presence. In more secular terms, it is an outlook that maintains underlying confidence in the givenness of things. As such, it is in conflict with the prophetic stance, which, secularized or not, must remain unrelentingly distrustful of all that a culture seeks to pass off as ultimate and fixed.

To reiterate: the relation between the prophetic and the sacramental can be seen to play itself out in a secularized form in the irreducible tension between subversive and affirmative impulses in the theory of interpretation. Before illustrating this claim with examples, we should note that it runs counter to the strenuous efforts of some critics to remove interpretive acts from any association with the religious. Edward Said, for example, has argued for a rigorous distinction between "religious" and "secular" critical theory. The former, according to Said, is subservient to absolutes and marked by appeals to "extrahuman" authority, while the latter is worldly and skeptical in its steadfast debunking of all "totalizing" systems.[6] Similarly, Jonathan Culler, calls for "oppositional" criticism that is unremitting in its secular enmity to the pious aura of the religio-humanistic cultural order.[7]

While Said and Culler write insightful criticism, their portrayal of the "religious" and the "secular" is tellingly one-dimensional. It reflects an uncritical acceptance of the attitude towards religion—presumably one is compulsively for or against it—predominant in our culture at large. It also reflects a certain kind of schizophrenia. It is the same academic schizophrenia evident in the work of Paul de Man, who, at one and the same time, could call religious questions "the most important ones," advocate "total" humility before the work, and yet reject anything smacking of the religious as outright critical contamination.[8] De Man, Said, and Culler have, of course, different things to say, but they are alike in avoiding a significant question: under what conditions do "oppositional," secular positions themselves become new forms of "totalization?"

For a less rigid perspective on these issues, I find critics such as Geoffrey Hartman, Susan Handelman, and Lynn Poland more tactful and engaging. Each shows how persistent, unconscious, and complex religious remnants can be. On the matter of "totalization," Hartman, in *Criticism in the Wilderness*, wonders aloud whether "pure secularism . . . is simply another religion [whose] ghosts or gods will appear at some point."[9] Writing elsewhere, he takes note of "the scandal of theological survivals in even the most secular thinkers."[10] He calls such ongoing affiliations a "scandal" after observing the fervor with which any trafficking between the religious and the secular is often resisted in critical circles. For my purposes here, it will be necessary to leave behind the dictates of secular puritanism in order to focus on hermeneutical aspirations which, unpurged of their ambiguity, show surprising interpenetrations of the secular and the religious.

Susan Handelman examines such aspirations in her work, *The Slayers of Moses* (1982). The subtitle of this study, "The Emergence of

Rabbinic Interpretation in Modern Theory," designates one area in which we can see "the return of theology into secular systems of thought."[11] Handelman selects several modern thinkers—including Sigmund Freud, Jacques Derrida and Harold Bloom—and shows how they are alike in drawing creatively upon their Jewish intellectual backgrounds. Specifically, they draw upon the rabbinic tradition of interpretation and its key principles: multiple signification, the inseparability of text and commentary, and endless interpretability. Through the influence of figures like Freud, Bloom, and Derrida, such principles have had a strong impact on contemporary literary theory. In some respects they have managed to shift recent critical practice to the ways of midrash, albeit in a secular guise. A work like Derrida's *Glas*, for example, takes an obvious turn in that direction; anyone familiar with a page of the *Gemara* or other commentaries on the Talmud will recognize correspondences to the format of multiple insets and to the style(s) of interpretation in *Glas*. The overall shift in literary critical thinking, however, is usually less overt. Bloom's kabbalistic criticism, Freud's psychoanalysis (as transformed poststructurally by Jacques Lacan[12]), and Derrida's deconstructive texts have all helped to instigate a movement away from unquestioned assumptions about identity, authorial purpose, and the stability of texts. In place of those former "givens," we find unabated emphasis on polyvalency, on intertextuality, on the opacity of writing, and, more generally, on playful modes of interpretation freed from chimeric searches for a text's single determinant meaning.

According to Handelman, this supposed "sea-change" in critical theory is hardly innocent. It is a recent manifestation of the age-old struggle between the Hebraic and Hellenistic world views. It is the same conflict Matthew Arnold once described between "Hebraism and Hellenism," the two dynamos of Western culture that Arnold wished could be "happily balanced."[13] Handelman, by contrast, eschews any reconciling ideal of "balance" in showing how "the agon of Hebrew and Hellene" reappears in the realm of criticism. For Handelman, we better understand important facets of the work of Freud, Bloom, Derrida, Emmanuel Levinas, and others, when we grasp their efforts to "de-Hellenize" modern thought. Handelman illustrates her point by comparing Harold Bloom's "tortuous anxieties of influence and dialectical poetic wars" with

Northrop Frye's "stately static schemata of archetypal criticism." Bloom's "openly avowed Hebraic bias," says Handelman, leads him to "Jewish esotericism, Kabbalah, and Gnosticism," the antithesis to "Frye's use of the Christian apocalyptic mode."[14] With greater philosophical elusiveness, such a counter-interpretive position is also taken up by Derrida, who employs rabbinic methods to dismantle the ordered, lucid logic hypostatized by "Greeks" and "Christians," the representatives of Western thought who, in late ancient times, adopted interpretive modes that privileged speech, that were prejudiced against writing, and which were, therefore, antagonistic to Jewish interpretive modes. Hence, it should not surprise us to find Derrida in our century doing battle against the onto-theological tradition of Western philosophy. Nor is it surprising that he wages that battle indirectly through the innuendo and excursus of differential "play." Much is at stake in this play if, as Handelman says, Derrida "is seeking to undo completely the Greco-Christian tradition of thought"[15] by replacing it with *ecriture*—writing as an endlessly productive signifying practice irreducible to some final, self-evident truth.

Throughout the 1970's and 1980's, Derrida's deconstructive philosophy was adopted by a number of critics fighting the vestiges of American New Criticism, the formerly dominant school of literary thought with its own theological affiliations. The most apparent affiliation was with T. S. Eliot, whose emphasis on unified sensibility (and neo-Catholic arguments generally) influenced the group in its hegemonic heyday. Yet, beyond Eliot's influential polemics, there were subtler connections among the agrarian, conservative, and Christian proclivities of the New Critics—John Crowe Ransom, Allen Tate, Robert Penn Warren, and Cleanth Brooks especially—that have emerged more clearly over time.[16] Such theological subtexts have proved to be more than a secondary matter of spiritual taste. If we seriously consider the scenario of interpretive conflict described by Handelman, the Christian bias of the New Criticism has been a formative factor over several decades of literary criticism. It is one key to understanding the reactions and the antithetical methods of contemporary "rabbinic" literary theories, and, no less, the animosity of surviving New Critics to the deconstructive enterprise.

Derrida's well-known claim that there is no "outside of the text"[17] seems less startling when the ancient rabbinic tradition of infinite interpretation is taken into account. Alternately, the anti-historical "close readings" of New Critical formalism look downright historical when the theological contexts of that movement are brought to light. In regard to New Criticism and its historical moment, Lynn Poland has pointed out parallels between the New Critics and this century's Protestant Neo-Orthodox theologians. Reflecting the concerns of the same cultural period, these seemingly incongruous groups show surprising affinities. As Poland puts it, both groups "tended to stress the ambiguities, conflicts and sometimes even meaninglessness in the modern historical situation, while seeking a norm and agency for human redemption in the autonomous, paradoxical Otherness of the literary or kerygmatic word."[18]

This theological parallel to Neo-Orthodoxy does not explain New Criticism. At the same time, Derrida's discourse cannot be reduced to rabbinic methods and ideas. On the other hand, the shaping impact of such religious facets on critical positions can hardly be excluded from the broader hermeneutical picture. In the case of Derrida, beyond the rabbinic influence, there are further religious and quasi-religious strains one could discuss, including the curious problem of his relation to "negative theology."[19] Such discussions do not produce final answers. They *do* show that the religious dimension of thought is more likely to go through unexpected transformations than simply to go away. They also show that interchanges between the secular and religious spheres generate a wide range of responses in critics, from hostile refutations of the validity of religion (here one thinks of Culler) to subtly coercive defenses of transcendent authority (recent claims of George Steiner come to mind[20]). The volatility of this situation, heightened by the constant push for more advanced theoretical positions, makes any attempt to trace the theological and secular permutations in critical thought somewhat precarious.

Restoring Meanings/Demystifying Illusions

Ricoeur's distinction between hermeneutical retrieval and suspicion offers a touchstone of sense in the midst of this interpretive strife. To repeat, his point is that interpretation can be understood, on the one hand, as "the manifestation and restoration of a meaning addressed to me in the manner of a message," and, on the other hand, as "a demystification, as a reduction of illusion." These impulses compose a double possibility funded by contrary motivations, "willingness to suspect, willingness to listen."[21]

This distinction of Ricoeur's is often cited by commentators because it offers a purview of a changing, conflictual scene in which critical models—structuralism, for instance—can rapidly rise and decline. The distinction is perhaps best viewed as a heuristic one alerting us to the intrinsic value of two opposed orientations—not in order to systematize differences between critical models, but to intimate a way of thinking that moves past tiresome rivalries and the fallacy of false alternatives.

One way of illustrating what Ricoeur means by "suspicion" is to turn to three adepts of the practice in our own century: Freud, Theodor Adorno, and Derrida. Although the latter two are not the examples discussed by Ricoeur, each of these figures can be said to have excelled at unmasking some ideological consensus society has wished to pass off as fixed. Freud's works lay bare the undignified biological drives that human culture hides while establishing itself upon rationalizations and denials. Adorno unrelentingly criticizes the principle of identity that co-opts all critical questioning and thus ensures the ease with which we comply with the barbarous machinations of the culture industry. Most recently, Derrida's inclusion of the unconscious and the absent as "present" effectively challenges the comfortable metaphysical closures behind the syndrome of consciousness-as-mastery. While their work cannot be reduced to these motifs, it is apparent that each sustains a radical interrogation and demystification of what we have come to do and think as second nature.

Alongside the names Freud, Adorno, and Derrida, one can place, for purposes of comparison, three historically parallel figures whose cultural hermeneutics have been motivated in a fundamentally alternate direction. In the thought of Carl Jung, Heidegger, and Hans-Georg Gadamer, the basic impetus has been toward the restoration of meaning rather than toward critical suspicion. We can see in Jung's investigations of the archetypal origins and primordial images expressed in a broad range of cultural creations the attempt to establish "a new organic syncretism"[22] offering paths of healing for the human psyche. Heidegger attempts to overcome the calculative thinking rooted in Western metaphysics and anthropocentrism in order to recover the quintessential question of the meaning of being. And Gadamer, in letting go of the ideal of prejudice-free, methodically secured guarantees of objective knowledge, emphasizes interpretation as an event of dialogue between past and present, an event which signals the belongingness of humans to the truth of being.

To note the restorative aspect in these latter three figures is not to deny their strong debunking tendencies. Nor do I wish to imply that Freud, Adorno, and Derrida do not renew cultural meanings in resourceful ways. The point is one of emphasis. The overall emphasis of these thinkers, however, also raises again the issue of "theological survivals." In Freud, Adorno, and Derrida, we see three figures who come from secularized Jewish traditions.[23] Jung, Heidegger, and Gadamer, on the other hand, stem from secularized Christian traditions. Such backgrounds do not tell all, but it is not mere coincidence that the tools of critical suspicion have been most radically developed by those of one background, while those accentuating some kind of recovery of meaning, often entailing the momentary letting go of critical consciousness, stem from the other.

These links warrant a closer look, for they can be highly nuanced. Yet, they are not always hard to reason out. Let me put it in shorthand this way: when intellectuals and thinkers of various stripes come from a tradition—even one that is thoroughly secularized—which says the *Christian* decisive event in history has *already* occurred, they are likely to trust culture and to view the presence of meaning in ways that are profoundly different from those who come from a tradition which says the decisive *Jewish* event in history has *not yet* occurred. This is especially so when, in the latter case, their tradition has been persecuted, systematically marginalized, and subjected to atrocity over the course of centuries, and often by envoys of the former. From the irrevocable antithesis between Christianity and Judaism—a topic, I should note, that carries a certain taboo—critical consequences follow.

Let me expand on these issues by first turning to the phenomenon of prophetic criticism. Radical cultural critique is rooted in the prophetic impulse, even when it announces itself as something entirely new. One can speak of that impulse in a general way, but also with a view to its historical manifestations. It is especially apparent in biblical prophetism, a development fostered by the unusual circumstances of ancient Israel and its experience of exile. In the form of social imperatives and a demand for universal justice, the Hebrew prophets fashioned critiques of Israel's own and neighboring idol-bound cultures.[24] Throughout Western history, the "sacred discontent" inducing such critiques has tended to find new formulations and to take different shapes, rather than to disappear entirely. It has come and gone and returned repeatedly, particularly as an element in Jewish existence. In secularized versions, it has persisted, as Carl Raschke says, in "the Hebrew passion for iconoclasm, for de-situating holiness and making it a temporal disclosure."[25] That concentration on temporality, and a corresponding de-emphasis on space, are remarked upon by Handelman as well. As she frames it, Hebrew iconoclasm coincides with the thematic of *displacement* in rabbinic interpretation—the "necessary re-vision and re-creation of a text which is the only anchor of a people displaced in space."[26]

space

Key thinkers with backgrounds in exiled Jewish life have, certainly since the Enlightenment, sustained prophetic consciousness and adopted its capacity to displace, to historicize, to demythologize and to undermine pseudo-sanctified conventions. In modern times, intellectual earthquakes have resulted, particularly in the area one might call "cultural hermeneutics." The terms of understanding and engagement in this broad field have been revolutionized by works of critical interrogation, above all those of Karl Marx (the critique of ideology), Freud (the critique of rationalization), Adorno (the critique of identity), and Derrida (the critique of false presence).

These critiques may be called prophetic because they demystify the auras around leading symbols and expose illusions that underwrite culture. Such critiques are animated by suspicion and marked by their deployment of doubt, but a kind of doubt that reaches deeper than, say, the Cartesian variety. The famous doubt exercised by René Descartes (and standardized by his followers) questions things and finds errors where certain facts need to be established. However, the knowing subject who exercises this methodical doubt does not really question the individual possession of autonomous consciousness. As Ricoeur puts it, "Descartes doubts things but leans on the fortress of consciousness"; he does not raise "the problem of false-consciousness," and that leaves his thought devoid of "a critique of culture whereby consciousness appears in itself as a doubtful consciousness."[27] To be consciously suspicious of false consciousness is, by contrast, the crux of prophetic criticism. And prophetic attacks on false consciousness—attacks which, it should be noted, finally expand rather than detract from consciousness itself—always find false consciousness nurtured at levels beyond or beneath those of autonomous intentions. Again, Freud finds it in our elaborate denials of unconscious desires, Derrida in the belief that language is entirely transparent to our meanings. Marx, who first elaborated the term "false consciousness," finds it based in the economic realm as he uncovers hidden connections between ideology and class domination. Marx also unveils those connections in the depth dimension of culture, where the "holy" turns out to be enmeshed with the fetish of money and with codes of submission. This discovery leads the young Marx to utter words that could be taken as a maxim of the prophetic task, ancient or modern: "The criticism of religion is the premise of all criticism."[28]

One could say, in a play on Marx's words, that the premise of understanding prophetic criticism is an awareness of its roots. I have just mentioned Freud, Marx, and Derrida, and their Jewish backgrounds. I have left out the figure of Nietzsche, whose familial background—fiercely rejected by him—is Protestant (a point I'll return to in a moment). Nietzsche is, of course, no less prophetic a critic of modern thought. Ricoeur, for one, includes him, along with Marx and Freud, in a discussion of nineteenth-century "masters of suspicion."[29] Nietzsche's critique is similarly powerful because it unveils masked consciousness under the discourse of dominant culture. In the form of a genealogical hermeneutics of the will, Nietzsche strives to undermine the reigning metaphysics and its mainstays, the concepts of being and truth. At the same time, his critique targets religion in a primary way. He shows prevailing spiritual values to be distortions, and he exposes the longing for suprasensible transcendence as "Platonism for the people,"[30] a disguised negation of life.

Nietzsche's proclamation of the "will to power" is accompanied by an anti-religious mannerism. His irreligious bent comes most alive in his critique of Christianity as a movement of *ressentiment*. It is also evident, but with greater ambivalence, when he re-invents the doctrine of "eternal recurrence"; he thereby endorses the infinite weight of every moment of time in refutation of the Christian world view, with its center in a fullness of time. Yet, his anti-religious challenges notwithstanding, prophetic streaks permeate Nietzsche's criticism, and they make his project acutely different in scope and character from any critique rational thought might undertake. Instead of doubting and measuring the world through the constructive criteria of the intellect, Nietzsche's ecstatic reason encounters life as a divine-demonic dynamic. In the process, he devises gestures that betoken an almost classic prophetic pose: he sets out to smash bourgeois idols, he speaks sometimes in paradoxical oracles, he registers the subterranean tremors of his time, he vents wrath upon "nihilism," he announces he is "out of season" with his decadent age, while yet believing himself to be standing at a dramatic moment in world history when something radically new can appear.[31]

These gestures do not arise out of a vacuum. They carry valencies of the prophetic and bear traces of other historical occasions of absolute "protest." However Nietzsche secularizes, re-creates, or deploys those traces in his prophetic attack, they may still reflect back upon his own religious roots and Protestant desire itself—that underlying historical move to break with all heteronomous religious closures in the name of a greater, life-giving principle.[32] By Nietzsche's day, of course, Protestant protest had become Lutheranism, and Lutheranism had consolidated into a new, middle-class heteronomy, a largely dogma-bound institution serving the national status quo by way of the now absolutized Word. Nonetheless, some element akin to biblical prophetism, as it had been recovered and transformed by the Reformers in their mandate for wholesale change, recurs in Nietzsche's thought. Since God has died, and the system of values supported by God has collapsed, that element can surface only in an "overturned," revaluated form. We can discern it, though, even after Nietzsche has put it to his own "uses"—in his Zarasthustrian utterances, for instance: "Spirit is the life that itself cuts into life."[33]

If Nietzsche's prophetic critique shows, in its overturning ways, a Protestant root or two, we may be looking at the factor which, in the long run, places his critique on a trajectory at odds with those inspired by secularized Jewish thought. In other words, what Karl Jaspers has called the negated "Christian"[34] side of Nietzsche's thinking may end up, despite that negation, recapitulating in part the disparity between Christianity and Judaism in their contrary approaches toward the issue of presence. For along with his critique of culture, Nietzsche moves toward myth, with its immanence of meaning, and in a way that is anathema to Hebraic thought.

Nietzsche's retrieval of myth stems from the side of his thought which affirms the "flux"—his unconditional yea-saying. Always in dialectical tension, that side accompanies his "enterprise of destruction."[35] At one level, Nietzsche demolishes metaphysical ideas, but at another level he substitutes for them the notions of play, interpretation, and sign. On the one hand, he criticizes the pernicious legends of Christianity, but on the other hand he anticipates the recovery of the will to power through elements drawn from other mythological narratives: the Overman, Eternal Recurrence, and Dionysus. Nietzsche tries to re-direct the significance of these "broken" mythic expressions toward the future, and he plays with their motifs creatively over the course of his career, but their mythic aspects remain. Allan Megill, in *Prophets of Extremity*, summarizes the matter this way: "[Nietzsche] is concerned in both his early and his late writings with attempting a 'return to myth'. Admittedly, the myth is in each case different, and in the late writings the very idea of myth tends to be undermined. But the fundamental concern with returning to myth, or to some simulacrum thereof, persists."[36]

Nietzsche's persistent retrieval of myth evinces what one might call his orientation to being. While he is known foremostly as the philosopher of becoming rather than of being, that label is a bit misleading. For as Heidegger points out in his study of Nietzsche, the "will to power" is, not least of all, an expression of the *being* of becoming. In Nietzsche's own words, it is the "closest approximation" to being.[37] But however Nietzsche may signify being and its power(s), that "interest" determines much. It connects his thinking to Greek mythopoesis. It leads him—despite his naturalistic, anti-romantic stance—to conceive ideas of biological struggle that, in our own century, have been seized upon (with horrifying distortion) by movements of political romanticism.[38] In another direction, it is also what leads him to abide by the circle as his formative symbol, and to embrace, courageously, the "always-already" while summoning, with monumental inconsistency, the "not-yet." For although in one vein of his thought Nietzsche calls for the new in history, the new for him can finally only happen within a segment of the circular movement of time.

For Being—and Against

Let me move on from Nietzsche with this observation: the orientation to being—rather than to critical consciousness—tends to emerge in thinkers of Christian background, even when, like Nietzsche, they have profoundly jettisoned the beliefs, contents, and formal trappings of that background. It emerges multifariously, for instance, in the writings of Jung, Heidegger, and Gadamer (mentioned above). And it appears in various spheres of twentieth-century literature, psychology and philosophy. In regard to Jung, one could show how his analyses of the instinctive strata of the human psyche correspond at key points with the presuppositions of Christianity. Or, in regard to the author of *Being and Time* (who received formal training in a Jesuit seminary), one could show how the categories of care, anxiety, and resoluteness bear a striking resemblance to those of pietism. But such correspondences are not really the point. The underlying bearing is the issue here, along with questions that arise concerning the hermeneutical limits of the turn towards being.

As stated before, differences abound in seminal thinkers like Jung, Heidegger, and Gadamer, yet they are alike in adhering more to the hermeneutics of affirmation than to indefatigable suspicion. Though they rely on the breakthroughs and insights of prophetic critics, their approach to meaning reflects, finally, a "sacramentality," an orientation to what's given with the world, and in its depth. Not that criticism is removed from their respective projects; for one thing, Jung, Heidegger, and Gadamer must all attack a mindset that in many respects propels modern culture and eradicates hermeneutical trust: namely, positivism. As Ricoeur notes, in opposition to positivism, "hermeneuts" of affirmation presuppose "that the 'true' and the 'real' cannot be reduced to what can be verified by mathematical and experimental methods but has to do with our relationship to the world, to other beings, and to being as well."[39]

Such relationship is bound up with semantic trust in the possibility that being is, somehow, "sayable." Where prophetic critiques expose the false consciousness that is mediated through language, sacramental perspectives release us from rigidly concluding that the inevitable medium of language cuts us off from "nonlinguistic existence."[40] Sacramental perspectives thereby counteract the disenchantment of the world, its artistic works, and cultural expressions. That is why we may feel an effect of re-enchantment, for example, when New Critical and phenomenological interpretations of a literary work are successfully carried out, for these readings tend to approach the work more to reveal its values than to suspect its deceptions. The intent behind such readings clashes, of course, with the demand for suspicion—with deconstructive readings, for example, which would expose a text's deferral of presence and indeterminacy of meaning, before dismantling it into its historical codes. Deconstruction has been adopted by prophetic criticism in its fight against new forms of idolatry, hegemonic models, the distorting potential of symbols, and unjustified assumptions about the plentitude of being. But we can expect to find sacramental criticism proceeding in the opposite way. We find it attending to words, images, and symbols not to uncover their false auras but for their participation in being beyond the function of signs. This does not mean sacramental criticism secretly longs for a triumphalist unity of being, though it is often caricatured as doing so. At its best, it is an openness to disclosures of being. In that mode, it perhaps comes close in spirit and purpose to a few words William Carlos Williams offers in a reflection upon his life in poetry. At the end of his *Autobiography*, Williams writes: "We catch a glimpse of something, from time to time, which shows us that a presence has just brushed past us, some rare thing."[41]

The *aporia* of being and questions of presence tend to form the axis (or vortex) around which the conflicts between prophetic and sacramental interpretation revolve. This is apparent in twentieth-century philosophy in the strife between Heidegger and Adorno. In what has become a Western tradition of bringing an end to Western metaphysics, the later Heidegger resolves "to think Being without regard to its being grounded in terms of beings," to "think Being without beings."[42] In conjunction with such thinking he envisions commentary on works of art that would be as unobtrusive and yet as revealing as snowflakes falling on a bell. For Adorno, on the other hand, the very notion of being is "mythological" subterfuge. Not surprisingly, then, at the heart of his *Negative Dialectics*, Adorno engages in a diatribe against Heidegger and offers a counter-aesthetic which refuses any unity of art and this life. In taking up such a position, Adorno may consider himself a secular intellectual battling a popular priest's dangerous adherence to the "gods." But, as Martin Jay points out, Adorno himself is a thinker whose refusal to name or describe the Other is more than a little "consistent with the Jewish taboo against uttering the sacred."[43] Adorno is a critic of culture, but also one who ends up calling, in *Minima Moralia*, for "the standpoint of redemption"[44] as our last hope. Such a concern makes his hermeneutical bearing as prophetic as that of his nemesis is sacramental.

In the orbit of modern psychology, a comparable enmity is apparent in the debates between Jung and Freud. Corresponding to the philosophical opposition between Heidegger and Adorno over the matter of being are Jung's and Freud's inverse approaches to the unconscious. Freud rediscovers the unconscious in terms of what he calls "the fact of consciousness"[45]; the blind mechanisms of instinct are scientifically analyzed in the stoical hope that through the controlling quality of conscious acceptance, humans can live in some degree of daylight despite their own irrational depths. Jung, by contrast, investigates those depths in terms of the psyche itself, since the unconscious for Jung, as Philip Rieff astutely points out, is really "all that consciousness can become."[46]

This means that in the process of recovering the archetypal powers from which Western humankind has become estranged, Jung tends to override critical consciousness. In short, there are reasons both he and Heidegger become connected (very briefly in the case of Jung, thoroughly involved in the case of Heidegger) to the politically romantic ideals of National Socialism.[47] In the extremity of their retrieval of being and of the unconscious from their suppression by the modern positivist mentality, critical consciousness in turn gets suppressed. This amounts to rather more than a passing intellectual occurrence, for in the nightmare of twentieth-century politics, that suppression takes the form of programs to annihilate those who represent critical consciousness.

In deference to Ishmael's dialectic, the other side of the coin should be mentioned here by noting that both Freud and Adorno have been criticized for their compensating one-sidedness. For instance, in regard to Freud (with whom he was closely associated for many years) Otto Rank could say that "the whole of psychoanalysis in its theoretical and practical aspects is actually an unparalleled glorification of consciousness and its power."[48] Similarly, Adorno's mentor, Siegfried Kracauer, questions

Adorno's hypertrophy of unfettered cultural criticism for its hidden utopian bent. The absolute rejection of any "ontological stipulation" in favor of an infinite negative dialectics is not sufficient, says Kracauer, since some ontological coordinates are needed "to imbue it with significance and direction."[49]

Gadamer Meets Derrida

While rejecting the need for any such "coordinates," Derrida, in contrast to Adorno, manages to confront a host of ontological problems. He does so by using a strategic counter-concept: *différance*. However "unthinkable" this notion is, and however ungrounded deconstruction may be, Derrida's stance is nonetheless prophetic in its submerged intent and in the hope it unexpectedly elicits.[50] In its radical opposition to dominant Western culture (logocentrism), it is comparable to Adorno's "immanent critique." The attacks unleashed by Adorno and Derrida are dissimilar in strategy and style, and yet, as Peter Dews points out, there is also a revealing affinity between these thinkers. It lies, says Dews, in their "opposition to Heidegger, insofar as both are profoundly suspicious of the vein of nostalgia, of longing for a pre-modern and pre-urban unity, which runs through Heidegger's thought." Derrida is deeply influenced by Heidegger, yet for him, as for Adorno, "even to talk of Being implies an unacceptable orientation towards unity."[51] Derrida overcomes that incongruity through a critical theoretical inversion: he makes difference "originary" rather than derivative. At the same time, he substitutes the word "text" after displacing the notion of being.

The hermeneutic theorist Gadamer, on the other hand, trusts heavily in the notion of being. He may be considered, so to speak, as Derrida's sacramentally inclined "other." Over and against Derrida's deconstruction and "dissemination" stands Gadamer's hermeneutic ontology with its "fusion of horizons." Interpretive fusion occurs, according to Gadamer, between person and text, or between person and person, as a mediating event in the process of understanding. Gadamer himself performs such a process in his landmark work, *Truth and Method*.[52] He conceived that work over years after assimilating Heidegger's writings and teachings. He integrates and builds on Heidegger's insights in a way that, contrary to Derrida, retains his teacher's insistence on the *primordial* nature of the human relation to being. For Gadamer, the experience of the truth of being occurs with language above all, for it is in language that being discloses itself.[53] But the experience of truth transpires no less in interpreting art and history. It occurs in these spheres when understanding is not covered over by the presiding human subject with its "methodological consciousness."

Gadamer's conception of art as "play," his recommendation of a dialogue between past and present, and his commitment to conversation in which fixed positions are transformed—these are all facets of an open-ended search for truth. It is a decidedly stable search, focusing less on crises in human life and thought than on persistence and solidarity. However, it is Gadamer's assumption of universality in human experience—in particular, the notion that there are fundamental conditions of the phenomenon of understanding[54]—that makes his account of truth and meaning suspect from Derrida's poststructuralist point of view.

Given the incommensurability of their standpoints, it is hard to summon surprise at the outcome of a much anticipated debate between Gadamer and Derrida in Paris in 1981. We find these men speaking at cross purposes. (Papers given by Gadamer and Derrida in connection with this inconclusive event have been collected in a volume entitled *Dialogue and Deconstruction*.[55]) The paper Gadamer presents at the colloquium, "Text and Interpretation," shows he expects to enter into a give-and-take conversation with Derrida on the basis of "the hermeneutics of good will." Derrida's talk and replies, on the other hand, take an indirect form; he addresses questions which place him "outside" the conversational frame in a position to resist co-optation of the deconstruction of literature and philosophy.

Following this rather tentative exchange of views in the early 1980's, commentators from the camps of Derrida and Gadamer have taken up and elaborated the terms of the dispute. For instance, the deconstructionists have claimed that what Gadamer calls "continuity" and "dialogue" in fact amounts to monologue. "Understanding," moreover, is an idealization concealing an imperial attempt at appropriation. The upshot of this claim is put concisely by Mark C. Taylor: "From a deconstructive point of view, . . . hermeneutics remains committed to a philosophy of presence that is repressive of otherness and difference."[56] Critics of deconstruction, on the other hand, have questioned Derrida's tendency to make a fetish of "disunity," and to do so by way of a kind of "calculated hesitation."[57] They ask, moreover, why the "other" is privileged for its de-centering power but denied a re-centering capacity with the potential to relocate meaning. From another angle, critics of poststructuralist thinking have pointed out, with Peter Dews, that "despite all appearances, *différance* is itself a powerful principle of unity."[58]

The debates touched on here do not fit tidy summaries, and the conflicts that underlie them are not about to ease up soon. I have suggested there is a correlation between profoundly critical and receptive modes of interpretation, on the one hand, and prophetic and sacramental trends in Judaism and Christianity on the other. If that is so, then a statement by Franz Rosenzweig in a key work of twentieth-century theology does not bode well for interpretive accord. In *The Star of Redemption*, Rosenzweig claims there will be "enmity between Judaism and Christianity at all times before the final redemption."[59] Most often it seems that way in the theory of interpretation too.

Yet, in adumbrating major orientations in interpretation, we lose sight of anomalies and counter-trends that sometimes tell another story. For interchanges between interpretive suspicion and interpretive trust also occur, though they are easily overlooked. For example, there are literary critical moments when the suspicious dismantling of a text ends up reanimating the work for us by preserving a trustful sense of its otherness. At the same time, a deeply sacramental approach to a work of art can become the most effective indictment of the pervasive instrumental reason that kills mystery in our culture.[60] Or, in a somewhat different vein, consider a work of feminist cultural criticism like Luce Irigaray's *Speculum of the Other Woman*: in the middle of this highly suspicious critique of "the economy of the Same," of the logic of phallocentric patriarchy that is underwritten by the "Judaeo-Christian tradition," we find a chapter, "La Mystérique," that points to mysticism, of all things, as intimating a "beyond" that can break through the logic of such domination.[61]

While the interweaving of antithetical human orientations may be uncommon in textual and cultural interpretation, we usually find it at the core of works of art that matter. If, in thinking to the year 2000, we avoid turning theory into a defense mechanism against literature, we might turn to particular literary texts, and there again focus upon the deeper structures and movements of thought—the impulse towards being and its sacramental "givens," and towards consciousness, and all it throws into question. The men and women who create literature are not an alternate species to those who theorize about it. Among both groups there are those who have "doubts or denials," but, as Ishmael says, also some who, along with them, "have intuitions."

NOTES

1. Theodor Adorno, *Minima Moralia: Reflections From Damaged Life,* tr. E. F. N. Jephcott (London: Verso, 1984), p. 67. Paul Ricoeur, *Freud and Philosophy: An Essay on Interpretation,* tr. Denis Savage (New Haven: Yale University Press, 1970), p. 27. Herman Melville, *Moby-Dick,* ed. Harrison Hayford and Hershel Parker (New York: Norton, 1967), p. 314.

2. Ricoeur refers to these opposed hermeneutical "styles" in slightly different ways throughout his work. Important treatments can be found in *Freud and Philosophy,* pp. 27-28, 341-343; "The Symbol Gives rise to Thought," *The Symbolism of Evil,* tr. Emerson Buchanan (Boston: Beacon, 1967), pp. 347-357; and, "The Critique of Religion," *The Philosophy of Paul Ricoeur,* ed. Charles E. Reagan and David Stewart (Boston: Beacon, 1978), pp. 213-22.

3. On the pervasiveness of metaphor see, for example, George Lakoff and Mark Johnson, *Metaphors We Live By* (Chicago: University of Chicago Press, 1980). For a critical discussion of the thoroughgoing linguisticality of our experience, especially its social and theological aspects, see Rebecca S. Chopp, *The Power to Speak: Feminism, Language, God* (New York: Crossroad, 1991). The embeddedness of "depth" metaphors in the "social-symbolic order" is apparent even in critiques of it. Note Chopp's description of that order as a "deep symbolic economy" (p. 111).

4. Robert Scharlemann, "Tillich's Religious Writings," in *Paul Tillich, Writings on Religion,* ed. Robert Scharlemann, Vol. 5 of *Main Works/Hauptwerke* (Berlin and New York: De Gruyter-Evangelisches Verlagswerk GmbH, 1988), p. 8.

5. Ricoeur, *Freud and Philosophy,* p. 28.

6. Edward Said, *The World, the Text, and the Critic* (Cambridge: Harvard University Press, 1983), pp. 21, 29.

7. Jonathan Culler, "Comparative Literature and the Pieties," *Profession* 86, p. 30-32. See also Culler's attack on an imagined "complicity of literary study and religion" in *Framing the Sign: Criticism and Its Institutions* (Oxford: Basil Blackwell, 1988), p. 79. Giles Gunn offers criticisms of the positions of Said and Culler in "On New Uses of the 'Secular' and the 'Religious' in Contemporary Criticism: Edward Said, George Steiner, and the Counter-Example of Erich Heller," *Morphologies of Faith: Essays in Religion and Culture in Honor of Nathan A. Scott, Jr.*, ed. Mary Gehart and Anthony C. Yu (Atlanta: Scholars Press, 1990), pp. 51-68. For a polemical, yet well-deserved, debunking of Culler's position, see David Lehman, *Signs of the Times: Deconstruction and the Fall of Paul de Man* (New York: Poseidon, 1991), pp. 262-5. Lehman points out that Culler's hostile rendering of religious discourse to the same status as sexist and racist belief amounts to a kind of "atheistic fundamentalism, as extreme in its way as the other kind of fundamentalism . . ." (p. 265).

8. J. Hillis Miller reports that Paul de Man "rather surprisingly, once said to me with great conviction, 'Religious questions are the most important ones'." See Miller's "Naming and Doing: Speech Acts in Hopkins' Poems," *Religion and Literature* 22 (Summer-Autumn 1990), p. 189. De Man mentions the need for "total" humility in relation to a work in conversation with Robert Moynihan. See "Interview with Paul de Man," *The Yale Review* 73 (1984): 586-7. De Man's equation of "theological" reading with the longing for determinate meaning can be found throughout his works, including "Time and History in Wordsworth," *Diacritics* (Winter 1987): 5. De Man's position of conclusive uncertainty and his "principle of disbelief" have been, in turn, called into question—especially in light of the collaborationist scandal that surfaced in the late 1980's. For critiques of de Man, see Kenneth Asher, "The Moral Blindness of Paul de Man," *Telos* 82 (Winter 1989-90): 197-205, and Lehman, *Signs of the Times*.

9. Geoffrey H. Hartman, *Criticism in the Wilderness: The Study of Literature Today* (New Haven: Yale University Press, 1980), p. 145.

10. Geoffrey H. Hartman, *Psychoanalysis and the Question of the Text* (Baltimore: Johns Hopkins University Press, 1967), p. 91.

11. Susan A. Handelman, *The Slayers of Moses: The Emergence of Rabbinic Interpretation in Modern Literary Theory* (Albany: State University of New York Press, 1982), xviii.

12. Handelman points out, of course, that Lacan is not Jewish (xvii). She notes, however, Lacan's recognition of "the relation of Freud to Rabbinic thought," and the impact of that recognition on Lacan's innovative psychoanalytic formulations (p. 154).

13. Matthew Arnold, "Hebraism and Hellenism," *Culture and Anarchy* (Cambridge: Cambridge University Press, 1948), p. 130.

14. Handelman, *The Slayers of Moses,* xiv.

15. Handelman, *The Slayers of Moses,* xiv. Handelman, it should be pointed out, is one of a growing number of commentators who have come to speculate on the nature of Derrida's relation to rabbinic thought. See also Kevin Hart, "The Poetics of the Negative," *Reading the Text: Biblical Criticism and Literary Theory,* ed. Stephen Prickett (Oxford: Basil Blackwell, 1991), p. 317. For another study of the relation between rabbinic interpretation and contemporary literary theory, see *Midrash and Literature,* ed. Geoffrey Hartman and Sanford Budick (New Haven: Yale University Press, 1986). Allan Megill also points to Derrida's "persistent fascination with Judaism and with the problem of its relation to a predominantly Greek and Christian culture. This fascination . . . is important for understanding the depth, rigor, and passion of the attack that he launches on the Western tradition." See Megill's *Prophets of Extremity: Nietzsche, Heidegger, Foucault, Derrida* (Berkeley: University of California Press, 1985), p. 276.

16. These connections are mentioned by Vincent B. Leitch, *American Literary Criticism from the Thirties to the Eighties* (New York: Columbia University Press, 1988), pp. 33, 59. See also Grant Webster, *The Republic of Letters: A History of Postwar American Literary Opinion* (Baltimore: Johns Hopkins University Press, 1979), pp. 100-102. Webster shows, for instance, how "Brooks' method" parallels the fundamentalist way of reading: "Like the Fundamentalist with his sacred scripture, the Formalist assumes an Ideal Poem, one in which there are no mistakes, where he subsumes what he must consider to be only apparent ironies and contradictions under one controlling figure or paradox" (p. 101). William K. Wimsatt and Cleanth Brooks themselves point out the ties between their literary theory and "the religious dogma of the Incarnation" in *Literary Criticism: A Short History,* Vol. 2, (Chicago: University of Chicago Press, 1957), p. 746.

17. Jacques Derrida, *Dissemination,* tr. Barbara Johnson (London: Athlone, 1981), p. 328.

18. Lynn M. Poland, *Literary Criticism and Biblical Hermeneutics: A Critique of Formalist Approaches* (Chico, CA: Scholars Press, 1985), p. 161.

19. Several works have appeared which discuss Derrida's parallels to—and profound differences from—negative theology. See, for example: Robert Magliola, *Derrida on the Mend* (West Lafayette, IN: Purdue University Press, 1984), Kevin Hart, *The Trespass of the Sign: Deconstruction, Theology, and Philosophy* (Cambridge: Cambridge University Press, 1989), and *Derrida and Negative Theology,* ed. Harold Coward and Toby Foshay (Albany: State University of New York Press, 1992).

20. In regard to Steiner, such claims can be found, in my view, in *Real Presences* (Chicago: University of Chicago Press, 1989). An example: " . . . any coherent account of the capacity of human speech to communicate meaning and

feeling is, in the final analysis, underwritten by the assumption of God's presence" (p. 3). See David Lyle Jeffrey's review of *Real Presences* in *Religion and Literature* 22 (Spring 1990): 101-10.

21. Ricoeur, *Freud and Philosophy*, p. 27. To my knowledge, Ricoeur does not relate these two hermeneutical orientations to the prophetic and sacramental, or to consciousness and being. My claim is that, while Ricoeur may not use those terms or delve into such roots, they are implicit in his distinction.

22. Edward F. Edinger, *Ego and Archetype: Individuation and the Religious Function of the Psyche* (Baltimore: Penguin, 1970), xiii.

23. Of these three figures, it is Freud especially whose thought has been studied in terms of its relationship to Judaism. See Yosef Hayim Yerushalmi, *Freud's Moses: Judaism Terminable and Interminable* (New Haven: Yale University Press, 1991), and Dennis Klein, *Jewish Origins of the Psychoanalytic Movement* (New York: Praeger, 1981).

24. To take note of something discernibly new in the prophetic movement within ancient Israel is not to deny the strong impact of syncretism on all aspects of Judaism. Biblical and classical scholars have tended for too long to portray Israel as battling for (good) ethical monotheism over the (bad) polytheism of its neighbors. But while such scholarly idealizations should be exposed, they do not preclude the fact that there is some element in the voices and writings of the prophets that pries Hebrew consciousness away from the milieu of ancient mythologies of origin. Herbert N. Schneidau attempts to delineate this process of differentiation in *Sacred Discontent: The Bible and Western Tradition* (Berkeley: University of California Press, 1977). He argues that inherent in the ancient Hebrew Bible is a liberating alienation experience stemming from the Hebrews' struggle against the place-bound cultures of their neighbors. Although mythology also flourished in Hebrew history, the fact of having a history lent to the mythology "a tendency to turn against itself" (p. 13), thus passing on to Western civilization a demythologizing consciousness which disturbs and eventually undercuts all conventions.

25. Carl A. Raschke, "From Textuality to Scripture: The End of Theology as 'Writing'," *Semeia* 40 (1987): 47.

26. Handelman, *The Slayers of Moses*, p. 223.

27. Ricoeur, "The Critique of Religion," p. 215.

28. Karl Marx, "Contribution to the Critique of Hegel's *Philosophy of Right*: Introduction," *The Marx-Engels Reader*, 2nd ed. , ed. Robert C. Tucker (New York: Norton, 1978), p. 53.

29. Ricoeur, "The Critique of Religion," p. 58.

30. Friedrich Nietzsche, *Beyond Good and Evil*, tr. Walter Kaufmann (New York: Vintage, 1989), p. 2.

31. Nietzsche writes: "We live at the turning point of human time—greatest happiness." Quoted from Karl Jaspers, *Nietzsche and Christianity*, tr. E. B. Ashton (New York: Henry Regnery, 1961), p. 42.

32. On the relation between the prophetic and Protestantism, see Paul Tillich, "The Recovery of the Prophetic Tradition in the Protestant Reformation," *Faith and Thought* 2 (Spring 1984): 3-38. To recall the figure of Marx for a moment, I add here a remark of Paul Ricoeur's that also points to the submerged affiliations between prophetic and Protestant thinking. In "The Critique of Religion," Ricoeur writes: "Marxism, let it never be forgotten, appeared in Germany in the middle of the last century at the heart of the departments of Protestant theology. It is, therefore, an event of western culture, and I would even say, of western theology" (p. 215).

33. Friedrich Nietzsche, *Thus Spake Zarathustra* (II 8) in *The Portable Nietzsche*, tr. Walter Kaufmann (New York: Viking, 1968), p. 216.

34. Karl Jaspers, *Nietzsche and Christianity*, tr. E. B. Ashton (New York: Henry Regnery, 1961). Jaspers writes: "[Nietzsche's] *opposition* to Christianity as a reality is inseparable from his *tie* to Christianity as a postulate . . . . His thinking had grown out of Christianity, spurred by Christianity's own impulses; and his fight against Christianity [sought] . . . to overcome and surpass it . . ." (p. 6). Jaspers quotes a number of passages from the German edition of Nietzsche's writings which show the ambivalence in Nietzsche's relation to Christianity, including this statement: "We are no longer Christians . . . . It is our very *piety*, more rigid and demanding, which today forbids us to be Christians still" (p. 7). Jaspers probably overemphasizes the contradictions in Nietzsche's thought, and Jaspers' reading of his precursor has certainly been surpassed. Yet existentialist philosophers like Jaspers, it seems to me, were able to grasp facets of Nietzsche's writings that have been overlooked in recent poststructuralist versions of him. In the new readings, Nietzsche's answers, his forthrightness about tragedy in life, and his own periodic spirit of "vengeance," are all downplayed. Poststructuralist readings are well represented in *The New Nietzsche*, ed. David B. Allison (Cambridge: MIT Press, 1985). In a fine essay in that collection ("The Will to Power") Alphonso Lingis makes the key point: "If Being . . . is not a ground, but an abyss, chaos, there is consequently in Nietzsche a quite new, nonmetaphysical or transmetaphysical understanding of beings, of things" (p. 38). Greater attention to this basic Nietzschean insight has provided a corrective to previous readings, and it has launched a liberating trend in contemporary hermeneutics by inspiring diverse modes of anti-foundationalism. But perhaps some of Nietzsche's more aristocratic positions have been too neatly disguised as "play" in the process. For a critical review of John Sallis' poststructuralist version of Nietzsche, see David Pan, "The Deconstruction of Tragedy," *Telos* 89 (Fall 1991): 141-54. A volume which, ironically enough, calls into question the new doctrinal

status of the poststructuralist Nietzsche is *Nietzsche and Modern German Thought*, ed. Keith Ansell-Pearson (New York: Routledge, 1990). Of the making of many Nietzsches there would appear to be no end.

35. Ricoeur, "The Critique of Religion," p. 218. Charles Taylor points out the *unconditional* aspect of Nietzsche's yea-saying in *Sources of the Self: The Making of the Modern Identity* (Cambridge: Harvard University Press, 1989), p. 489.

36. Allan Megill, *Prophets of Extremity: Nietzsche, Heidegger, Foucault, Derrida*, p. 35. Megill makes an interesting comparison to Derrida on this score: "In Derrida . . . I see nothing of this mythic moment. If Nietzsche is an ironic mythmaker, Derrida seems only ironic: the radicality of his irony undermines any pretension to myth" (p. 333).

37. Martin Heidegger, *Nietzsche*, Volumes One and Two, tr. David Farrell Krell (San Francisco: HarperCollins, 1991), p. 7. See Krell's "Analysis" of Volume One, p. 233. Heidegger makes his point in reference to aphorism # 617 of Nietzsche's *Will to Power*. In the translation of that passage by Walter Kaufmann (New York: Vintage, 1968), Nietzsche writes: "To impose upon becoming the character of being—that is the supreme will to power. . . . That everything recurs is the closest approximation of a world of becoming to a world of being:—high point of the meditation" (p. 330).

38. Writing in 1932 on the eve of fascism in Germany, Tillich makes some interesting remarks on this issue. "Political romanticism," he observes, "appeals frequently to Nietzsche, and not without justification. . . . There is hardly an intellectual weapon of political romanticism that he did not forge, or at least sharpen. And yet he does not really belong to this movement. . . . He would never have recognized as the harbingers of the future the resentment-laden petit bourgeois groups that stand behind political romanticism." See *The Socialist Decision*, tr. Franklin Sherman (New York: Harper & Row, 1977), pp. 38-39.

39. Paul Ricoeur, "Psychoanalysis and Contemporary Culture," *The Conflict of Interpretations: Essays in Hermeneutics*, ed. Don Ihde (Evanston: Northwestern University Press, 1974), p. 145.

40. David E. Klemm makes this point in *Hermeneutical Inquiry*, Vol. II (Atlanta: Scholars Press, 1986), p. 183.

41. William Carlos Williams, *Autobiography* (New York: New Directions, 1967), p. 360.

42. Martin Heidegger, *On Time and Being*, tr. J. Stambaugh (New York: Harper & Row, 1962), p. 2.

43. Martin Jay, *The Dialectical Imagination: A History of the Frankfurt School and the Institute of Social Research*, 1923-1950 (Boston: Little, Brown, 1973), p. 262.

44. Theodor Adorno, *Minima Moralia,* p. 247. The statement reads as follows: "The only philosophy which can be responsibly practised in the face of despair is the attempt to contemplate all things as they would present themselves from the standpoint of redemption. Knowledge has no light but that shed on the world by redemption: all else is reconstruction, mere technique. Perspectives must be fashioned that displace and estrange the world, reveal it to be, with its rifts and crevices, as indigent and distorted as it will appear one day in the messianic light."

45. Sigmund Freud, *An Outline of Psycho-Analysis,* tr. James Strachey (London: Hogarth Press, 1973), p. 14. Ricoeur, in *The Conflict of Interpretations,* discusses this emphasis of Freud's: "What Freud wants is for the patient to make the meaning which was foreign to him his own and thus enlarge his field of consciousness, live better, and, finally, be a bit freer and, if possible, a bit happier. One of the most important homages rendered to psychoanalysis speaks of the 'cure through consciousness'. Correct—as long as we realize that analysis wants to substitute a mediating consciousness under the tutelage of the reality principle for immediate and deceptive consciousness" (p. 150).

46. Philip Reiff, *Freud: The Mind of the Moralist,* 3rd. Ed. (Chicago: University of Chicago Press, 1979), p. 35.

47. On Heidegger's involvement in National Socialism, see Michael E. Zimmerman, *Heidegger's Confrontation with Modernity: Technology, Politics, and Art* (Bloomington: Indiana University Press, 1990) and Richard Wolin, ed., *The Heidegger Controversy* (New York: Columbia University Press, 1991). On Jung's involvement, see Vincent Brome, *Jung* (New York: Atheneum, 1978), and Farhad Dalal, "The Racism of Jung," *Race and Class* 29 (Winter 1988): 1-22.

48. Otto Rank, *Truth and Reality,* tr. Jessie Taft (New York: Norton, 1978), p. 6.

49. Siegfried Kracauer, *History: The Last Things Before the Last* (New York: Oxford University Press, 1969), p. 201.

50. Christopher Norris, amongst others, has argued for the "ultimately ethical nature of [Derrida's] enterprise" evident in deconstruction's labor of "rigorous demystification." See his *Derrida* (London: Fontana, 1987), pp. 230 and 236. Eve Tavor Bannet claims Derrida's move from ontology to grammatology is highly liberating in that it destroys "nothing less than the ethno-centrism and self-referentiality of the West: the 'mythology of the white man' who takes his own logos for the universal form of reason, who transforms his own consciousness into a universal form of appropriation, who makes everything and everyone the 'same' as himself . . . ." See *Structuralism and the Logic of Dissent: Barthes, Derrida, Foucault, Lacan* (New York: Macmillan, 1989), p. 222. Richard Bernstein also emphasizes the liberating intent of Derrida in "Serious Play: The Ethical-Political Horizon of Jacques Derrida," *Journal of Speculative Philosophy* (forthcoming). For

a contrary view, see Charles Taylor's discussion of the "poverty" of Derrida's position in *Sources of the Self*, pp. 488-89.

51. Peter Dews, *Logics of Disintegration: Poststructuralist Thought and the Claims of Critical Theory* (London: Verso, 1987), p. 43.

52. Hans-Georg Gadamer, *Truth and Method*, 2nd. Rev. Ed. , tr., rev. Joel Weinsheimer and Donald G. Marshall (New York: Crossroad, 1991). For Gadamer's discussions of the "fusion of horizons," see pp. 306, 374, 576-77.

53. For Gadamer, as for Heidegger, being discloses itself only in our historically conditioned language. As Gadamer puts it in *Truth and Method*, "Being that can be understood is language" (p. 475).

54. See Gadamer's essay, "The Universality of the Hermeneutical Problem," in which he states: "What I am describing is the mode of the whole human experience of the world. . . . There is always a world already interpreted, already organized in its basic relations . . .". This essay is collected in *Hermeneutical Inquiry*, Vol. I, ed. David E. Klemm, p. 188. I am indebted to Klemm's fine Introduction to Gadamer in this volume (pp. 173-77).

55. *Dialogue and Deconstruction: The Gadamer-Derrida Encounter*, ed. Diane P. Michelfleder and Richard E. Palmer (Albany: State University of New York Press, 1989).

56. Mark C. Taylor, *Tears* (Albany: State University of New York Press, 1990), p. 135. For an attack along these same lines in *Dialogue and Deconstruction*, see John D. Caputo, "Gadamer's Closet Essentialism: A Derridean Critique," pp. 258-64.

57. Frank Kermode uses this term in "Endings Continued," *Languages of the Unsayable: The Play of Negativity in Literature and Literary Theory*, ed. Sanford Budick and Wolfgang Iser (New York: Columbia University Press, 1989), p. 76. Kermode also seems to have Derrida in mind when he speaks of the "vested interest in . . . interminable deferral" (p. 91). Gary Brent Madison offers an interesting critique of Derrida from a Gadamerian perspective in *The Hermeneutics of Postmodernity: Figures and Themes* (Bloomington: Indiana University Press, 1988), pp. 106-22.

58. Dews, *Logics of Disintegration*, p. 43.

59. Franz Rosenzweig, *The Star of Redemption*, tr. William W. Hallo (Notre Dame, IN: Notre Dame Press, 1985), p. 415.

60. David Tracy makes this point in relation to the religious dimension of culture. "The great mystics," he notes, "have also fashioned powerful hermeneutics of suspicion." See *Plurality and Ambiguity: Hermeneutics, Religion, Hope* (San Francisco: Harper & Row, 1987), p. 111.

61. Luce Irigaray, *Speculum of the Other Woman*, tr. Gillian G. Gill (Ithaca, NY: Cornell University Press, 1985), pp. 191-202.

"A NEW INTERIORITY"

Feminist Theologians, Women Writers, and Question of Salvation

Judith Lee

> We know that our old self was crucified with him so that the sinful body might be destroyed, and we might no longer be enslaved to sin. (Romans 6:6)

> I look on life as a revelation.
>
> Isak Dinesen[1]

Many different voices may be heard among feminist theologians who are committed to taking into account cultural and gender differences in formulating doctrine and liturgy. The publication of several essay collections during the past decade illustrates the wide range of issues that are at the center of this theological debate: essay collections such as *The Politics of Women's Spirituality* (1982), *Womanspirit Rising* (1979 and 1992) and its companion volume *Weaving the Visions: New Patterns in Feminist Spirituality* (1989), *God's Fierce Whimsy: Christian Feminism and Theological Education* (1985), *Feminist Interpretations of the Bible* (1985), *Christian Feminism: Visions of a New Humanity* (1984), *With Passion and Compassion: Third World Women Doing Theology* (1989), *Feminist Theology: A Reader* (1990), and *After Patriarchy* (1991).[2] These essays suggest that there are two major directions in feminist revisionary theology: there are those theologians who embrace non-Christian traditions of spirituality, such as Carol P. Christ, who argues that "women need the Goddess" because only by replacing the male-centered Christian symbolic system can women find representations for their spirituality, and Mary Daly, who celebrates a "metapatriarchal journey of exorcism and ecstacy."[3] Other theologians, such as Rosemary Radford Ruether, Dorothee Soelle, Sallie McFague, and Delores S. Williams, continue in the activist tradition of spiritual writers who have sought renewal within the Jewish and Christian traditions, either by criticizing traditional theology or by offering new theological concepts that encompass socio-political conditions.[4]

These revisionary theologies challenge us to look anew at the dialectic between theology and narrative. By insisting upon the interdependence between the spiritual and material dimensions of our consciousness, they shift the boundaries between theology (which takes as its province the non-narratable) and narrative (which extends the notion of "world" to include all that can be represented). That is, by identifying the *theological* problem to be a problem of *representation*, these theologians deliberately blur the difference between the non-narratable relation that is theology's subject and narrated experience: the narrative, they imply, is not mere analogy or metaphor, but actually determines the way we experience our (non-narratable) spirituality.

The significance of this shift is exemplified in feminist theological writings on salvation because changing our doctrines of salvation involves inventing a new conversion narrative—telling a different story about what constitutes meaningful action and representing differently our relation to divinity and, by implication, to what we call "the world." Indeed, the question of salvation takes us to the heart of the problem of representation that theology and narrative share; the conversion narrative, one might argue, marks the boundary between what can be narrated and what cannot. After a brief overview of the feminist salvation theories, I will look at how several modern writers have negotiated with this boundary in response to traditional Christian models for salvation, with particular attention to several tales by Isak Dinesen.

Feminist critiques of traditional Christian redemption theories center on three subjects: the male imagery used to refer to God and the Christ, the body/spirit dualism that is the basis for concepts of sin and transcendence and that implicitly denigrates the feminine, and the paradigm of salvation as solitary atonement.[5] Recent debate has centered on two interrelated questions. The first has to do with the fact that women have traditionally been identified as the occasion of sin and the obstacle to redemption, whether mythologically in the figure of Eve or more generally in being associated with sexuality and material desire. As a result, some feminist theologians argue, we must reformulate our definition of sin by differentiating between the moral dilemmas facing men and women. Having done this, we can replace the idea of atonement with the idea of healing in a paradigm that reflects spiritual parity between men and women.

Valerie Saiving introduced this line of argument in a 1960 essay, "The Human Situation: A Feminine View." Pointing out that concepts of the self are culturally determined, Saiving argued that traditional theological theories of both sin and salvation are based upon assumptions that may accurately characterize the moral dilemmas confronted by men but do not address those that are specific to women:

> For the temptations of woman *as woman* are not the same as the temptations of man *as man*, and the specifically feminine forms of sin—"feminine" not because they are confined to women or because women are incapable of sinning in other ways but because they are outgrowths of the basic feminine character structure—have a quality which can never be encompassed by such terms as "pride" and "will-to-power." They are better suggested by such items as . . . lack of an organizing center or focus; dependence on others for one's own self-definition . . . in short, underdevelopment or negation of the self.[6]

Other feminist theologians have extended Saiving's argument. Judith Plaskow has proposed that "sin" involves *failing* to turn toward oneself, and Dorothee Soelle urges us to recognize that complicity in unjust social systems constitutes sin.[7] Rosemary Radford Ruether has perhaps been the most outspoken theologian to argue that sexism is "the root expression of sin" because in denying women's equivalent personhood with men, sexism engenders systemic structures that falsify the relation between God and humankind, normalizing and perpetuating the alienation traditionally identified with sin.[8] In working toward a systemic theology in an ecological context, Sallie McFague identifies sin with the plunder and pollution of "the body of the world."[9] Emphasizing instead the importance of making our relatedness the basis for our theology, Catherine Keller has explored the interdependence between the theology of sin and those conceptions of God that presuppose a hierarchical relationship and division between human and divine:

> Thus the God of the fathers, or God the Father, reveals a pure structure of reflexive selfhood: self-knowing

> rendered infinite and exact by his own immutability.
> Because he cannot be affected, he is the perfect object to
> himself: his self-objectification circulates around the
> eternal self-enclosure of his self-identity. But a bizarre
> double standard confronts us here: The traditional God is
> the absolute instance of traditional sin.[10]

Because we have in effect deified self-sufficiency and separatist individuality, Keller argues, changing God-language is not an adequate response to the limits of traditional Christian theology; instead, drawing upon Whitehead's doctrine of mutual transcendence, she proposes that we replace the idea of solitary selfhood with what she calls "relational spirituality." Within this framework, "God-talk" would presume the interdependence between creator and creature, and moral questions would derive from our sense of relatedness.

These feminist redefinitions of sin do not generate theories of salvation that merely celebrate the body and the sexuality that are devalued in traditional theology. Rather, assuming that spirituality and social responsibility are interdependent, many feminist theologians argue that we must replace self-transcendence with healing as the metaphor for salvation. All these redemption theories involve conceptions of identity that involve the body and relatedness. Daphne Hampson explains, "Rather than breaking the self, women, it may be suggested, need to come to themselves. . . . If women's ills have been the result of an undervaluation of the self, then their healing must consist in self-actualization. . . . Salvation in these circumstances is to come to have self-worth."[11] Sallie McFague succinctly summarizes the conceptual changes that are involved in changing to this model: by presuming that the health of bodies is a condition for other kinds of well-being, it diminishes the split between body and spirit so important in traditional Christian redemption theories; since "health" involves achieving a balance both within oneself and in one's relations, this model calls attention to one's ethical responsibility to others; it represents a process that may be lengthy rather than a "quick cure"; and finally, it emphasizes our individual responsibility to participate actively in "making whole again the ruptured body of the world," work that cannot be done by some other (paradigmatic) persons.[12]

With their differences, feminist theories of redemption are thus ministerial rather than sacrificial, shifting the center from a surrogate to individual agency. Pointing out that African-American women's surrogacy roles make traditional Christian models of redemption problematic, for example, Delores S. Williams replaces the traditional Christian sacrificial model with a ministerial model based upon the wilderness experience that is central to African-American religious traditions:

> The image of Jesus on the cross is the image of human sin in its most desecrated form. . . . Jesus, then, does not conquer sin through death on the cross. Rather, Jesus conquers the sin of temptation in the wilderness (Matthew 4:1-11) by resistance. . . . In the wilderness he refused to allow evil forces to defile the balanced relation between the material and the spiritual, between life and death, between power and the exertion of it.[13]

Jesus' resistance and endurance in the wilderness present a narrative paradigm in which salvation involves acting in the world, "righting relations" through ethical speech, healing touch, militant resistance, prayer, and compassion.

This connection between healing and social change underlies Rosemary Radford Ruether's argument that thinking about salvation must center on our worldly (socio-political) relations:

> We cannot split a spiritual, antisocial redemption from the human being as a social being embedded in socio-political and ecological systems. But neither can we imagine a reconstructed social order without converted selves. Feminism recognizes sinfulness as an expression of precisely this splitting and deformation of our true relationships with all the networks of being with which we are connected. . . .
>
> Thus a feminist liberation spirituality, while seeking a new, nonsexist social order, cannot neglect the cultivation of a new interiority. . . . We must enter into a process in which the liberated self and the transformation of social systems are interconnected.[14]

Ruether thus advocates political change brought about not by acting on the world but by acting in the world—affirming our worldliness.

The "new interiority" of which Ruether speaks is the subject of all feminist reflections upon theology and spirituality as we explore and experiment with ways to grow spiritually through being-in-the-world rather than by transcending it, embracing our relationships as the origin and occasion for our spirituality. From this point of view, it is imperative that we invent new representations that will bring into being and make available new relations and new processes of transformation.

Recent scholarship has suggested that Native American spiritual traditions provide a framework for doing this. Different Native American traditions share the beliefs that the physical world is sacred, that humans participate in a non-hierarchical relationship with non-humans and have with them a divine responsibility for continuing the process of creation. With these assumptions, "conversion" involves an initiation into the mysteries of our relationship to our fellow-creature in the physical world. At the risk of oversimplifying, Paula Gunn Allen points out the fundamental difference in Christian spirituality: "[T]he Indian universe moves and breathes continuously, and the Western universe is fixed and static. The Christian attitude toward salvation reflects this basic stance: one can be "saved" only if one believes in a Savior who appeared once and will not come again until "the end of time."[15] The experience of immanence and relatedness that is at the center of all Native American spiritual traditions implies that conversion is a return, recuperating what has been forgotten (though not lost) and integrating one's pleasure and pain as opposed to transcending them.

In *Daughters of Copper Woman*, a collection of fables, myths, poems and tales told by women belonging to a secret society among the Nootka Indians living on Vancouver Island, Anne Cameron proposes a model of conversion based upon this non-Christian spirituality. Although Cameron makes no mention of religious belief, she suggests a correspondence between reading, relatedness, and conversion that calls for reimagining what constitutes meaningful action and for renegotiating the boundaries of the narratable.

There are several different discourses in *Daughters of Copper Woman*. The first ten pieces are tales about a mythical past told from the point of view of an anonymous storyteller; they describe the arrival of Copper Woman on the island where the Nootka now live, the origin of the human races, the emergence of Old Woman, and the evolution of women's rituals based upon these myths. The second nine pieces are narrated by a young woman named Ki-Ki who is transcribing stories told by her grandmother. Cameron intersperses poems among these tales, and she frames them with a preface and an afterword in which she writes as a witness who has been granted a special trust: "These women shared their stories with me because they knew I would not use them without their permission. . . . The style I have chosen most clearly approaches the style in which the stories were given to me."[16] Thus, although Cameron claims responsibility for the text, she disavows any authority that it might bring to her. In the afterword, she urges the reader to turn away from the book itself and to practice the way of reading that the tales have exemplified: "Anyone who appropriates these stories by re-telling or adapting them is betraying the trust in which they were offered. Look instead into your own history/herstory: what you need is in the stories of your sisters, mothers, aunts, grandmothers, foremothers."[17] The private act of reading, she hopes, has brought a spiritual awakening to the gifts and responsibilities of our earthly and human bonds.

In two very different accounts, the transformation of Old Woman, which is the central mystery of this mythology, becomes a metaphor for a way of reading that will be a conversion experience because it involves a confrontation with the non-narratable. In "Qolus the Changeable," Copper Woman's transformation into Old Woman contrasts to the apparently instantaneous transformation of a goddess into man, and it explains the origin of the matrilineal culture within the Nootka. Qolus, queen of heaven, surrenders her supernatural powers to become First Man when she tires of heaven and desires to participate in earthly events; Qolus does not retain her feminine nature in her transformation; she *becomes* male. However, Copper Woman does not entirely change into Old Woman; rather, Old Woman becomes visible in Copper Woman. The transformation is described in language that locates mystery in Copper Woman's *physical* change, and reading her new body-text becomes a paradigm for the kind of reading/conversion that Cameron's book itself proposes:

> Then the daughter [one of Mowita's daughters, a Child of
> Happiness] with the green eyes, whose name is known

> only to the initiates, lay down on a bed of skins, and Old
> Woman, hidden in the skins, became pregnant. From this
> the green-eyed daughter lived as part of Old Woman, who
> was also part of and in her. And there is no easy answer to
> the questions and puzzlement that comes with being told
> this, the answer lies within each of us, and we much each
> find that answer for ourselves.[18]

Copper Woman both is and is not Old Woman; Old Woman both is and is not a physical being. She is an entity, a spiritual principle, and a state into which some women evolve. The grotesque image is an unreadable text signifying the sacredness and mutability of the body; it is a riddle that makes sense only if we turn *away* from it and surrender our need for certitude.

Another transformation occurs in "The Face of Old Woman" as part of the narrator's own initiation as a writer. After Granny tells Ki-Ki to write down the stories she has told because the sacred knowledge should be kept secret no longer, Old Woman suddenly manifests herself in Granny:

> Her face was hard-edged, her mouth looked like the top of
> a drawstring bag that's been pulled shut, all puckered and
> lined, and thousands of years old. I stared into the face of
> Old Woman, and felt the chair under me start to melt
> away, the table disappear, until there was just Old Woman
> talking with my Granny's voice, but Granny's voice
> altered, just Old Woman and me, alone in a place that
> wasn't the kitchen of the house I live in.[19]

Like the descriptions of Copper Woman's transformation into Old Woman, this passage shows both the physical nature of Granny's transformation and the absolute presence of Old Woman. Granny both is and is not Old Woman.

More particularly, Ki-Ki's initiation involves being able to *read* Granny's face, a text that has suddenly become strange, and with that reading comes the understanding that her writing will restore the spiritual community of women now dispersed throughout the world: "And I knew then, and know now, that what we have protected on this island is not complete, the knowledge is scattered, and if we offer all women what we know, the scattered pieces can start to re-form, and those who need to find courage, peace, truth and love will learn that these things are inside all of us, and can be supported by the truth of women."[20] Engendered by Granny/Old Woman in the same way that Old Woman entered Copper Woman and women of subsequent generations, Ki-Ki's poems, songs, and fables can be decoded only by readers who already have a knowledge they have forgotten.

Daughters of Copper Woman thus offers a conversion narrative that centers on the earth, the body, and human relationships. Ki-Ki's conversion is a turning toward a world she had previously devalued, a world so irreparably flawed that any spiritual life could be sustained only in isolation and in fantasy, and Cameron offers the book itself as a means by which readers can return to relationships and stories they may have ignored. The spirituality underlying this alternative model for redemption is perhaps best exemplified in the story "Tem Eyos Ki." This story takes place many generations after the emergence of Old Woman and before the arrival of the Europeans. Women had complacently turned their attention exclusively to educating the children and nurturing the spiritual life of the community, leaving decisions about governance to the men, who then began to dominate. One day, Tem Eyos Ki came from the waiting house (where the women went during their "sacred time" each month) singing a song that filled the other women with such profound longing that they left their homes and tasks to follow her. When the men saw the women following Tem Eyos Ki, they became angry and threatened to silence her, but Tem Eyos Ki flew away in a magic dugout sent by Qolus the Changeable. The men and women then resolved to live once again as Copper Woman had taught them, but each woman continues to experience a longing that she cannot express. Like the song of Tem Eyos Ki, *Daughters of Copper Woman* brings not certainty but longing, and it expresses the salvific power of the desire and sense of displacement at the core of human relationships.

Although Cameron makes no reference to Christian theology and does not frame her narratives in terms of theological questions, her attention to the connections between gender, representation, and spirituality places her work among that of feminist theologians and writers who have responded more explicitly to Christian paradigms. She calls for a "new interiority" that centers on our discovery of our earthly relatedness rather than on a mystical union with a transcendent godhead. As Elizabeth A.

Johnson has put it, "The category of conversion [in feminist re-visions] receives a description somewhat different from that of classical theology where it typically connotes the process of disowning oneself or divesting oneself in order to be filled with divine grace. . . . It involves a turning away from demeaning female identity toward new ownership of the female self as God's good gift."[21]

In the context of these reflections upon gender and spirituality, a woman-centered revisionary mythos would not represent an individual act of atonement or sacrifice, nor would it center on a moment of *turning away* from the mundane and the material. This would not be a story about a crisis of the body, nor would it depict an escape from the bonds and bounds of one's relationships. Re-presenting healing and world-transformation, this narrative would replace a single act or a single moment of revelation with a sequence of discoveries and constructions, culminating in an open, perhaps inconclusive, ending. Mary Catherine Bateson, for example, deliberately offers an alternative to what she calls the "pilgrimage" model of a life in her memoir *Composing A Life*, proposing that women's lives exemplify the new "compositions" that we must create out of changing working patterns and revised personal expectations.[22] We also find versions of this alternative to "confession" in May Sarton's memoirs and journals, which do not follow a teleological model or celebrate significant actions in tracing the quiet processes of self-discovery through living with illness and in relation; similarly, Madeleine L'Engle's three-part autobiography *The Crosswick Journal* weaves together reflections and anecdotes in a non-linear form within its chronology.[23]

The novels of Virginia Woolf and Doris Lessing show the narratological experimentation required and made possible by shifting to a woman-centered conversion narrative even without drawing upon any Christian pre-text. In Woolf's *Mrs. Dalloway* and *To The Lighthouse*, for example, epiphanies constitute brief and temporary illuminations of a woman's psycho-sexual wholeness, made possible by her relationship with an uncomprehending Other and experienced in the distance and difference that make that relationship otherwise problematic; and in her novels of the sixties and seventies (particularly her Martha Quest novels), Doris Lessing displaces contemporary psychological models that secularize and trivialize women's spirituality.[24] Margaret Atwood's novel *Surfacing* transforms the mythos of the fall into a woman's journey literally into the earth, culminating in a grotesque bodily transformation that is a sign of spiritual apotheosis.[25]

Other modern writers have drawn upon the New Testament to write conversion narratives that celebrate women's experience. In very different re-visions, for example, H.D. (Hilda Doolittle) and Clysta Kinstler have made Mary Magdalen the central character of the gospel story, and Rachel Ingalls has written a comic story about a modern Annunciation in "Blessed Art Thou."[26] In this story, a young monk has intercourse with a young man who has wings, and afterwards gradually turns into a pregnant woman. The presence of a woman and her overt sexuality cause more trouble in the monastery than the theological questions raised by this second Annunciation.

Alice Walker has experimented with alternative conversion narratives by insisting upon the distinction between the patriarchal institution of Christianity that justifies domination and the spiritual teachings of Jesus that are compatible with pagan and matriarchal teachings. The epistolary structure of *The Color Purple* recreates the non-linear and oft-interrupted process of a woman's spiritual life. Comprised of a series of letters from the abused and longsuffering Celie to God and to her sister Nettie, it traces Celie's loss of faith in a God she imagines to be male and her recovery of faith through experiencing a more pantheistic spirituality. We know Celie's conversion has occurred when she begins her final letter to God, written after she has been reunited with her sister and her family, as follows: "Dear God. Dear stars, dear trees, dear sky, dear peoples. Dear Everything. Dear God."[27]

In her more recent novels, Walker more explicitly contrasts this kind of conversion to the traditional Christian model. Her purpose is particularly clear in *The Temple Of My Familiar*, when Celie's daughter Olivia describes the "conversion" undergone by her own family while they worked as Christian missionaries in Africa:

> We had begun to see, in Africa—where people worshiped many things, including the roofleaf plant, which they used to cover their houses—that "God" was not a monolith, and not the property of Moses, as we'd been led

> to think, and not separate from us, or absent from
> whatever world one inhabited. . . .
> The religion that one discovered on one's own was a
> story of the earth, the cosmos, creation itself; and
> whatever "Good" one wanted could be found not down
> the long road of eternity, but right in one's own town,
> one's home, one's country. *This world.* After all, since
> this world is a planet spinning about in the sky, we are all
> of us *in heaven* already![28]

Throughout this novel, Walker refers to the matriarchal religions in Africa
and South America that were repressed and replaced by patriarchal
religions—primarily Islam and Christianity—but vestiges of which can be
found in the alternative spiritual practices invented by women of color.
The "Gospel According To Shug," for example, is a re-vision of the
Beatitudes, a series of aphorisms describing a relational spirituality that
involves both autonomy and compassion: "Helped are those who love the
stranger. . . . Helped are those who are content to be themselves. . . .
Helped are those who love others unsplit off from their faults. . . . Helped
are those whose every act is a prayer for harmony in the Universe."[29] The
pamphlet on which this "Gospel" is written becomes an analog for the
novel itself, a "temple" that is, like other churches formed by black women,
"not a building or any kind of monument, but simply a few words . . . like
spiritual rice grains."[30]

Walker returns to these ideas in *Possessing the Secret of Joy*, showing
the inadequacy of the Christian redemption myth in accounting for the
suffering of the oppressed. The central character, Tashi, realizes this in a
conversion that affirms the reality and injustice of her own suffering
during the years following her clitorectomy:

> I am a great lover of Jesus, and always have been. Still, I
> began to see how the constant focus on the suffering of
> Jesus alone excludes the suffering of others from one's
> view. And in my sixth year as a member of Adam's
> congregation I knew I wanted my own suffering, the
> suffering of women and little girls, still cringing before the
> overpowering might and weapons of the torturers, to be
> the subject of a sermon. Was woman herself not the tree
> of life? And was she not crucified? Not in some age no
> one even remembers, but right now, daily, in many lands
> on earth?[31]

Tashi's conversion, like Celie's and Olivia's, involves an affirmation both of her own selfhood and of her relatedness with others; by rejecting the belief that her suffering is private and individual, Tashi discovers both the suffering and the beauty of her fellow beings. She turns away from the transcendent Christ and turns toward this world and time.

The tales of Isak Dinesen are very different revisionary conversion narratives. Both the Old and New Testaments are important subtexts in Dinesen's tales, and in her fiction, essays, and letters she engaged in an ongoing dialogue on Christianity in which she addressed the same issues as are at the center of the current feminist theological debate (assumptions about the female body, sin,and transcendence). Particularly important for our discussion is Dinesen's insistence upon the complementarity of theology and narrative: she rejected the subordination of story that is implicit in traditional distinctions between secular and sacred texts and in narrative's analogical function for theology, but she did not claim for narrative itself the transforming power that has been implied by recent feminist theological discussion. For Dinesen, both theology and story derive from the same desire—to believe—and they mark out the same ontological uncertainties that she called "the gifts and mysteries of this life."[32]

Dinesen's main objection to Christianity was the authority vested in what she considered "a collection of mythological notions and tales."[33] More precisely, she rejected the certitude offered by the Christian doctrine of atonement. She wrote in *On Modern Marriage*:

> One immerses oneself in the history of the salvation-bringing Church with increasing wonder at its ability to make human beings sacrifice their own and others' dearest wishes and vital necessities merely by its assurance that they will thereby receive salvation. In the end one asks: "And were they saved?" . . . and is answered: "No, probably they were not saved, but through these enormous sacrifices they did manage to be more satisfied than you seem to be."[34]

Encouraging a relation of dependence and the abdication of personal responsibility, the Christian doctrine of atonement offers mere escapism, according to Dinesen; more importantly, it encourages hypocrisy. She wrote to her sister Ellen in 1928:

> For two thousand years human beings have felt gratitude to Christ because he "sacrificed himself" for them; but I really think there would be very few who would not, if they were offered the chance this very afternoon,—even if they were directly confronted with flaming Hell and eternal damnation,—rush up and say: for Heaven's sake do not take that upon yourself.[35]

Indeed, Dinesen objected more strongly to what she saw to be Christianity's bourgeois complacency than to its moral ideology. As she put it in a speech she gave on her sixty-fifth birthday: "Has not Christianity excluded the enthusiasm over the gifts and mysteries of this life, renounced and repressed our sensuality? And thereby blocked us out of the spiritual world on the only conditions that we have?"[36]

But Dinesen also objected to using the Christian redemption narrative as a fictional subtext on aesthetic principles as well. In a 1949 essay on a novel by H. C. Branner (*The Riding Master*), she explored the disjunctions between myth and mystery. Branner's novel is flawed, she argues, because it centers on an idealized Christ figure whose sacrifice gives the novel a closure that is too predictable. Branner thereby ignores, and implicitly denies, the desire that underlies the gospel—the desire animated by the *promise* of salvation: "The promise of salvation through blood recurs in untold ages of man and among innumerable peoples. And deep in the mind of manifold ages of man and peoples has lain the faith and the expectations of the miracle: the solitary figure who is able to redeem everyman by himself assuming the guilt of everyman."[37] By assigning divinity to the historical Jesus or by idealizing him in secular narratives, she argues, both theologians and novelists "make capital of him" and offer "redemption by anaesthesia."[38] Dinesen insists upon restating the Christological paradox: if we say that God became human, then the ministry of Jesus was like any other labor; as such, it exemplifies the miracle of *human* love, not of divine love.

Dinesen returns repeatedly to this paradox in her fiction. "Sorrow-acre" and "Alkmene," two of her most complex and ambiguous tales, are particularly important to our discussion because in each one Dinesen treats ironically the New Testament's authority as a mastertext by positing the kind of connection between gender, textuality, and reading that informs *Daughters of Copper Woman* and, like Walker's novels, each centers on the opposition between denying and sacralizing the world. "Sorrow-acre" explores the necessary incertitude that comes from reading metaphorically—from assuming that there is an unreadable, non-narratable gap between text and meaning; "Alkmene," in contrast, explores the implications of reading literally.

"Sorrow-acre" is based on two versions of a Jutland folk tale about events taking place during a flood that occurred in 1634. In Dinesen's version of the tale, a young man, Goske, is accused of setting fire to the lord's barn, and the lord agrees not to press charges if Goske's mother, Anne-Marie, will harvest a rye field between sunrise and sunset. During the day, the lord and his nephew Adam argue about the justice and morality of the lord's bargain with Anne-Marie; she accomplishes her task but collapses in her son's arms when she has finished, and it is unclear whether or not she knows that she has successfully redeemed her son.

Named after the grandmother and mother of Jesus, echoing the figure of Demeter figure as she goes back and forth across the field, Anne-Marie clearly signifies a shift from a patriarchal to a matrilineal myth.[39] She is a disturbing redemptive figure, however. For one thing, she is no idealized mother. Rumor has it that she long ago had a child whom she killed, and since Goske is her only means of survival she is motivated as much by self-interest as by maternal love. And because his innocence or guilt is never established (he is accused by two men who resent and suspect him for other reasons), her act has no moral significance whatsoever. The final scene, in which Anne-Marie falls into her son's arms "like a sheaf of corn that falls to the ground" mirrors the scene of Jesus cradled in Mary's arms.[40] The Pieta represents the Christ's paradoxical nature as divine and human; the image of a death that is not a death, it represents the unfathomable joy and grief brought by the crucifixion. When Anne-Marie simply touches her son's cheek and feels his tears, giving no sign that she has understood the lord's pronouncement that Goske is free, she embodies an uncertainty about the value of human action diametrically opposed to the idea of redemption signified by Pieta. While the Pieta is a figure for the mystery of divine love, this tableau is a figure for the mystery of *human* relationships.

Dinesen does not merely replace the divine Father-and-Son with a flawed human mother-and-son and substitute the mother's sacrifice for the son's, moreover. Her metaphors of textuality challenge the authority of Scripture itself. One of the tale's important subtexts is the opening line of the Gospel of John ("In the beginning was the Word . . ."). The debate between the lord and Adam about the justice of Anne-Marie's labor centers on their different readings of this line. Reading it literally, the lord bases his own authority on the belief that Scripture is the origin of all human order and stability; he argues that his own word has an equivalent power and authority to determine all social relations upon which the culture is based. Adam, on the other hand, argues that even the scriptural Word itself originates in human desire and imagination, disruptive powers far greater than (human) law.

Dinesen treats ironically the lord's claim to power, and by extension the belief in the divine authority of Scripture, by opening the tale with two "texts" that oppose the "word" that authorizes him. She uses metaphors of textuality in a long description of the landscape to locate the origins of culture in primal forces and desire anterior to human consciousness and language. In the beginning was not "the Word" but a landscape with a "timeless life, to which language was inadequate."[41] The design of meadows, windmills, and buildings is a hieroglyph of human desire: "writing in the sky [that] solemnly proclaimed continuance, a worldly immortality."[42] Juxtaposed against this text (which a child could read "like a book") is the unreadable text of a woman's body; for the legitimacy of the (patrilineal) culture depends upon the unverifiable word of women, "who carried the future of the name in their laps and were, like dignified and debonair caryatides, holding up the houses."[43]

In the end, these cultural texts are themselves subordinated to the incomprehensible pattern of relations that constitutes creation. Adam experiences a conversion in which he recognizes that this system of signs is itself the Word:

> He saw the ways of life, he thought, as a twined and
> tangled design, complicated and mazy; it was not given to
> him or any mortal to command or control it. Life and

> death, happiness and woe, the past and the present, were
> interlaced within the pattern. Yet to the initiated it might
> be read as easily as our ciphers—which to the savage must
> seem confused and incomprehensible—will be read by the
> schoolboy. And out of the contrasting elements concord
> rose.[44]

Adam's conversion thus involves the ability to *read* the text of the world itself. That is, the World is the Word, of mysterious origin and with an undecipherable signature. This subordination of both transcendent Word and patriarchal Scripture to the polyvalent world-text is continued in the tale's epilogue, where we are told that the lord had a stone marker inscribed with a sickle erected in the field; afterward, the peasants named the field "sorrow-acre," the name by which it is known "a long time after the story of the woman and her son had itself been forgotten."[45] The lord's sign becomes separate from the story, which itself eventually disappears. We are left with a field, a stone, and a name—signs of the inescapable earthly origins of both story and doctrine.

In "Sorrow-acre," then, Dinesen treats the Christian theory of ransom ironically by representing a redemptive bargain that undermines certitude and sacralizes the world. From this point of view, even though both doctrine and story express the human desire for order, it is through story that we glimpse the sacred, unreadable and destabilizing mystery of living-in-the-world. In "Alkmene," the title character herself is ultimately an unreadable text because she literally enacts the Christian belief in the need for atonement. Alkmene is a strange girl of unknown parentage who is adopted by a parson and his wife, Jens and Gertrud Jesperson; the narrator of the tale is Vilhelm, whose father owns the estate on which Jens and Gertrud live. Alkmene unaccountably inherits a fortune, which upon some reflection Jens agrees to accept for her, despite recognizing the temptation it poses, because he believes that he will live on in the good works she will perform with the money. After he dies, however, Alkmene uses the money to buy a sheep farm that she runs with Gertrud, becoming legendary for her solitary and parsimonious way of life.

Alkmene represents the possibility of redemption to Jens, Gertrud, and Vilhelm because she fulfills their "expectation of a miracle." She seems to be a sign of Providence: named after the mother of Hercules, she promises the"earthly immortality" of a heroic lineage; arriving after Gertrud had despaired of having children, she is a reminder that God blessed Sarah and Abraham with the birth of Isaac; and her mysterious past makes her a kind of fairy-tale princess. When she refuses to conform to their expectations by being silent, moody, and restless, she embodies a female subjectivity for which they have no language.

One of Alkmene's most disturbing characteristics is her insistence upon interpreting literally the doctrine of atonement. Soon after her father's death, she asks Vilhelm to accompany her to Copenhagen so that she can witness the execution of a notorious murderer. She repeats the question that Jens himself had posed about sin: "And who can say of himself: of this deed I could never have been guilty?" This execution, she explains to Vilhelm, is "a warning to the people who may be near to doing the same thing themselves, and who will be warned by nothing else."[46] Following literally the code that all human beings share inherited guilt, Alkmene admits not that she has murderous intentions but that she is capable of murder. The episode might be glossed by Dinesen's remark much later in "H. C. Branner: *The Riding Master*": "What an impressive admission the suffering and dying thief on the cross makes when he recognizes that 'we are indeed here justly, for we receive the due rewards of our deeds,' and exclaims, 'Jesus, remember me when thou comest into thy kingdom!'"[47] If we are to take the doctrine of atonement literally, saying that Jesus substituted for each of us in assuming our guilt, then we must recognize in ourselves not only the ability to endure crucifixion but the capacity to commit acts that would warrant it. This is what Alkmene does. She does not follow the other observers, who dip cloths in the blood of the corpse in the belief it would cure "the falling sickness" (a reference to epilepsy that ironically refers to the "sickness" of believing in a "fall" that would be "cured" by the Redeemer's blood). By literally living in atonement for her own complicity with forces of evil that exist before and beyond her agency, Alkmene contradicts a doctrine of atonement that would alleviate her responsibility. In doing so, she provides a view of the world as a place from which there is no exit, a dangerous place where mystery may not have meaning.

Not all of Dinesen's tales are as austere as these, however, and many of those tales that turn on an ironic view of Christian moral principles treat female sexuality and healing with a wry humor. I want to discuss two of these. "The Heroine" (also in *Winter's Tales*) is a parody of the Christian redemption story in which a woman's body is as sacred as the body of Christ, and "The Cardinal's Third Tale" (in *Last Tales*) draws upon the healing metaphor to represent salvation ironically. In these tales, as in "Alkmene," Dinesen assigns to female protagonists a position equivalent to that of the Christ in the Christian narrative: just as idealizing Jesus dehumanizes the historical figure because it denies his capacity for choice, idealizing women dehumanizes them because it denies their subjectivity.

Early notes for "The Heroine" suggest that it originated in Dinesen's queries about the Christian redemption narrative: "If he [Jesus] could, by dying in captivity [without enduring the crucifixion], relieve all the captives of the earth, would he do it?"[48] Heloise, the tale's redemptive figure, is one of a group of tourists stranded at the French/German border when the Franco-Prussian war begins. The German officer in charge announces that all their lives will be spared if Heloise will come to him naked. Refusing to be an object of exchange or a sacrificial victim, however, Heloise asks her companions to decide what she should do; they adamantly protest that their lives are not worth such a price, and they are released in any case. Several years later one of the group returns to Paris, where Heloise stars in a popular musical review called "Diana's Revenge." When they meet, Heloise admits that she turned to her companions on that day because she knew they would never allow her to do what the German officer asked. Not only does she save her own life by challenging them to sacrifice it but, paradoxically, she "redeems" them by refusing to be their redeemer. She explains: "They would have made me do it, to save their lives, if he had put it straight to them at first, or if they had been left to themselves. And then they would never have got over it. They would have repented it all their lives, and have held themselves to be great sinners."[49]

By substituting a female body for the Body of Christ here, Dinesen dismantles the traditional religious identification between sin and female sensuality. If the body is a "temple," then it is not merely a *sign* of the sacred but is itself as sacred as the Body of Christ. It is specifically because of her physical beauty that Heloise assumes a divine presence and brings about a spiritual awakening in those who observe her. Before going their separate ways, the small company shares "a hurried, spare meal of bread and wine" to honor Heloise: "Heloise was still the central figure of their communion, but in a new way, as an object infinitely precious to them all. Her pride, her glory was theirs, since they had been ready to die for it."[50] This final "eucharist" celebrates their mortality and relatedness, their sacred and redemptive relationships with each other.

In "The Cardinal's Third Tale," Dinesen's use of the healing metaphor anticipates current feminist theologies in more complex ways.[51] The Cardinal describes the adversarial relationship between the arrogant and sophisticated Lady Flora and the humble village priest Father Jacopo, who engage in a series of debates on the nature of human existence and salvation. Lady Flora is disdainfully impatient with Father Jacopo's idealistic vision of human and cosmic harmony, while he is both mystified and horrified at her irreverence. The daughter of a philandering man who taunted his wife because she was unusually large (as she herself is), Lady Flora resolves to remain celibate and solitary. Just before leaving Rome after a period of convalescence for an injured ankle, however, she contracts syphilis when she kisses the foot of the statue of Saint Peter just after another pilgrim has done so. The Cardinal describes her at their last meeting, at a resort for syphilitics, where she had taken her place comfortably among a human company she had previously shunned and where she had acquired a sense of humor: ". . . a new joviality, a mirthful forbearance with and benevolence toward the frailty of humanity. . . . [M]ystically, she had become a maiden—an old maid."[52]

In the end, among an exiled and fallen (infected) body of people, Lady Flora achieves in her bodily disfigurement "a new interiority" and thus presents the tale's true paradox: ". . . even persons of true genuine dullness will *know* every body and soul in our universe to be infinite!" (emphasis added).[53] Body *and* soul are infinite and, implicitly, sacred. Lady Flora has discovered the "true humanity" that Father Jacopo had described: "[T]here exists a true humanity, which will ever remain a gift, and which is to be accepted by one human being as it is given to him by a fellow human. The one who gives has himself been a receiver."[54] She has given and received, of course, a sign of love that would have horrified Father Jacopo.

By ending the tale with Lady Flora's own unanswered question about her sore, Dinesen transforms the sign of sickness, sexuality, and bodily decay into a sign of redemptive self-realization: "To what, I thought, does this bear a likeness? To a rose? Or to a seal?" Lady Flora restates the paradox of the Song of Songs that Father Jacopo had used as proof of the divine origins of all creation ("Aye, and does not the rose clearly exhibit to our eyes the signature of the workshop from which she is issued?").[55] Lady Flora's question inverts Father Jacopo's analogy: if, as in the Song of Songs, we celebrate sexuality as a figure for mystical love, then we establish an equivalence in which the reverse holds: sexual love is as sacred as mystical love, and the sign of one equally signifies the other. Unlike Father Jacopo, Lady Flora sees mystery in the rose/sore because it is an *illegible* "signature." Indeed, by her name she embodies the riddle her experience presents to her. This "flower" is herself a sign of what cannot be explained—the disturbing and inescapable mystery of the pain and dis-figuring to be endured in salvific healing.

These theological and narrative re-readings of the Christian conversion narrative provide a model for negotiating between what I find to be the self-denying materiality of post-structuralist feminist theories on the one hand and body-denying essentialism of more traditional theology on the other. Whatever their disagreements, feminist theologians affirm the substantiality of the "I," and they assume that personhood is not incompatible with relatedness or with effecting social change. Indeed, it is in their insistence upon the transforming power of our individual stories and spirituality that their models of healing differ from the idea of *jouissance* and *ecriture feminine*—which make the body into an animated object that cannot be possessed but that has no interiority. At the same time, these writers' insistence upon the difference between story and doctrine, between myth and mystery, provides a model for "depatriarchalizing" the Christian myth without secularizing it.[56] If we allow ourselves to tell our stories in our own time, we can do two things: we can recontextualize theology to account for the specific cultural conditions that inform our spirituality, and we can also recontextualize our interpretation of narratives to account for the spirituality—the interiority—they cannot represent.

NOTES

1. Quoted by Thomas Dinesen in *My Sister, Isak Dinesen*, tr. Joan Tate (London: Michael Joseph, 1975), p. 58.

2. Ed. Charlene Spretnak, *The Politics of Women's Spirituality: Essays on the Rise of Spiritual Power Within the Feminist Movement* (New York: Doubleday, 1982); ed. Carol P. Christ and Judith Plaskow *Womanspirit Rising* (1979; New York: Harper and Row, 1992), and *Weaving the Visions: New Patterns in Feminist Spirituality* (New York: Harper and Row, 1989); ed. The Mud Flower Collective, *God's Fierce Whimsy: Christian Feminism and Theological Education*, (New York: Pilgrim Press, 1985); ed. Judith Weidman, *Christian Feminism: Visions of a New Humanity* (New York: Harper and Row, 1984); ed. Virginia Fabella & Mercy Amba Oduyoye, *With Passion and Compassion: Third World Women Doing Theology*, (Maryknoll, NY: Orbis Books, 1989); ed. Ann Loades, *Feminist Theology: A Reader*, (Louisville: Westminster/John Knox, 1990); ed. Paula M. Cooey, William R. Eakin, & Jay B. MacDonald, *After Patriarchy*, (Maryknoll, NY: Orbis Books, 1991).

3. Carol P. Christ, "Why Women Need the Goddess: Phenomenological, Psychological, and Political Reflections," in *Womanspirit Rising*, pp. 273-87; Mary Daly, *Gyn/Ecology: The Metaethics of Radical Feminism* (1978; Boston: Beacon Press, 1990). "The Metapatriarchal Journey of Exorcism and Ecstasy" is the title of Daly's introduction. For a useful overview of these responses to Christianity and new insights into their importance see Charlene Spretnak, *States of Grace* (San Francisco: HarperCollins, 1991).

4. See, for example, Rosemary Radford Ruether, *Sexism and God-Talk* (1983; Boston: Beacon Press, 1993); Dorothee Soelle, *The Window of Vulnerability: A Political Spirituality* (Minneapolis: Fortress, 1990); Sallie McFague, *Models of God* (Minneapolis: Fortress, 1987); and Delores S. Williams, *Sisters in the Wilderness: The Challenge of Womanist God-Talk* (Maryknoll, N.Y.: Orbis Books, 1993).

5. It is clearly beyond the scope of this essay to include a comprehensive review of feminist salvation theories. Two invaluable discussions of the issues involved, including excellent bibliographies, are by Elizabeth A. Johnson, *She Who Is: The Mystery of God in Feminist Theological Discourse* (New York: Crossroad, 1992) and Anne E. Carr, *Transforming Grace: Women's Experience and Christian Tradition* (San Francisco: Harper & Row, 1988). Letty M. Russell places feminist perspectives on sin and salvation among other liberation theologies in *Human Liberation in a Feminist Perspective—A Theology* (Philadelphia: Westminster, 1974), as does Elisabeth Moltmann-Wendel, *A Land Flowing With Milk and Honey: Perspectives on Feminist Theology*, tr. John Bowden. (New York: Crossroad, 1986). For an excellent poststructuralist analysis of feminist theologies of sin and salvation see Mary McClintock Fulkerson, "Sexism as Original Sin: Developing a Theacentric Discourse," *Journal of the American Academy of Religion* LIX/4 (1992): 653-75.

6. Valerie Saiving, "The Human Situation: A Feminine View," in *Womanspirit Rising*, p. 37.

7. Judith Plaskow, *Sex, Sin, and Grace: Women's Experience and the Theologies of Reinhold Niebuhr and Paul Tillich*, cited in Catherine Keller, *From a Broken Web: Separation, Sexism and Self* (Boston: Beacon Press, 1986), p. 40; Dorothee Soelle, "The Gospel and Liberation," *Commonweal* (December 22, 1972).

8. Rosemary Radford Ruether, "Feminist Theology and Spirituality," in *Christian Feminism: Visions of a New Humanism*, p. 27. Mary Daly also develops an analysis of sexism as the primal sin in *Beyond God the Father: Toward a Philosophy of Women's Liberation* (1973; Boston: Beacon Press, 1985).

9. Sallie McFague, "The Ethic of God as Mother, Lover and Friend," in *Feminist Theology: A Reader*, pp. 261, 263. This essay is a valuable introduction to McFague's argument, which is developed more fully in *Models of God*.

10. Keller, *From A Broken Web*, pp. 37-38.

11. Daphne Hampson, *Theology and Feminism* (Cambridge, MA: Basil Blackwell, 1990), pp. 127-28.

12. McFague, *Feminist Theology: A Reader*, pp. 261-9.

13. Williams, *Sisters in the Wilderness*, p. 166. By placing the cultural and social experience of women of color at the center of her redemption theory, Delores S. Williams enters into dialogue with both white feminist theologians and African-American male theologians. Susan Brooks Thistlethwaite offers a useful analysis of the differences between womanist and feminist theologies in *Sex, Race, and God: Christian Feminism in Black and White* (New York: Crossroad, 1991). See also Jacquelyn Grant, *White Women's Christ and Black Women's Jesus* (Chico, CA: Scholars Press, 1989).

14. Ruether, "Feminist Theology and Spirituality," pp. 25, 26.

15. Paula Gunn Allen, *The Sacred Hoop* (Boston: Beacon Press, 1992), p. 59. Although Allen does not discuss conversion narratives, she argues that Native American writers have drawn upon their spiritual traditions to write narratives than cannot be interpreted in terms of Western ontological and aesthetic assumptions; see pp. 51-184.

16. Anne Cameron, *Daughters of Copper Woman* (Vancouver: Press Gang Publishers, 1981), Preface.

17. Cameron, Afterword.

18. Cameron, p. 40. This symbiotic relationship between Copper Woman and Old Woman is a variation on the "twin sisters" of many other North American Indian traditions: the Maya Cihuacoatl (Serpent Woman) and Coatlicue (Serpent Skirt); the Navajo Changing Woman and White Shell Woman; the Algonquin Matchikwewis and Oshkikwe; the Keres Nau'ts'ity (Sun Woman) and Ic'sts'ity (Corn Woman or Yellow Woman). Paula Gunn Allen provides a valuable introduction to different Native American matriarchal traditions in *Grandmothers of the Light* (Boston: Beacon Press, 1991).

19. Cameron, p. 145.

20. Cameron, pp. 146-47.

21. Johnson, *She Who Is*, p. 64.

22. Mary Catherine Bateson, *Composing A Life* (New York: New American Library, 1990).

23. Madeleine L'Engle, *The Crosswick Journal*, 3 vols. (San Francisco: HarperCollins, 1992). The three volumes were originally published separately: *A Circle of Quiet* (1972), *The Summer of the Great-Grandmother* (1974), and *An Irrational Season* (1977).

24. Virginia Woolf, *Mrs. Dalloway* (New York: Harcourt Brace Jovanovich, 1925) and *To The Lighthouse* (New York: Harcourt Brace Jovanovich, 1927). Doris Lessing develops these themes most fully in *The Four-Gated City* (New York: New American Library, 1964) and *Summer Before the Dark* (New York: Knopf, 1973).

25. Margaret Atwood, *Surfacing* (New York: Simon and Schuster, 1972). Carol P. Christ and Charlotte Spretnak discuss the relevance of Atwood's and Lessing's novels to the possibility for new representations for women's spirituality in "Images of Spiritual Power in Women's Fiction," in *The Politics of Women's Spirituality*, pp. 327-43.

26. H. D. (Hilda Doolittle), "The Flowering of the Rod" in *Trilogy* (1946; New York: New Directions, 1973)); Clysta Kinsler, *The Moon Under Her Feet* (San Francisco; HarperCollins, 1991); Rachel Ingalls, "Blessed Art Thou," in *I See A Long Journey* (New York: Simon and Schuster, 1985), pp. 87-141.

27. Alice Walker, *The Color Purple* (New York: Washington Square Press, 1982), p. 249. Catherine Keller uses this novel as the paradigm for her concept of relational spirituality in "Feminism and the Ethic of Inseparability," in *Weaving the Visions*, pp. 256-65.

28. Walker, *The Temple of My Familiar* (New York: Pocket Books, 1990), pp. 144-5.

29. Walker, *The Temple of My Familiar*, pp. 287-9.

30. Walker, *The Temple of My Familiar*, p. 295.

31. Walker, *Possessing the Secret of Joy* (New York: Pocket Books, 1992), pp. 275-6.

32. Quoted by Aage Henriksen in "The Empty Space Between Art and Church," tr. Annette Wernblad. In Henriksen, *Isak Dinesen/Karen Blixen: The Life and the Work*, tr. William Mishler (New York: St. Martin's Press, 1988), p. 180.

33. Quoted by Judith Thurman in *Isak Dinesen: The Life of a Storyteller* (New York: St. Martin's Press, 1982), p. 374.

34. Isak Dinesen, *On Modern Marriage*, tr. Anne Born (New York: St. Martin's Press, 1977), pp. 58-9.

35. Isak Dinesen, *Letters From Africa*, ed. Frans Lasson, tr. Anne Born (Chicago: University of Chicago Press, 1981), p. 347.

36. Quoted by Henriksen, p. 180.

37. Isak Dinesen, "H. C. Branner: *The Riding Master*," in *Daguerrotypes and Other Essays* (Chicago: University of Chicago Press, 1979), p. 171.

38. Dinesen, "H. C. Branner: *The Riding Master*," p. 175.

39. Susan Hardy Aiken explores the significance of this displacement in "Dinesen's 'Sorrow-acre': Tracing the Woman's Line," *Contemporary Literature* 25 (Summer 1984): 156-86.

40. Isak Dinesen, "Sorrow-acre," in *Winter's Tales* (New York: Random House, 1941), p. 69.

41. Dinesen, "Sorrow-acre," p. 29.

42. Dinesen, "Sorrow-acre," p. 30.

43. Dinesen, "Sorrow-acre," p. 32.

44. Dinesen, "Sorrow-acre," p. 63.

45. Dinesen, "Sorrow-acre," p. 69.

46. Dinesen, "Alkmene," in *Winter's Tales*, p. 218.

47. Dinesen, "H. C. Branner: *The Riding Master*," pp. 175-6.

48. Quoted in Donald Hannah, *Isak Dinesen/Karen Blixen: The Mask and the Reality* (New York: Random House, 1971), p. 171. Although Hannah notes the correspondence between this tale and the aesthetic principles that Dinesen later presented in "H. C. Branner: *The Riding Master*," he has a very different perspective on her treatment of the doctrine of atonement.

49. Isak Dinesen, "The Heroine," in *Winter's Tales*, p. 86. Dinesen here is retelling the De Maupassant story "Boule-de-Suif," in which a prostitute gives herself to a Prussian officer in order to save the lives of a group of morally self-righteous upper-class people who then shun her for what she has done.

50. Dinesen, "The Heroine," p. 81.

51. According to Thurman (p. 364), Dinesen told her friend Mogens Fog that she intended "The Cardinal's Third Tale" to be a response to members of the *Heretica* group who had affirmed their belief in an ethical Christian redemption. This tale was written during 1952-53 when, according to her assistant Clara Svendsen, Dinesen was particularly interested in theological questions.

52. Isak Dinesen, "The Cardinal's Third Tale," in *Last Tales* (New York: Random House, 1957), p. 96.

53. Dinesen, "The Cardinal's Third Tale," p. 97.

54. Dinesen, "The Cardinal's Third Tale," p. 87.

55. Dinesen, "The Cardinal's Third Tale," p. 85.

56. The term "depatriarchalize" was coined by Phyllis Trible in *God and the Rhetoric of Sexuality* (Philadelphia: Fortress Press, 1978).

LITERARY IMAGINATION, THEOLOGICAL THINKING, AND CHRISTIAN PRAXIS

Werner Jeanrond

Theology, at least in Europe, is under threat from many sides now. Representatives of authoritarian church structures on the one hand, and defenders of fundamentalist approaches to the Bible on the other hand consider critical theology to be a nuisance. But academic theology is also treated increasingly as an enemy by all those self-proclaimed liberative forces who believe that any second-order reflection on human experience is, by virtue of its theoretical nature, at best superfluous and at worst oppressive. What is most alarming, however, is the news of a grand coalition between both of these otherwise conflictual forces, that is, the conservative traditionalist lobby and the advocators of a non-reflective liberative praxis. In my native Germany this bizarre coalition can be seen at work in its effort to close down a good few long-established theological faculties. Critical theology is clearly on the defensive today.

I have two reasons for mentioning this contemporary scenario at the beginning of a reflection on the possible connections between the literary imagination and theological thinking: First of all I would like to counteract any possible fear that by subscribing to a literary interest in theology one more theologian might wish to abandon the *critical* demands of a necessarily theoretical approach to religion by embarking on a road to a literary exile in order to escape the wrath of the above-mentioned anti-theological coalition. And secondly I would like to reconfirm my strong commitment to the reflective and critical nature of theological thinking. Christian theology in my understanding is and remains theoretical, critical, and self-critical in its approach to the transformative possibilities of Christian praxis. Theology, then, is a theory for a better praxis.

In this essay I would like to examine how theology thus defined could benefit even more from a closer study of the literary imagination than has been established to date. Thus, my starting-point is firmly theological, which means that my analysis is motivated by the systematic and conceptual methods of theological thinking, supported by the insights of the general hermeneutical debate today, but concerned with the possibilities of a transformative Christian praxis.

One may wonder why further reflection on this general theme of literary imagination and Christian theology is undertaken at all after a number of books recently ploughed that field so thoroughly and seem to have described every possible connection between our two areas of study. For instance, Terry Wright's book *Theology and Literature* (1988)[1] and David Jasper's *The Study of Literature and Religion* (1990),[2] the opening work for the series "Studies in Literature and Religion," each provide us with a fine analysis of the mutual enrichment arising from this interdisciplinary concern. Yet, with regard to my understanding of theology as a theory for a better praxis I have a problem with both of these works, and that has at first nothing to do with their understanding of literature and of literary criticism, but with their open and silent assumptions about the nature of theology. In order to draw attention to the crucial point of my misgivings I would like to state my conclusion first and then argue for it in some detail.

We ought to distinguish between two approaches to theology: one approach sees theology as a way of *understanding* the nature of Christian faith, that is as an exercise in clarification of one's existential or communal set of convictions about God, the self, other selves, and the universe. The other approach sees theology as a way of developing enlightened strategies for transforming our present relationships between the self, other selves, God and the universe. Obviously, the latter approach cannot function without the former, but unfortunately, much theology remains committed only to the former.

The problem which I would like to tackle here is this: how can we redescribe the connection between literary imagination and theology once theology is understood to be not only concerned with understanding the world, but also with transforming the world? Thus, if theology is a theory about Christian praxis in this world, how can its work be helped by the study of literature, but also, vice versa, how can the study of literature be influenced by this redescribed theology?

In a first section I shall argue in more detail for this need to redefine the partners in our interdisciplinary project of the study of literature and Christian theology. In the second section I shall discuss how theology may be challenged by the literary imagination within the Christian tradition. And in my third section I shall try to study and illustrate the possibility of a mutually critical relationship between literary imagination and theology.

What Kind of Theology Is Interested in the Study of Literature?

The recent debate among Christian theologians on the proper method of contemporary theology is of greater importance to the study of literature and theology than has been generally realized. Moreover, by subscribing heavily to the crucial debate on interpretation in our so-called postmodern period, literary critics and theologians interested in literary criticism have invested most of their energies in hermeneutical pursuits and reduced the problem of theological method to the question of the proper understanding of biblical, doctrinal, literary, and other texts. In spite of the critique of metaphysics and of any form of ontological conviction, in spite of the critique of any claim to be able to identify the meaning of a text once and for all, in spite of the insights into the hidden and open ideologies involved in our interpretative efforts, many of the literary critical and theological participants in this grand international and interdisciplinary debate on interpretation theory have lost sight of the world whose various literary manifestations they intended to study once their literary methodology had been suitably purified.

However, interestingly enough, hardly anybody of this great assembly of critics ever returned to the intricate problems of this world. Only two groups of theological participants whose interests in liberation and emancipation were too strong to have evaporated in the process of meta-methodological purification managed to assert their transformative projects, namely the feminist and the liberation theologians. Yet, some of their supporters have already opted out of the metacritical effort and decided that, on the basis of solidarity with the victims of oppression, only a liberative praxis itself would lead to a radical transformation both of the people concerned and of the structures of injustice which cause oppression.[3]

This gap between theologians involved in theological metacritique and theologians involved directly in so-called liberative praxis is not new in Christian history. The various movements of radical Christianity throughout the history of the Christian church point to this kind of radical difference between those Christians involved in the theoretical reflection of Christian faith and those who have become too impatient to be engaged in the task of a thorough, and at times painful, reflection upon Christian faith-praxis in this world.

The theological debate on method has therefore rightly turned again today to the relationship between the different disciplines within theology. Fundamental Theology, that is, the theological discipline in which theology reflects upon its methodological options, is not really contested in this debate except by some radical Barthians who (unlike Barth) believe that they can do theology without ever thinking about what they are doing when they are doing it. But the much more interesting question is the one of the relationship between the systematic account of Christian faith and its practical application, that is, between Systematic Theology and Practical Theology. Let me make two brief comments on this debate. The first concerns the relationship between understanding and transformation, the second the relationship between systematic reflection and Christian praxis in theology.[4]

Understanding and Transformation

Hans-Georg Gadamer must be given credit for paying renewed attention to the dimension of application as an integral part of the process of understanding.[5] But at the same time Gadamer considers application only in so far as it has an effect on human consciousness. "Application does not mean first understanding a given universal in itself and then afterward applying it to a concrete case. It is the very understanding of the universal — the text — itself. Understanding proves to be a kind of effect and knows itself as such."[6] Thus, Gadamer concludes that every interpreter moves within the framework of historically effected consciousness. Within this framework, understanding achieves at best a fusion of horizons. But this approach to understanding never leaves the level of consciousness; the horizons to be fused in the act of understanding are not discussed in terms of their ethical-political dimensions. Rather

Gadamer discusses the problem of application in hermeneutics and the ethical dimension of hermeneutics with reference to Aristotle's concern with *phronesis*, because he wishes to exclude the possibility of any technical/methodical approach to understanding. Understanding is "a modification of the virtue of moral knowledge . . . . This knowledge also is not in any sense technical knowledge or the application of such. The man of the world, the man who knows all the tricks and dodges and is experienced in everything there is, does not really have sympathetic understanding for the person acting: he has it only if he satisfies one requirement, namely that he too is seeking what is right — i.e., that he is united with the other person in this commonality."[7]

Following Gadamer, the theologian David Tracy also points to the ethical-political dimensions of understanding. Moreover, he acknowledges the transformative qualities present in every classic text, but he fails to say how they influence more concretely the theological reflection both on the Christian project and on concrete strategies for its realization.[8] As long as theologians continue to make a split between the task of understanding the Christian project and the task of developing adequate strategies for its realization they are in danger of ignoring what one might call the institutional context of Christian theology.[9]

Umberto Eco once defined the difference between his literary and his philosophical activities in terms of accountability. He explained that as a writer he can afford to entertain possibilities and options, but as a philosopher he is accountable for his stand point and decisions and must be able to argue in public for the particular decision he has taken.[10] The same is true, of course, of the theologian. She or he is accountable for their particular assessments of a text or context (used here in the widest sense of the terms). They must be prepared to argue in public for their reflective action. But, unlike the philosopher, the theologian is also committed to a very particular public, namely to the Christian movement and its aspirations of helping to assist in the transformation of the world.

This commitment to the church must not be understood in any narrow confessional or denominational sense. Rather, it is a commitment to the institutional dimension of Christianity in the widest sense. But it is a commitment, and, as such, one dimension of the theologian's activity, in addition to his or her commitment to two other dimensions, namely society and academy.[11] Moreover, this commitment to the concrete Christian project of transforming the relationship between self and God, self and other selves, self and self, and self and universe demands from the theologian what one could call (for want of a better phrase) an ethical-political imagination. Thus, it is this commitment to transformative action in our history that makes it necessary for the theologian not to confine her or his energies only to the hermeneutical task of retrieval and suspicion.

Theory and Praxis in Theology

The separation between systematic theology as the theoretical reflection on Christian faith and Christian praxis as the practical application of this reflection has proved to be inadequate because, on the one hand, the needs of Christian praxis have not always been appreciated by those theologians who are more concerned with the nature of their second-order reflection itself. On the other hand, Christian practitioners have not always been so concerned with theological labor because they have felt that they alone have been doing the "real" thing, namely transforming the world according to God's (or what they have uncritically understood to be God's) will. Hence, in my view Christian theology must overcome this split and redefine itself as a critical reflection upon Christian praxis in this world. This reflective task includes the dimensions of understanding and explanation, but also the dimension of assessment.[12] We need some such theory of concrete praxis which is guided by the critical understanding and explanation of all human experience of God's creative project.

While one can distinguish these dimensions of Christian theology, one must not separate them. In other words, I think that the division of theological labor in systematic and practical theologies is not adequate. In fact it has allowed many systematic theologians to isolate themselves from the world in which and for which they are to reflect publicly and responsibly on more adequate strategies of global transformation. Furthermore, it has encouraged many liberation theologians to neglect critical and self-critical methodological reflection. Instead the Christian interpretation of biblical and other texts itself ought to be motivated by this search for more adequate models of Christian praxis.

What has all of this to do with my topic of the possible connection between literary imagination and theology? First of all, my reflections so far show that the theological interpretation of texts, biblical or literary, as I understand it, follows a certain openly declared interest; it is neither value-free nor otherworldly. Rather, it follows a definite ethical-political line of argument. Secondly, these reflections point to a gap in the traditional relationship between the study of literature and the study of Christian religion. Let me explain what I mean by this.

Both T. R. Wright and David Jasper have contributed very richly to the interdisciplinary study of literary texts. Yet both, though to a different degree, are guided by an understanding of theology which focuses predominantly on the hermeneutics of retrieval and suspicion, rather than on the need for a better theory of a better Christian praxis. Both authors have achieved a significant clarification of the mystical side of literature and theology. By this I mean they have been able to elucidate patterns of theological reflection on God in literary and biblical texts. But the prophetic side, the side concerned with ethics, with human praxis, with the struggle for more adequate strategies of transformative and liberative action, has not been sufficiently elaborated in ways which seem both possible and desirable to me as a theologian.[13]

T. R. Wright describes the central tension between systematic theology and literature like this:

> In literature, meaning is never fixed; any "complete" interpretation would render the literary "work" redundant (both the artefact and the imaginative processes involved in its production, its writing and its reading). Interpretation of literature is always a temporary illumination, never, fortunately, a "final solution." There will always, therefore, be a tension between conceptual and creative discourse. Systematic theology will continue the necessary attempt to impose clarity and consistency upon language while literature will no doubt maintain its equally necessary task, to explore, to complicate and to enrich the apparent security of theological concepts.[14]

David Jasper must have been somehow aware of the limits of such a purely systematic understanding of theology when, however briefly, he addresses Moltmann's theology of hope in his short chapter entitled "The

Limits of Formalism and the Theology of Hope," though he restricts himself to merely pointing out the existence of this other dimension: "For Ricœur, and perhaps the New Critics, as I have described them, a literary work does not refer directly to a given reality, but to a 'possible world' created by the syntactic and semantic structures of the text."[15] The pragmatic potential of the reception of such possible worlds and the ethical dimension of this process are, however, not explicitly considered.

However, I agree with Jasper's conclusion to this chapter of his book:

> This discussion has illustrated . . . how in one particular manner, a serious commitment to literary critical method may, sometimes paradoxically, lead us back to truths which theology has forgotten or has failed to articulate; that the forms of literature and art can often quite spontaneously illuminate in startling ways the divine work of creation and redemption; and that theology, critically and rigorously pursued, in its turn, continues to offer a systematic and necessary reminder of the things of ultimate concern to literature and literary criticism.[16]

Therefore, in what follows I wish to offer some thoughts on the role of the literary imagination in a redefined Christian theology and on the mutually critical relationship between literature and this more praxis-oriented theology.

The Literary Imagination in the Christian Theological Tradition: The Call for a Narrative Theology

The debate on theological method since the late 1960s has clearly confirmed the narrative dimension of Christian theology, and the debate on literary hermeneutics this century has produced many reasons in favor of a theological participation in both the global conversation on interpretative methodology generally (i.e., hermeneutics) and the study of narrative modes of communication more particularly.

Among the theologians who have recently re-emphasized the importance of narrative forms of communication for theological thinking is the German Johann Baptist Metz.[17] He deserves particular attention, not only because he was (together with the linguist Harald Weinrich) the first in Europe to introduce this topic into contemporary theology (1973), but also because his proposals for a reform of theological thinking have to do with his discussion of the role of narrative in theology.[18] Thus, Metz's proposals are of significance for our considerations here. Since Metz's work is not mentioned in the otherwise excellent chapter of Wright's *Theology and Literature* which deals with "Narrative Theology: The Stories of Faith,"[19] it seems appropriate here to list some of Metz's proposals and then assess their significance for our discussion. As will be clear from the discussion, Metz's attention to narrative theology, however much in need of clarification, does include an ethical-political dimension. The absence of Metz's proposals from Wright's book offers, I think, further support to my thesis that the concern for the ethical-political dimension of theology has not been prominent hitherto in the pioneering works on the study of literature and theology.

The context for Metz's reflections on theological method is the crisis of religious language. His experience is that the salvific center of the Christian message can be proclaimed adequately only through an anamnetic narrative soteriology and not through a purely argumentative explication.[20] What is needed today is a continuous recovery of the dangerous and liberating memory of Jesus Christ: the *memoria passionis, mortis et resurrectionis Jesu Christi.*[21] This memory calls for a supportive argument. Such thought must, however, not be used to "sublate" the history of human suffering into a theological dialectic of a Trinitarian soteriology.[22] Only memory and narrative provide the necessary challenge to all systematic, conceptual, and argumentative attempts at reconciling God's offer of salvation with the history of human suffering. Any such mediation leads according to Metz "either into a dualistic gnostic perpetuation of suffering in God or to a devaluation of suffering into a concept; *tertium non datur.*"[23] Thus, Metz concludes, a new theological method is required which speaks of God's offer of salvation without destroying it or the reality of human suffering: a narrative theology is necessary. Its basic categories are memory, narrative, and solidarity.[24]

Memory is understood by Metz as the mediator between a priori reason and truth on the one hand and the history of human freedom on the other. Memory calls for the narration of that history. Therefore, Metz argues, the Christian community is not primarily a community characterized by interpretation and argumentation, but by memory and *narrative.* "The linguistic content of Christianity must be understood as a macro-narrative, which of course, contains and produces argumentative elements and structures—but not vice versa."[25] Memory and narrative are categories of a practical fundamental theology, but only in conjunction with *solidarity*, a solidarity with all human beings, past, present and future.[26] According to Metz, only narrative strategies can succeed in communicating anew today the foundational experiences of Christianity. These strategies demand the involvement of every Christian and discredit any effort to maintain a theoretical-academic distance over against the truth of the foundational stories. "The critical-liberating power of such stories cannot be proven a priori or reconstructed. One has to encounter them, listen to them and possibly spread them by narrating them to others."[27] Hence, remembering, narrating, and acting in solidarity are socio-political activities which constitute a new human praxis, a praxis which transforms the identity of Christians in this world. Such a praxis, then, has an epistemological significance because it conditions the continuous retelling and reception of these narratives in the Christian community as well as this community's practical self-understanding in this universe.[28] Thus, Metz wishes not only to retrieve narrative strategies from early Christianity, but to address at the same time the question of the truth of the Christian narratives. Metz rejects any objectivist ("subject-less") concept of truth. Truth is for him not the result of purely theoretical reason. Rather "that is true, which is relevant to all subjects—even to the victims and the dead."[29] Truth becomes a practical concept: it describes and assesses the transformation of both Christian community and the world at large.

Assessing Metz's argument in favor of narrative theology we may appreciate his effort to bridge the gap between ancient story and modern times by appealing to the transformative power of narratives in a community, but we have to ask 1) whether the appeal to narrating really solves the epistemological problem of theology; that is to say, whether narrative mediates *critical* insight; 2) whether Metz's concept of narrative is adequate; and 3) whether his concept of truth can stand up to critical inquiry. In a way, even these questions would be subject to Metz's critique of theology as a theoretical discipline in so far as they presuppose a reflective distance over against the actual narrative praxis in Christianity. In fact, it seems to me that Metz has confused Christian praxis and Christian reflection on Christian praxis. Even by arguing in favor of what he calls a narrative theology, he himself has been involved in argument, reflection and critique. "Narrative theology," then, is really a misnomer; especially since Metz himself has repeatedly promoted the argumentative defense of the foundational narratives, the narrative process, and its reception in Christianity.

What concept of narrative is employed by Metz? In fact, he never defines the concept of narrative which he uses. Instead he points to the primary task of safeguarding the possibility of narrating in our Western culture. Although he calls for "competent" narrating,[30] he does not enlighten us as to what that means. Obviously for him narrative is precritical, preinterpretative and therefore preferable to traditional theological interpretation and argumentation.[31] However, Metz seems to have overlooked a) that all forms of narrative communication contain, as we have seen already, interpretative elements, take sides, portray particular perspectives, are ambiguous, and thus, need critical assessment; and b) that the "bourgeois situation" which he criticizes, but in which we in the West continue to live, narrate and think, causes significant problems also for the act of narrating in our culture. Once religion is marginalized, the simplistic appeal to the power of narrative will not yet redress the failure of Christianity to communicate its liberating and transformative gospel to the world. This is not to argue that narrative forms of communication ought not to be tried. Rather, I wish to state that they need to be considered in a wider context of communicative theory and praxis. Moreover, the strong emphasis on narrative in Metz promotes the further neglect of the great host of other forms of religious and theological thought and communication.

In spite of these criticisms one must grant that Metz has contributed to the rediscovery of the power of literary discourse in Christianity itself and has challenged theology to pay closer attention to it. Moreover, though he concentrates only on narrative, Metz has at least implicitly defended the need for interruption of our theological discourse by expressions of literary quality, and he has charged theology with the task of helping to create a climate in which narration becomes a real possibility again, a possibility which may lead to transformative and liberative action in church and world. But most significantly for our discussion here, Metz has shown how the reappraisal of narrative in Christian theology can help to redescribe the theological task itself as a theory for a better praxis.

In my next section I wish to examine how the literary imagination generally points us into the same direction of retrieving the ethical-political dimension of theological thinking.

The Literary Imagination as a Challenge to Theology

As T. R. Wright, David Jasper, and others have shown and illustrated with the help of many examples, literary texts can function as challenges to the Christian thinker by pointing to forgotten and neglected dimensions of the divine-human relationship. But they can do even more: precisely by disturbing the discursive activity of theologians they may not only offer new material for more and different doctrinal systems or question the point of doctrinal systems altogether; they may also redirect the very focus of the theological exercise to the aims of Christian praxis. Let me give a few examples.

Both parts of Goethe's *Faust* have provided powerful challenges to the bourgeois religious imagination and of its theological *Überbau* of either the neoscholastic or the traditional Liberal Protestant variety. When Margarete at the highly dramatic end of Part I refers to her prison as a "holy place"[32] in spite of the presence of Mephistopheles and the opposite perception of prisons in the popular mind, then the theological interpreter will not only be forced to conclude that he or she now understands that Goethe's drama favors in fact a cosmic theology according to which all places can be seen to be sacred (as has been maintained by the late Mircea Eliade[33]); but the further conclusion is also possible, namely, that if even the company of the devil and the surroundings of a prison cannot take away from God's presence, then Margarete's entire life story, and ours as well, needs to be reconceived. Thus, Goethe's challenge to a certain dualistic cosmology may have profound implications for our reflection upon how we live in this world as Christians.

Or, to stay with *Faust*, when at the end of Part II the Chorus Mysticus sings that the eternal feminine draws us onward,[34] then Goethe's literary imagination projects a vision of God which differs radically from many theological approaches to gender, then and now, and demands a reexamination of the male imagery of God in the entire Christian project and hence a reexamination of the corresponding visions of life in God's presence.

Similarly, countless plays, poems, and novels confront us theologians with the emphasis on the salvific presence of God in this cosmos and thus challenge the whole set of doctrinal claims according to which either only a direct intervention by God in one historical instance or only a sophisticated ecclesial administration can provide the necessary mediation of salvation. In his study *Stellvertreter Christi? Der Papst in der zeitgenössischen Literatur* [*Vicar of Christ: The Pope in Contemporary Literature*] (1980), Karl-Josef Kuschel examines the literary challenges to the past and present Vatican understanding of the petrine office in the church.[35] He points explicitly to the practical-political aims of plays such as Bertold Brecht's *Leben des Galilei* and Rolf Hochhuth's *Der Stellvertreter*. Kuschel discusses these plays in relation to the ongoing debate on what kind of papacy and, more generally, what kind of church government Christians should develop in view of their particular eschatological spirit. Thus, Kuschel's interpretation not only aims at an *understanding* of a literary work with particular regard to its challenges to traditional doctrinal systems, but includes an assessment of the possibilities for transformation of the Christian project which the work in question has to offer.[36] Kuschel's interpretations of contemporary drama exemplify well how a relationship between literature and a more comprehensive theological reflection can work. A connection between only a "systematic" theological imagination and literature would have missed many of the ethical-political challenges to contemporary theology present in Brecht's and Hochhuth's works.

A mere systematic-theological interpretation of Dostoyevsky's Grand Inquisitor story in *The Brothers Karamazov*[37] which would only emphasize that the point of Jesus' life, death, and resurrection has been understood by the Grand Inquisitor but rejected for ecclesiastical reasons, would miss too much. It may grasp the irony that in the name of Jesus an ecclesial system has been established in which Jesus could only be considered as disturbing. But such an interpretation may not necessarily advance to the ethical-practical conclusion that an ecclesial system such as described by Dostoyevsky may be in need of change. In other words, an interpretation which stops at the level of understanding and explanation is not satisfactory from a more comprehensive theological point of view.

Rather, a theological interpretation must include the reflection on how we can redescribe the entire Christian project in this world; it must include the ethical-political dimension of Christian praxis.

In a programmatic article entitled "Theology and Literature: A Mutual Challenge,"[38] Hans Küng states that "theology examines whether literature, which is autonomous and not committed to any authority or rule (other than the aesthetic), opens possibilities of a new integration of religion and modern consciousness,"[39] a new coalition to defend the human being against any kind of idolatry of the powers of modernity and for a postmaterialistic view of life and way of life.[40] While I agree, of course, with Küng's interest in the defense of life as the common agenda of literature and theology, I would like to go one step further. Is it not the imaginative possibility of radical surprise, of radical otherness through which literature does at times challenge theological thinking? Is it not the possibility of seeing God's presence in new ways which gives certain literary texts their power of disclosure, and is it not the possibility of seeing our human relationship to God, to one another, to nature and to oneself in a new and surprising light which opens the way of conversion, emancipation, and transformation?

Adequate *theological* reactions to such literary challenges can never be a mere, "Oh, I never thought it could be like this," but must also include, "Oh, we have never thought it possible to respond to God's initiatives in such a way." Thus, the question of responding to literature theologically does not only involve the question of ethics in terms of being a responsible reader,[41] but also the question of ethics in terms of being an attentive theologian, one who is prepared to reconsider both the various dimensions of the project of Christian faith and all kinds of strategies devised so far for its realization.[42]

Obviously, only that kind of theology will be challenged by the literary imagination which is in fact prepared to reconsider its own set of theories of divine human relationship and of Christian praxis in this world in the light of new expressions of possible and actual human experiences with God and God's creative project in this universe. Such an approach to theology leads to what David Tracy and Edward Schillebeeckx have named a "correlational theology."[43]

A correlational approach to theology reckons with the possibility of revelation, of insight into the mystery of this world, of disclosure of some dimensions of the divine mystery, of God, not only in the traditionally canonized documents of Jewish and Christian religion, but also in every possible aspect of our cosmos. It reckons with the possibilities of an analogical imagination, that is, an imagination which sees correspondences and differences, an imagination which guides the transformation of all the human relationships discussed above.

A correlational approach to theology is therefore by design well disposed to the disclosure of the manifestation of the sacred in all kinds of natural or artistic expressions, and that includes the many different expressions of the literary imagination. But it offers also another challenge to theology: theologians willing to engage in this mutually critical correlation with reflection on works of art have to become engaged themselves in the debates on adequate theories of literary criticism in order to become professionally aware both of the structural, formal and generic aspects of literary composition as well as of the various dimensions and problems of reading. This latter challenge has indeed been accepted by an increasing number of theologians. More theologians than ever are involved in the multifaceted debates on interpretation theory. But here again the philosophical and metacritical interests have often taken over to the detriment of attention to the actual objects of literary concern, that is, the literary works themselves and the visions of life which they portray.

The challenge of a closer attention to the connection of literature and religion in literary criticism and theology must, of course, be a mutual one. Unfortunately, however, there are still literary critics who continue to ignore the religious dimension present in many literary works and other manifestations of contemporary culture.[44]

There can be no doubt that it is essential for correlational theologians to be involved in the hermeneutical and philosophical search for better methods of reading. But there can equally be no doubt that this entire search for more sophisticated methods can also represent a temptation, namely to escape from the challenge which the possible worlds depicted by literary works represent and into the relatively safer realms of metatheory.

Conclusion

Thinking to 2000 demands from correlational theologians, then, a readiness to accept a twofold challenge from the literary imagination: the call to develop more adequate theories of literary communication and the call to consider alternative proposals for Christian praxis. It would seem that we have already attended sufficiently to the former, but on the whole neglected the latter. Yet our world and our Christian communities are very poor in terms of vision.

I began my reflections with a reference to the different threats to theology today. I wish to return to this scenario here at the end of my study. It seems to me that the theological interest in literary manifestations of experience of the divine-human relationship must not be restricted to what used to be called systematic theology. Rather, it must be open to the horizon of a properly praxis-oriented theological reflection. By "properly praxis-oriented reflection" I do not mean a tyranny of this or that political program, but rather a genuine Christian concern with change in this world. Between the Scylla of a purely philosophically oriented theology and the Charybdis of a purely action-minded theology a properly critical and self-critical theology has a hard time nowadays. Yet it is here in the narrow passage between the two that the future of Christian theology will be decided: either theology will become irrelevant because it has no interest in the development of ethical-political theories of Christian action or it will become irrelevant because it cannot offer any longer a critique of existing forms of Christian praxis. Thus, if theology wants to avoid either destiny it must be careful to attend to the institutional dimensions of Christian faith which require prophetic vision while not giving up its mystical-philosophical inclinations. It seems to me that theological attention to the work of the literary imagination could prevent theology from neglecting the world as well as from neglecting the sacred; because literature can offer new, surprising and interruptive visions and possibilities, it can also remind the theologian of forgotten visions even in his or her own most sacred texts. In short, literature keeps our image of alternative ways of existence alive. And most of all, it reminds us theologians of the joy and the suffering of people, of death and birth, of chaos and cosmos, that is, the different dimensions of life whose mysterious dynamic can never be fully grasped by any concept or theory for praxis.

NOTES

1. T. R. Wright, *Theology and Literature.* Signposts in Theology (Oxford: Blackwell, 1988).

2. David Jasper, *The Study of Literature and Religion.* Studies in Literature and Religion (London: Macmillan, 1989).

3. See for example Katherine Zappone, *The Hope for Wholeness: A Spirituality for Feminists* (Mystic: Twenty-Third Publications, 1991), pp. 3-6. Zappone dissolves the dialectical relationship of theory and praxis in favor of the priority of action over critical reflection. Action is the first step, reflection the second.

4. For a discussion of the development of theological subdisciplines see Edward Farley, *Theologia: The Fragmentation and Unity of Theological Education* (Philadelphia: Fortress, 1983). Farley shows how "practical theology" developed as a discipline of mere application. He argues against such a split between theoretical and practical, and instead wishes to promote a unified approach to theology "as a habitus of understanding" pp. 193f.

5. Hans-Georg Gadamer, *Truth and Method,* 2nd revised ed. Joel Weinsheimer and Donald G. Marshall (New York: Crossroad, and London: Sheed & Ward, 1989), pp. 308-9: "The fact that philological, legal, and theological hermeneutics originally belonged closely together depended on recognizing application as an integral element of all understanding. In both legal and theological hermeneutics there is an essential tension between the fixed text—the law or the gospel—on the one hand and, on the other, the sense arrived at by applying it at the concrete moment of interpretation, either in judgment or in preaching."

6. Gadamer, *Truth and Method,* p. 341.

7. Gadamer, *Truth and Method,* pp. 322-3.

8. David Tracy, *The Analogical Imagination: Christian Theology and the Culture of Pluralism* (New York: Crossroad, 1981), pp. 115-24 and p. 145, n.75. See also my critique of Tracy's treatment of the ethical dimension in hermeneutics in Werner G. Jeanrond, *Text and Interpretation as Categories of Theological Thinking,* tr. Thomas J. Wilson (Dublin: Gill and Macmillan, and New York: Crossroad, 1988), pp. 135-40.

9. For a more detailed argument of this point see my article "Biblical Criticism and Theology: Toward a New Biblical Theology," in *Radical Pluralism and Truth: David Tracy and the Hermeneutics of Religion,* ed. Werner G. Jeanrond and Jennifer L. Rike (New York: Crossroad, 191), pp. 38-48.

10. Eco offered these observations in the course of a public discussion at University College Dublin in the Autumn 1991.

11. I am following here David Tracy's distinction of the three publics to which the theologian is committed, namely academy, society, and church. See *The Analogical Imagination,* pp. 3-46. Apart from these reflections Tracy has remained remarkably silent on the public of the church.

12. This point is further developed in my *Text and Interpretation as Categories of Theological Thinking,* pp. 64-72.

13. For an illuminating discussion of the prophetic and the mystical dimensions of religion see David Tracy, *Dialogue With the Other: The Inter-Religious Dialogue* (Louvain: Peeters, 1990), pp. 94-123.

14. Wright, *Theology and Literature,* pp. 12-3.

15. Jasper, *The Study of Literature and Religion,* p. 104.

16. Jasper, *The Study of Literature and Religion,* p. 106.

17. In the following discussion of Metz's contribution to narrative theology I use some material from an article previously published in *Proceedings: 7th European Conference on Philosophy of Religion* (Utrecht University 1988): 156-70.

18. Johann Baptist Metz, "Kleine Apologie des Erzählens," *Concilium* 9 (1973): 334-41; Harald Weinrich, "Narrative Theologie," *Concilium* 9 (1973): 329-34. Both articles appeared in English in *The Crisis of Religious Language, Concilium* 85 (Edinburgh: T.&T. Clark, 1973). Metz continued to reflect on the narrative dimension of theology and presented his thoughts in his book *Glaube in Geschichte und Gesellschaft: Studien zu einer praktischen Fundamentaltheologie* (Mainz: Grünewald, 1977 [*Faith in History and Society: Toward a Practical Fundamental Theology,* tr. David Smith (London: Burns and Oates, 1980)].

19. See Wright, *Theology and Literature,* pp. 83-128.

20. Metz, *Glaube in Geschichte und Gesellschaft,* p. 189: "Wo Theologie ihr narratives Grundwesen ächtet oder es sich absichtsvoll verbirgt, geschieht dies aber am Ende zum Schaden beider, des 'Arguments' wie der 'Erzählung' in der Theologie."

21. Metz, *Glaube in Geschichte und Gesellschaft*, pp. 78-9.

22. Metz, *Glaube in Geschichte und Gesellschaft*, pp. 118-9.

23. Metz, *Glaube in Geschichte und Gesellschaft*, p. 118 (my translation).

24. Metz, *Glaube in Geschichte und Gesellschaft*, p. 159.

25. Metz, *Glaube in Geschichte und Gesellschaft*, p. 193 (my translation).

26. Metz, *Glaube in Geschichte und Gesellschaft*, pp. 204-5.

27. Metz, *Glaube in Geschichte und Gesellschaft*, p. 187 (my translation).

28. See Dermot A. Lane, *Foundations for a Social Theology: Praxis, Process and Salvation* (Dublin: Gill and Macmillan, 1984), esp. pp. 6-24.

29. Metz, *Glaube in Geschichte und Gesellschaft*, p. 57 (my translation).

30. Metz, *Glaube in Geschichte und Gesellschaft*, p. 182.

31. Metz, *Glaube in Geschichte und Gesellschaft*, p. 193.

32. Goethe, *Faust*. ed. Erich Trunz (München: Beck, 1972), p. 144 (verse 4603).

33. See Mircea Eliade, *The Sacred and the Profane: The Nature of Religion*, tr. Willard R. Trask (New York and London: Harcourt Brace Jovanovich, 1959), pp. 20-65.

34. *Faust*, p. 364 (verses 12110f.): "Das Ewig-Weibliche zieht uns hinan."

35. Karl-Josef Kuschel, *Stellvertreter Christi? Der Papst in der zeitgenössichen Literatur*, Ökumenische Theologie 6 (Zürich and Köln: Benziger, and Gütersloh: Gerd Mohn, 1980).

36. See Kuschel, *Stellvertreter Christi?*, pp. 171-202.

37. Fyodor Dostoyevsky, *The Brothers Karamazov*, tr. David Magarshack (Harmondsworth: Penguin, 1983), pp. 288-311.

38. Hans Küng, "Theologie und Literatur: Gegenseitige Herausforderung," in ed. Walter Jens, Hans Küng and Karl-Josef Kuschel, *Theologie und Literatur: Zum Stand des Dialogs* (München: Kindler, 1986), pp. 24-9.

39. Küng, "Theologie und Literatur: Gegenseitige Herausforderung," p. 26.

40. Küng, "Theologie und Literatur: Gegenseitige Herausforderung," p. 29.

41. See in this regard the helpful study by Wayne C. Booth, *The Company We Keep: An Ethics of Fiction* (Berkeley and Los Angeles: University of California Press, 1988).

42. See my general comments on Christian praxis in my article "Theory and Praxis: A New Career for Ethics?," in ed. Seán Freyne, *Ethics and the Christian* (Dublin: Columbia Press, 1991), pp. 9-23; and in *Text and Interpretation*,pp. 64-71.

43. See my discussion of correlational approaches to theology in my *Theological Hermeneutics: Development and Significance* (London: Macmillan, and New York: Crossroad, 1991), pp. 174-6. Karl-Josef Kuschel prefers the "method of structural analogy" to the "method of correlation" because the latter leads to a perception of both correspondences and alienations. See Karl-Josef Kuschel, "*Vielleicht hält Gott sich einige Dichter . . .": Literarisch-theologische Porträts* (Mainz: Grünewald, 1991), pp. 384-5. While I agree with Kuschel that both perceptions are important dimensions of any adequate method of literary-theological thinking, I fail to see why the method of correlation is supposed to exclude the perception of alienations.

44. For a more recent example of this neglect of the religious dimension in literary and cultural criticism see the editor's introduction in ed. Thomas Docherty, *Postmodernism: A Reader* (Hemel Hempstead: Harvester Wheatsheaf, 1993), pp. 1-31.

EMERSON AND NIETZSCHE ON HISTORY
Lesson for the Next Millennium

Irena Makarushka

Reflecting on the unanticipated uniqueness implicit in the historical character of human experience, the narrator in Louise Erdrich's novel, *Love Medicine* observes, "So many things in the world have happened before. But it's like they never did. Every new thing that happens to a person, it's a first." The significance that events acquire when they happen to us is worthy of consideration as we reassess our world at the end of the twentieth century. Many, if not most, of the socio-political and environmental issues that concern us today "have happened before." What is unique about these issues, what lends them a sense of newness—if not urgency—is that now they are happening to us. In recognizing their impact on our lives, we become aware of our own moment in time. We begin to see that we can choose to define our place in history by taking responsibility for its unfolding. History, after all, is the sum total of our decisions and actions which determine the kind of world we leave for future generations who will also confront these issues again as though for the first time. The idea that history is the task of every individual and that the creation of the future is everyone's moral responsibility are among the lessons to be learned from Emerson's 1841 essay "History"[1] and from Nietzsche's 1874 essay "On the Uses and Disadvantages of History for Life."[2]

This essay offers a reassessment of the interpretation of history proposed by Emerson and Nietzsche and focuses on the connection they make between history and the individual as creator. If for Feuerbach we are what we eat, for Emerson and Nietzsche, we are the history we create. For Emerson, history was the record of the workings of the universal mind instantiated in actions of every individual (9). Nietzsche insisted that balanced between memory and forgetfulness, history was necessary "for the sake of life and action" (59). For each thinker, history was not about the past, but about the ways in which the present stands in relation to the future. In each case, history represented the process of coming to terms with the past by appropriating it into one's present in order to create a more just and harmonious future. As individuals engage in "doing" history, they transcend the particularity of the moment as well as the discreteness of their own experience and create the possibilities promised in time.

Near the end of his essay, Emerson noted, "History walks incarnate in every just and wise man" (41). Bracketing the culturally sanctioned exclusion of women from history, Emerson's observation can serve as a useful reminder of our task as we "think to 2000." History is not something apart from who we are, rather it is a reflection of the kind of individual we choose to become. The future is circumscribed by our desire to overcome the cynicism of the late twentieth century as well as by our desire to be just and wise. In *The Critique of Cynical Reason,* a particularly insightful description of our times, Peter Sloterdijk writes,

> Wherever deceptions are constitutive for a culture, wherever life in society succumbs to a compulsion for lying, there really speaking the truth has an element of aggression, an unfriendly exposure. Nevertheless the instinct for disclosure is stronger in the long run. Only a radical nakedness and bringing things out in the open can free us from the compulsion for mistrustful imputations. Wanting to get to the "naked truth" is one motive for desperate sensuousness, which wants to tear through the veil of conventions, lies, abstractions, and discretions in order to get *to the bottom* of things.[3]

Both Emerson and Nietzsche wrote about history in order to get to the bottom of things. They addressed the limits and self-deceptions of their own times and provided us with models for engaging in the creation our present as well as our future.

Emerson wrote "History" three years after his rejection of Unitarianism for which the address he delivered before the 1838 graduating class of Harvard's Divinity School provided a public forum. In substance, the "Divinity School Address" was a critique of Christianity, of its misrepresentation of Jesus and of its inability to appreciate the metaphoric nature of language and meaning. Emerson's "Address" anticipated Nietzsche's more acerbic critique in *The Anti-Christ.* The significance of Emerson's critique is far reaching and informs his reconsideration of history. His refusal to accept metaphysics and theology as the framework for belief about the nature of history and significance of human actions is informed by his refusal to be determined, defined and constrained by the law of the Father/s. For Emerson, the displacement of transcendence by immanence—of the divine by the human—was the condition for the reclamation of freedom and desire. He created a kind of erotics and politics of choice. As a result of his new freedom, unleashed from patriarchal bondage, he turned his intellectual and creative energies to writing "History" and other important essays such as "Self-Reliance," "The Over-Soul" and "Circles" published in the collection *Essays: First Series,* whose common theme is the primacy of the individual.

Emerson's rejection of Christianity and consequently of Western metaphysics is reflected in his attitude toward history. Devoid of idealist trappings and no longer interpreted as salvation history which perhaps had its last and most elaborate systematic justification in Hegel's philosophy, for Emerson, and later for Nietzsche, history became the moral obligation of every individual. The refusal to accept patriarchal values as normative allowed both Emerson and Nietzsche to read theories of history with suspicion. Nietzsche, for example, was highly critical of Hegel's theory of history which he saw as merely an extension of his Christian theology (96). After all, theory is connected to the presuppositions of Western philosophy and theology. The *theo* of theory is the same as the *theo* in theology.[4] In each case the grounding assumption is that knowledge and judgment are contingent on a metaphysical referent. Theory announces itself as mastery over that which is placed before it as subject. Emerging out of a Baconian understanding of the task of science, the position of theory in relation to its objectified subject is that of domination, power, force, and control.[5] With regard to history, the refusal of Emerson and Nietzsche to be determined by a theological/metaphysical worldview allowed them to replace theory with critical thinking as their interpretative practice. Their reading of history focused on the active participatory practice of individuals whose creative engagement with life and history creates the future. By insisting that values and meaning are not the manifestation of God in time and history but are created by individuals, they reconnected the aesthetic with the ethical. In other words, once they credited individuals with the power to create, the idea that creation is inscribed with the values implicit within the culture of the creator followed logically.

History and critical discourse are effected by the critique of Christianity and metaphysics proposed by Emerson and Nietzsche. Their desire to disclose the limits of the dominant models of authority illustrates the ways in which critique is a judgment about judgments which denies them their absoluteness, their colonizing power, their control and domination. Contemporary critical discourse—whether it is from a feminist, African-American, gay and lesbian, "third/fourth" world, or environmental perspectives—functions in our cultures in the same disclosive way. Effectively, the end of metaphysics signals the end of "His-story." Once the connection between God and world is sundered, "His-story" is replaced by a plethora of stories. The end of "His-story" becomes the condition for the recovery of the stories of those who were told that they had no stories to tell.

Critical discourse, in Sloterdijk's terms, attempts to "get at the 'naked truth'" by tearing through "the veil of conventions, lies [and] abstractions . . . ." Just as Emerson and Nietzsche chose to free themselves from the constraints of a monomythic system of power, so contemporary critical discourse is primarily a discourse of liberation, the discourse of the act of self-creation. It claims the right to access the power implicit in words and language, the right to be heard and taken seriously. The critical discourse of those who have been confined to the margins is the discourse of desire and freedom. It is an attempt to recover the power lost to the hegemony of the dominant, white, patriarchal theo-ries and theo-logies. The refusal to be subjugated by the laws of the fathers, politicians, scientists, theoreticians is the condition for engaging in the creation of a polymythic and polysignificant future. Rejecting the truth-claims of cultural monomyths, critical discourse celebrates Durkheim's insight that all religions are true, no religion is false.[6] Analogously, all myths as explanatory cultural narratives are significant and meaningful.

The attempt of contemporary critical discourse to recover the voices that had been suppressed in the past reflects Emerson's notion that reading and understanding history has only one goal: to better understand who we are today. Describing the proper way to approach history, he writes, "The student is to read history actively and not passively; to esteem his own life the text, and books the commentary" (13). The significance and meaning of history, therefore, emerges in the process by which it becomes meaningful to me and illuminates my life, my moment in time, my desires and my choices. It is useful to recall that in "Book One" of *The Will to Power*, Nietzsche used the terms passive/active to distinguish between two varieties of nihilism. Passive nihilism or pessimism described as "decline and recession of the power of the spirit" (WP §22)[7] signifies a culture's self-forgetfulness and which lead to its demise. Active or radical nihilism described as "increased the power of the spirit" (WP §22) is the condition necessary for the transvaluation of values. Insofar as it generates change, it is necessary for life and the future.

The importance of reading history actively, as Emerson suggests, echoes through Nietzsche's critique of Hegel's concept of history (105). Nietzsche argues that Hegel's theory of history is "an idolatry of the factual" leading to an "accommodation of the individual to the facts." The "religion of the power of history"—the religion of the monomyth such as that of Hegel—denies the power of the present and, therefore, disallows the creation of the future. Over against the Hegelian monomyth of the factual, Nietzsche proposed increasing the awareness of history as an artifact, as a narrative that emerges out of the ambiguity of human experience and which recalls the complexity of human existence.

Emerson also recognized the narrative aspect of history and insisted that history does not provide an objective record of the past. Rather, reflecting on Napoleon's question, "What is history? . . . but a fable agreed upon" (15), in a remarkable tribute to the primacy of the subject, Emerson writes, "All history becomes subjective; in other words there is properly no history, only biography" (15). Nietzsche echoed these sentiments with regard to philosophers in *Beyond Good and Evil* where he wrote, "Gradually it has become clear to me what every great philosophy so far has been: namely, the personal confession of its author and a kind of involuntary and unconscious memoir. . . ." (BGE §6).[8] The notion that history, and in Nietzsche's case philosophy, is biography strengthens the argument that the "here and now" and individual engagement are the primary focus of Emerson's interpretation of the meaning and significance of history.

Acknowledging that history is both biography and artifact, Emerson insisted that the universal truths of history are narrated by the poets. "The advancing man," observed Emerson, ". . . finds that the poet . . . that universal man wrote by his pen a confession true for one and true for all. His own secret biography he finds in lines wonderfully intelligible to him, dotted down before he was born" (33). His fascination with subjectivity and the centrality of individual desire and creative spirit is set within the context of the larger cultural moment. This contextualization saves Emerson from slipping into mere solipsism.

The interconnectedness of individuals and the ethical implications that follow from it are evident in Emerson's claims that "A man is a bundle of relations, a knot of roots, whose flower and fruitage is the world. His faculties refer to natures out of him and predict the world he is to inhabit . . ." (39). History, therefore, is relived in the experience and choices of every individual. In his recognition of the importance of taking the long view of history when thinking about the effects of actions, Emerson's attitude is not unlike that of Native Americans who believe that tribal decisions must be made for the sixth generation.[9] Adumbrating the significance of the relationships between human beings and nature voiced by contemporary environmentalists, Emerson insisted that we "cannot live without a world" (39).

For Emerson, nature and culture are not separate but inform one another. History, nature, and individuals collaborate in the reconfiguration of the past and the creation of the future. Being attentive to richness of ordinary experience, artists re-imagine the world. Emerson interpreted the similar patterns of architectural ornamentation found among different cultures as proof of the undeniable connection between the individual creative spirit and communal human creative spirit, between cultural artifact and nature, between a culture's history and individual's history. The result of such connectedness, he noted, is that ". . . all public facts are to be individualized, all private facts to be generalized. Then at once History becomes fluid and true, and Biography deep and sublime" (25).

History as fable, just as history as biography, becomes a story told and retold by one who has access to power and speaks with authority. The "fable" comes to be identified with power and its claims about its own objectivity and truth become culturally normative. Emerson argued that history as an agreed upon fable is only significant if it is interpreted through an individual's experience. Merely as a fable about the power of the past, history fails to animate the present. Emerson insisted that reading history makes the past present not by classifying the parts under objective categories but by a deep personal understanding of the inner coherences, the common ground and unity of cause and variety of appearance (17-8). The tensive relationship between surface and depth, form and content is fundamental to Emerson's notion of history and prevents it from falling into the category of the merely subjective. Nietzsche was also very clear about the importance of the interconnectedness of individuals, history and culture. As a result of ungrounded subjectivity, he wrote, "one widens the dubious gulf between content and form to the point of complete insensitivity to barbarism" (79). For both Emerson and Nietzsche, the task of readers and interpreters of history is the disclosure of its unity in diversity which effectively speaks to the complexity of human nature.

Emerson praised the harmony that he saw in ancient Greek culture wherein a balance was struck among the various elements constitutive of life; namely, history, culture, nature, and the individual. The aesthetic sense of measured order and grace represented for him, as it did for Nietzsche, a triumph of the natural and ordinary in human experience. He saw creation in this ancient culture balancing the "energy of manhood with the engaging unconsciousness of childhood" (30). Like the third transformation into the Heraclitean child playing with draughts announced by Nietzsche's Zarathustra, Emerson's vision of history celebrates the presence of the past in the present wherein the ancient traditions are reborn in the moment. Anticipating Nietzsche's eternal recurrence, Emerson wrote, "When a thought of Plato becomes a thought to me,— when a truth that fired the soul of Pindar fires mine, time is no more" (30). Emerson insisted that we interpret history out of our own lived experience—the past is re-presenced in our present. As he did in the "Divinity School Address," Emerson argued that "our own piety explains every fact, every word" (31) attributed to Jesus. Therefore, his teachings, like those of other teachers of wisdom such as Moses and Zoroaster among others, are not about the moral life of antiquity but of our own world.

Emerson's insights are unabashedly positive and optimistic, teeming with the exuberance of his own sense of freedom and his desire to extend to all the possibility of being self-reliant. He wrote, "To the poet, to the philosopher, to the saint, all things are friendly and sacred, all events profitable, all days holy, all men divine" (17).[10] In "History," Emerson offered a highly charged and consummately hopeful vision for the future, as did Nietzsche in "On the Uses and Disadvantages of History for Life," wherein he argued for the primacy of life and the future (59). For Emerson, freedom and desire with regard to history are interpreted as the engagement of the individual subjectivity in the universal historical consciousness. The past and the future meet in the present in the creative drive of individual. Though the creative will of the individual is at the core of the relationship between the individual and history, Nietzsche was also concerned with surfacing the complex and ambiguous elements of human nature. In his view, the creative and decreative are one and the same impulse expressed as the creative interpretative will.[11]

Nietzsche's interpretation of history, as the title of the essay suggests, focused on its ambiguous character. We need history for life, he argued, yet a surfeit of history is harmful (63-4). He identified three species of history and argued that they fail to provide a balanced rendering of history. The first species, namely, monumental history, looked back on the triumphs and greatness of individuals (68); the second, critical history, "cruelly trampled over every kind of piety" (76); and finally, antiquarian history regarded all aspects of the past with equal reverence. Nietzsche insisted that history must be narrated and interpreted in ways that reflect the inescapably ambiguous nature of human experience. Monumental history, therefore, was inadequate because it merely glorified the winners and forgot the losers. The disproportionate emphasis on and remembrance of the triumphs of the past is harmful because it creates an image that does not correspond to ordinary experience and invites self-destructive choices. Concerned about the effects of monumental history on culture, Nietzsche wrote, "Monumental history deceives by analogies: with seductive similarities it inspires the courageous to foolhardiness and the inspired to fanaticism . . . ." (71).

A balanced attitude toward history was also lacking in critical history which erred on the other extreme by focusing on the negative and destructive. In order to provide an interpretation that reflects the ambiguity of human experience, Nietzsche saw the need for critical history to become more forgiving and accepting of the past in order to prevent a paralysis of the will. Paraphrasing Paul and Augustine, he observed, "What happens all too often is that we know the good but do not do it, because we also know the better but cannot do it" (76). The same problem of imbalance was part of the perspective of antiquarian history. By venerating the past for its own sake, neither the present nor the future were given appropriate attention. Summing up his critique, Nietzsche wrote, "Antiquarian history itself degenerates from the moment it is no longer animated and inspired by the fresh life of the present" (75). Although all three species or modes of interpretation are necessary if history is to serve life and the future, Nietzsche insisted that their value and significance is determined by the degree to which they reflect the ambiguity of human experience.

Nietzsche's critique of the three species of history is informed by his fundamental commitment to life and the future. Looking critically at the ways in which history had been represented as offering objective or factual knowledge, following Emerson, Nietzsche overturned the claim of objectivity and focused on the role of the individual in the interpretative process. The substance of his argument was based on the *plastic power* defined as "the capacity to develop out of oneself in one's own way, to transform and incorporate into oneself what is past and foreign, to heal wounds and to recreate broken moulds" (62). Recalling Coleridge's secondary imagination which "dissolves, diffuses, dissipates in order to re-create,"[12] the *plastic power* was reconfigured as the creative will to power in his later writing. The creative will to power constituted the core of Nietzsche's philosophy and animated his religious imagination.

With regard to history, Nietzsche wrote, the *plastic power* permitted individuals

> to assimilate and appropriate the things of the past; and the most powerful and tremendous nature would be characterized by the fact that it would know no boundary at all at which the historical sense began to overwhelm it; it would draw the past into itself, its own and the most foreign to it and, as it were transform it into blood (63).

For Nietzsche, as for Emerson, the capacity to re-create the past and to re-imagine the future was developed to the greatest degree in artists. Art became the counterpoint to the abuses of historical consciousness which was blind to the ambiguities of experience. Nietzsche argued, "Artists alone are capable of learning from . . . history in a true, that is to say life-enhancing sense" (71). The creative will of artists, therefore, has both an aesthetic as well as an ethical dimension. Artists create in order to guarantee the future of humankind. Nietzsche's faith in the creative will of artists is similar to Emerson's belief that "artist[s] attain . . . the power of awakening other souls" (21) by their capacity to appropriate history in a self-transformative way.

Emerson argued that the genius of a culture is manifest in a variety of forms: art, literature, history, architecture. Nietzsche saw the highest development of culture, what he described as true culture, in the ancient Greek world wherein culture was "a new and improved *physis* without inner or outer, without dissimulation and convention, culture as the unanimity of life thought, appearance and will" (123). For both these thinkers, culture and history were incontrovertibly contingent on the creative will of artists. A similar view is expressed by Iris Murdoch in a remarkably prescient 1970 essay titled "Existentialists and Mystics." She observes,

> We are, apparently, entering an untheological time. Even the theology of Marxism has lost some of its charm. The old assumptions appear in different guises an in attenuated forms and begin to seem less satisfactory. But we are not left entirely without moral symbolism or without an intelligible relation to the past. . . . The writer has always been important, and now is *essential*, as a truth-teller and as a defender of words. . . . It may be that in the end the novelist will be the savior of the human race.[13]

The notion that the novelist or artist can play a salvific role in history is among the more strongly held beliefs of Emerson and Nietzsche. Emerson saw poets speaking all that is universal and eternal in human nature and experience (33) as they recount their own lives. Nietzsche argued that "history is the antithesis of art: and only if history can endure to be transformed into a work of art will it perhaps be able to preserve" (95) the *plastic power*—the inner drive to create.

The recent events in eastern Europe have affirmed the faith Emerson and Nietzsche have in art and artists as they have corroborated Murdoch's perceptive analysis. Vaclav Havel embodies the praiseworthy qualities of the artist committed to life and the future. Speaking as an artist who has faith in the politically transformative power of language in his 1989 speech "Words on Words" accepting the "Peace Prize of the German Booksellers Association," Havel writes,

> In the beginning was the Word . . . . What is meant . . . is that the Word of God is the source of all creation. But surely the same could be said, figuratively speaking, of every human action? And indeed, words can be said to be the very source of our being . . . .[14]

Havel sees the possibility of the disclosure of truths critical for the the future in the primacy of words. The moral symbolism which Murdoch associates with the language of novelists and Havel sees in the creative power of language mirrors the attitudes of Emerson and Nietzsche. Murdoch's faith that the writer can perform the task of redeemer resonates with their perception concerning the possibility of the future as being contingent on the creative engagement of artists and poets as truth-sayers.

Following Nietzsche, who believed that humanity is endowed with a creative will, the redemptive work of artists is the responsibility of all individuals. Emerson insisted that each individual is held responsible and is ethically and morally bound to create history. Each individual as a participant in nature and culture writes history out of an affinity for justice and wisdom by way of a creative imagination vested with the metaphoric and symbolic power of language. Facts, Emerson reminded us, are to be considered as symbols (42). Our history is to be written broader and deeper, "from an ethical reformation, from an influx of the new, ever sanative conscience,—if we would trulier express our central and wide-related nature, instead of the old chronology of selfishness and pride . . ." (43), we would write new history.

At the end of the twentieth century, as we consider the legacy we have created for those who will follow us, it may be instructive to bear in mind the words of Paul D, a freed slave in Toni Morrison's novel *Beloved*. As he recalled his time of bondage in Alfred, Georgia, dreaming the possibility of a different future, he said that what he wanted most was ". . . to get to a place where you could love anything you chose—not to need permission for desire—well now, *that* was freedom."[15] The freedom to desire is the legacy of Emerson and Nietzsche. Their interpretations of history stress the role and responsibility of the individual who desires a different future. Moving beyond the cultural monomyth of Western metaphysics, their reading of history creates the condition for seeing the world as a more wholistic and harmonious place. Access to the power of words and the right to tell one's story no longer needs to be determined by the categories of gender, race, class, sexual orientation, age or any other arbitrary classification that benefits those who have the power to discriminate. The cynicism so prevalent in these times is ultimately a denial of both desire and freedom. It is the cynicism of Nietzsche's pessimist who signifies the self-destructive impulse in culture. If, as Emerson suggested, history is incarnate in the just and the wise, and, as Nietzsche suggested, history is the task of creative individuals who value life and the future, then we can begin to see traces of a history that has an ethical as well as an aesthetic significance where desire and freedom are part of the experience of all individuals.

NOTES

1. Ralph Waldo Emerson, "History," in *Essays: First and Second Series* (Boston and New York: Houghton Mifflin Company, 1883), pp. 9-43. Parenthetical page numbers refer to this edition.

2. Friedrich Nietzsche, "On the Uses and Disadvantages of History for Life," in *Untimely Meditations*, tr. R. J. Hollingdale (Cambridge: Cambridge University Press, 1983), pp. 57-124. Parenthetical page numbers refer to this edition.

3. Peter Sloterdijk, *Critique of Cynical Reason*, tr. Michael Eldred (Minneapolis, MN: University of Minnesota Press, 1987), xxxviii.

4. For a detailed postmodern reading of the interconnectedness of history, theology, and theory, see Mark C. Taylor, *Erring: A Postmodern A/theology* (Chicago & London: The University of Chicago Press, 1984), chap. 3, "End of History."

5. For an analysis of the gendered aspect of the language of Baconian science which establishes itself as the accepted scientific lexicon, see Evelyn Fox Keller, *Reflections on Gender and Science* (New Haven: Yale University Press, 1985), chap. 2, "Baconian Science: The Arts of Mastery and Obedience."

6. Emile Durkheim, *The Elementary Forms of Religious Life*, tr. Joseph Ward Swain (New York: The Free Press, 1965), pp. 14-5.

7. Friedrich Nietzsche, *The Will to Power*, tr. Walter Kaufman and R. J. Hollingdale (New York: Vintage Books, 1968). Cited as WP with section number.

8. Friedrich Nietzsche, *Beyond Good and Evil*, tr. Walter Kaufman (New York: Vintage Books, 1966). Cited as BGE with aphorism number.

9. Oren Lyon and Bill Moyers, *The Faithkeeper*, video.

10. In "Translator's Introduction," to Friedrich Nietzsche, *The Gay Science*, tr. Walter Kaufmann (New York: Vintage Books, 1974), p. 7, Kaufmann notes that this quotation appears as the epigraph of the first edition of Nietzsche's *Die fröhliche Wissenschaft*.

11. Irena Makarushka, "Nietzsche's Critique of Modernity: The Emergence of Hermeneutical Consciousness," *Semeia* 51 (1990): 193-214.

12. Samuel Coleridge, *Biographia Literaria or Biographical Sketches of My Literary Life and Opinions* (London: Dent, 1965), p. 167.

13. Iris Murdoch, "Existentialists and Mystics: A Note on the Novel in the New Utilitarian Age," in *Essays and Poems Presented to Lord David Cecil*, ed. William Wallace Robson, (London: Constable & Co., Ltd., 1970), p. 181.

14. Vaclav Havel, "Words on Words," in *Writings on the East* (New York: The New York Review of Books, 1990), p. 7.

15. Toni Morrison, *Beloved* (New York: Alfred A. Knopf, 1987), p. 162.

HISTORY IN THE POSTMODERN ERA

Bernard Zelechow

Who's afraid of history? Apparently, from the anthropological and historical record, the answer is almost everyone.[1] "Primitive" cultures fled from the anxiety of historicity while the ancient Egyptians labored to deny its existential reality.[2] The latest onslaught against historical consciousness resides in structuralism and deconstruction. These movements recognize, in their critique of European civilization, that the grounds of European culture rest in a cluster of ideas that include historicity.

The irony is that modernity and the crisis of postmodern culture presuppose historical knowledge. The profoundly unhistorical eternal forms of modernism and the critique of modernism by postmodern thought are impossible without historical knowledge. Yet, in contemporary culture history is a much maligned and misunderstood realm of understanding. The discipline of history is accused of either imposing the dead weight of the certain past, political and cultural, on the present or of being concerned with the fleeting ephemera of culture and by that failing to attain scientific and philosophical certitude (identity).[3]

Despite the contempt for history, modernity used historical knowledge to distil its profoundly antihistorical worldview. Modernist ideology viewed the historical record from the Renaissance to the mid-nineteenth century as a linear exposition and disclosure of formal autonomy in all areas of knowledge and the arts. Once achieved, modernism declared the end of history. In this respect modernism shared the prejudice inherent in the history of philosophy. The philosophical mind disparages historical insight in favor of canons of permanence, certitude, and timelessness. Only Hegel dared to grapple with the then-now problematic of historical truth. And Hegel's motivation was theological rather than purely philosophical.[4]

Postmodernism, particularly in the arts, appears to reinstate the historical in the discourse of the contemporary world. It attacked modernism in its most vulnerable spot, that is, in the premise that the formal rules of modernism are timeless and unchanging. However, postmodernism too often reduces history to the trivial. Its attachment to the historical reeks of parody and cliché. It makes a virtue of historical anachronism.[5]

The values inherent in the historical enterprise are unexamined and taken for granted. Irrespective of the multiplicity of tropes employed by historians the content of history is always the story of human purposes. The corollary is that history is the story of human freedom. And finally history is invariably contemporary history.[6] The historical is at the center of existential reality. Without the notion of historical consciousness, psycho-social personal alternation and cultural and autobiographical transformation is unthinkable. Historical consciousness breathes life into possibility, the paradox of freedom, liberation, and the concept of social revolution.

The question is: what causes the ambivalent rejection and embrace of historical consciousness and knowledge? That is, why have European thinkers had such difficulty in accounting for history? Why does Dilthey's Kantian project falter? Several factors contribute to the theoretical barrier to historical understanding. First, historians were deflected by the inheritance of the Greek tradition of philosophy. The logical canons of identity and certitude were employed inappropriately in place of existential norms. Second, the Enlightenment suppression of the relationship between modernity (historical consciousness) and the biblical tradition mystifies the grounds of historicity.

The theological and biblical bases of history are repressed in the modern academy. This results from the theological authoritarian appropriation of historical discourse in the past. As a reaction to this arrogation, the academic rhetoric of history resides exclusively in the metaphors of facticity, causality, and tropes of historicism. The academic discipline seeks historical justification for its stance in ancient Greek models. Neither theological confiscation nor the mystification of history by the appeal to Thucydides and Herodotus does justice to historical critique, redeeming power, and validity of historical communication in the postmodern world.

A rehearsal of the appeal to Thucydides is warranted on two levels: first, because of the reverence paid him by academic historians, and second, because the problems Thucydides exposes still confound many twentieth-century thinkers about historicity. The first leads to a discussion of fact and objectivity, the second raises the issue of eternity, significance and meaning.

Recently, Simon Schama in *Dead Certainties* displays traditional historical critical erudition dressed fashionably anew as deconstruction.[7] Schama presents two case studies to make his deconstructive point. Finally, his work is a direct but off the mark attack on Thucydides. The first probe examines the death of General Wolfe on the Plains of Abraham and in Benjamin West's pictorial death notice. The second study—exhibiting the Harvard preoccupation with itself—investigates a celebrated murder of a Harvard University professor. The murder coincidentally links twentieth-century historical "undecidability" to the nineteenth-century "scientific" historian George Parkman.

In the first historical report Schama demonstrates that "the myth" of Wolfe's death takes precedence over the "reality." In the second example Schama illustrates the fact that eye-witness reports of events are often dubious and unreliable. Although the evidence was inconclusive, John Webster was convicted of murder. Schama's point is that the historical record is ambiguous, replete with lacunae, and uncertain. The object of the exercise is to convince the reader that contemporary standards of history inspired by Thucydides lacks credibility in light of deconstructive scrutiny. Therefore since he must choose, he prefers the scatological, imprecise, gossip monger Herodotus.[8]

From his dedication of this book to the late Harvard professor of History, John Clive, Schama makes clear that deconstruction is proof positive that history is fiction rather than science. He writes "In memory of John Clive for whom history was literature." He subtitles the work "unwarranted speculations." Unwarranted speculations indeed. There is no quarrel with Schama's rejection of Thucydides or his assertion that history is a form of fiction.[9] The problem is Schama's failure to explicate why he rejects Thucydides and what he means by history as fiction.

Schama's attack on Thucydides is motivated by the unreflective attitudes of his colleagues toward the worthy classical Greek thinker. For the profession the litany runs that Thucydides and Herodotus are the fathers of the discipline of history. The irony in this professional article of faith is that Thucydides may have thought that he was doing history, although that is doubtful, but he was indisputably a great literary artist.

It is fair to say that Thucydides understood little or nothing about what we understand by history. He begins *The Peloponnesian Wars* with a telling disclaimer. He abjures the rehearsal of ancient reports of the Greek city-states. Thucydides's reasons superficially have a "modern" scientific ring. The reports are shrouded in fantastic legends. Therefore, these accounts are untrue and untrustworthy. More conclusively for Thucydides is the argument that all narratives from the past are untenable. The past is gone, and therefore inaccessible; and because it is gone, it can never be known. But if this is the case, how is history possible?

The historian, whatever else he/she does is concerned with the past in relation to the present with an eye to the future. But this goal does not deter Thucydides's project. In fact the question does not even arise for Thucydides. He skirts the issue strategically by presupposing the implications of a "natural" or cosmological definition of time. If the past is unrecoverable and the future is not yet, Thucydides reasons that he must concentrate on the present. To carry the argument to its logical end, Thucydides states forcefully that he will inscribe only those happenings that he witnesses directly.

From Thucydides's announcement it appears that he aspired to first-rate journalism. Presumably the historians' guild has sanctified Thucydides because of the integrity of his journalistic ethic. The commitment to report only what he sees has won him the title of father of historical objectivity. For the moment an appropriate definition of historical objectivity can be postponed. It is only necessary to show that Thucydides had no interest in what we would call the objectivity of investigative reporting. The professionals should take another look.

Thucydides reports speeches by illustrious protagonists in the wars against Sparta. Everyone in this room knows or knows of Pericles's eloquent funeral address. Thucydides may or may not have heard the speech that he reports. In most disarming fashion Thucydides, matter of factly, tells us that he has not always been present when various prominent people orate. But no matter. After all generals always say what generals say. Politicians always say what politicians say.

There are three significant implications to be drawn from Thucydides's disclosure: 1) he has an inadequate concept of facticity; 2) Thucydides lacks a notion of persons with all the uniqueness that the term implies, and he presupposes category archetypes, students, teachers, generals, etc.; and 3) there is nothing new under the sun. All action is reaction. Determinism and fate are equivalences. If Thucydides is the father of anything, it would be political sociology.

There is one further attribute of Thucydides's artistry that deserves comment. It is the most poignant aspect of his attempts to understand the terrible times he lives in. Although Thucydides knows that the upheaval that he witnesses is enormous, he remains incapable of attributing meaning to the events. Trapped as he is in the presupposition that human action is exclusively a category of the circle and cycle of nature, Thucydides cannot generate an idea of historical significance. The Peloponnesian Wars are merely big wars among the cycle of war and peace.

There is a melancholy logic to Thucydides position that ties the conception of temporality to the inability to generate a notion of the significance of events. Thucydides's horizons are limited by the idea of nature as the total meaning system. Therefore, history is the chronicle of measurable circular time, and meaning is a description of successive happenings. His conception of history is coherent but one that is meaningless to those who consciously or unconsciously work with the presuppositions of biblical culture.

A much greater thinker, St. Augustine, reports in *The Confessions* that he struggled with the problem of temporality in trying to understand memory. Like Thucydides Augustine believed that the past is past and is unrecoverable, the future is not yet and therefore unknown. St. Augustine had much more difficulty because of the tensions generated by the collision of biblical insights with the cosmological tradition. St. Augustine knew in a theological way the importance of eternity for temporality. But, as close as Augustine came to formulating a concept of history he never disentangled himself from Greek premises.

The stumbling block for Thucydides and Augustine resides in the concept of temporality. From the ancient Greeks to the nineteenth-century historicists, history was implicitly defined as the measurable and grammatical form of time.[10] The denotation was cast in the universal grammatical form of the tenses of past, present, and future. Defined as the form of time, historical knowledge is logically impossible. The past is gone and cannot be reclaimed and the future is not yet. The present is a succession of equal states of now. Essentially, a profound adherence to Platonism and its variant Aristotelianism bolstered the prejudice against the immeasurable subject matter of history, the sphere of the existential. What makes history history is the concepts of significance and meaning, ideas that defy empirical measurement.

That is, how is history possible? Kant never asks this question implicit and pregnant in the *Critique of Pure Reason*. But, in little more than a century, the question becomes crucial for European thinkers. Wilhelm Dilthey, successor to Hegel in Berlin, posed the question anew in his aborted *Critique of Historical Reason*. Between Kant and Dilthey European thinkers discovered that they could neither avoid history or live with it. Hegel alone among philosophers attempted to tame the power of historical insight. His powerful conceptualization of the problem of history dominated the discourse but also deflected the discussion from the essential foci of historical concern. His presupposition of realizable totality foundered on the dynamic infinity of historical development.

A mere generation after Hegel's profession of a philosophy of history, Kierkegaard launched his polemical attack on Hegel and historicism. Paradoxically, *Concluding Unscientific Postscript* begins with the scathing condemnation of history but concludes with a Christian project as an autobiographical version of historical self-consciousness. Nietzsche repeats the Kierkegaardian project substituting secular self-becoming for historicism.

The quirkiness of historical study itself contributes to the paradoxical positions held by Kierkegaard and Nietzsche. Historical consciousness is uncertain. It lacks a secure theoretical structure. It reflects the ambiguity and anxiety of human life. History is concerned with change and difference. It embraces the paradox of existence in defying the law of contradiction. Instead of the logical either/or, historical consciousness incorporates being and becoming simultaneously. Because of this quirkiness, historicity does not observe the logical canons in the house of modern scholasticism. Rather, historicity is a mode of existential communication. But both Nietzsche and Kierkegaard were appalled by the historicist strategies employed to mask the existential qualities of historical consciousness. It is these straight-jacket canons of explanation that are the targets of modern anti-historical attacks by Kierkegaard, Nietzsche, and Franz Rosenzweig.

Modern historicists transcend theoretically the ancient problem of the logic of grammatical time. They assimilate the conceptual notion of temporal development through a notion of distance. This creation of historical distancing occurred during the Renaissance. Its "discovery" parallels the development of perspective in painting.[11] The Renaissance integrated the form and content of the classical past without much reflection on its relational meaning.[12] Distancing—necessary for the construction of objects—without relation profoundly alienates the investigator. The process detaches historical content from historical beings. However, this alienation did not safeguard historicism from a variant of the ancient problem of the logic of the form of time.

For modern historicists the issue is one of values and judgements. How can historical judgements about eternal values be made from within contingent history? Is there an extrinsic standard of judgement that applies? The scientific agenda of historicism requires a negative answer. According to historicism values are culturally determined. Therefore, the past could not be judged in light of the present; the present could not be understood in the perspective of the not yet. Theoretically, historical explanation is reduced to descriptive statements locating events in time and space.

The historicist dilemma merges with the bias of the Enlightenment tradition. A case in point is Habermas's musings about history. Habermas's work relies on the historical, and he knows that history is possible. He knows that the nineteenth-century idea of historicism is inadequate. Its standard was the chronological account of how the present came into existence. The canon of historical explanation is met in locating the time and place of past events. Habermas recommends Benjamin's *Ten Theses on History* as the appropriate canon for the discipline. Yet, he maintains he does not know how Benjamin arrives at his insight.[13]

Walter Benjamin, secularist and Marxist, drew ironically from the deepest recesses of Jewish tradition the conception of historicity so admired by Habermas. Benjamin offers a transhistorical conception of history in which the present generation is accountable for past events with the responsibility for the gestating future. Benjamin's categorical imperative demanded that not only the winners in the past must be remembered but the losers must be redeemed also. In short, Benjamin's idea of history incorporates the biblical imperative of bearing witness.

Habermas's response and Benjamin's solution leads us back to Augustine's struggle and beyond. Until the biblical texts transformed Augustine, memory as a transtemporal category eluded him. The biblical texts alone display an historical notion of time based on something other than cosmological measurement. St. Augustine did not reconcile the two ideas successfully. For a coherent view of historicity we must return to the Hebrew Bible. Historicity, the singularly original contribution to modern and postmodern consciousness, is uniquely biblical. No other culture presents a worldview that embodies historical consciousness so comprehensively.[14]

To warrant so sweeping an assertion about the power of history a few distinctions distinguishing history from other modes of cultural memory are necessary. Every people has a past. Every people has a chronicle. But until recently most cultures lacked historical consciousness. Such consciousness is subversive of traditional culture. Thucydides was partly right to reject the past. He was sceptical enough to be suspicious of what the reports of the past promoted. But he refused to or could not draw out the implications of the ancient descriptions. The past as presented as a past represents the official ideology. It is the collective myth that seals totalitarian cultural desires to insure an unquestioned agreement to agree.[15] An unexamined past is a repressed past. Like repressed personal memory, repressed cultural memory is a burden, an uncontrollable, irrational,reactive burden. It is a forgetting which is not forgotten.

Historical consciousness provides the environment for forgetting to find its proper place in the cultural scheme. It is dialectically ironic that the instrument of forgetting is the active notion of remembering. Only by remembering—locating and incorporating the forgotten in the consciousness of the present—can the present be liberated for the future and the past be laid to rest.

Significantly, *zachor*, the verb to remember occurs more than five hundred times in the five books of Moses.[16] To remember is an essential component of historicity. However, by itself, as Augustine testifies, remembrance does not provide all the components that make history possible. For a conception of history to emerge: 1) a category of existence other than nature must exist; 2) an articulated expression of freedom must be present; 3) a concept of meaning and significance must be operative (4) the idea of critique must be embodied; and 5) transhistorical time and human consciousness must be understood in symbiotic terms.

From the opening lines of Genesis, the biblical writers announce a plane of reality that has priority over nature. The biblical God, the creator of nature, is first the God of history.[17] God, upon surveying creation, deems it good. But the culmination of God's creation is the sanctification of the temporal, the Sabbath. As A. J. Heschel has put it, the sabbath is God's temple in time.[18]

The biblical God does not manifest God's self in visual terms. God's presence is embodied in speech. The speaking God calls out to humankind in the same manner that God called to nature. However, whereas nature has no answer, humankind engages in discourse with God by virtue of God's having created humankind in his image. But what is especially significant for this essay is that God encounters humankind existentially in time. This encounter transforms human existence so that it is consistent with sanctified time. For God's meeting with humankind endows the human experience with meaning and significance. There is a reciprocity in the bond between the Creator and God's creatures. The link is announced metaphorically in the story of the tree of knowledge of good and evil. The tale expresses the acknowledgement of the emergence of the human community. It figuratively announces the terrifying reality of human freedom. The story unfolds to reveal the human task involved in reciprocity. The world is the human paradise in which human beings are enjoined to sanctify existence temporally and paradoxically eternally in partnership—albeit unequal partnership—with God.

It is far from coincidental that in biblical Hebrew the term *olam*, the world, also means eternity. Nor is it accidental that in the language of scripture there is a play on God as Presence and the temporality of the present. The name of God is in some vague way associated with the verb to be. But the Name is not synonymous with the Greek category of Being. It does not mean "I am that I am." Characteristic of Hebrew thinking, the name *Ehyeh Asher Ehyer* translates imprecisely into a temporal presence.

It means "I was always present I am present and I will always be present as the Presence."[19] In other words God's name is synonymous with sacred history. The link between God's name and human history is also the bond linking immediacy (experientially the present) and permanence (experiential self-conscious presentness of the past). The bond sets the task of knowing God's word and doing it. To remember is to take part in eternity. This conception of *zachor* embodies a transportation of the past out of pastness into the present for present and future redemption.

This human eternity finds its expression in what becomes the structure of historicity. For the biblical writers insist that all here are present/were present at Sinai. The epiphany is transhistorical. The biblical injunction in the *Sh'ma*, Hear O Israel, is that one must remember one's presence and one must teach it to the children that they remember their presence. The linkage between remembering and teaching distinguishes the biblical injunction from the Greek notion of recollection, literally to recollect. To recollect is a contemplative act while to teach the remembrance is an action in the world.

Active remembrance would be meaningless if it were not bound to a possibility of transformation and redemption. Therefore, ransom/release/liberation makes up the third element in the structure of biblical thinking binding Creation and Revelation into a whole.

But how and why are redemption or human liberation necessary and possible? The rationale is paradoxical as is the activity itself. Central to the human project is the biblical assertion that revelation is God's story. By definition God's story presupposes an absolute platform that makes all other storytelling possible. The absolute quality of the divine platform provides the standard whereby every other narrative can be judged. This unique angle of vision is responsible for the profoundly dynamic, subversive, and liberating quality of revelation. If God's standard is absolute, all human culture in relation to that standard is insufficient and inadequate. Hence, inherent in the notion of God's story are the powerful weapons of infinite critique and prophecy. The notion of critique is powerful enough that revelation itself, from within itself, is subject to the standards of prophetic critique.

The idea of absolute platform has two other profound implications. God's perspective makes human history possible. God's story cannot be told without the narration of the human story. God's standard cannot be realized without human participation. This symbiosis of human and divine stories is reflected in the paradox of human freedom and God's omniscience. In setting in motion consciousness and morality, God loses control of human action. But God sets out the plan of creation, revelation, and redemption (the game plan so to speak). The result is that human beings lack the mastery over the conditions and consequences of their actions. How and when, if and in what way the ultimate meaning of history will unfold is the historian's quest.

Further, the idea of divine absolute platform provides the clue to how to overcome the historicist dilemma of justifying the making of value judgements. The issue goes beyond the historicist concern for the relativity of values. For from within history, without distancing oneself from history historical judgement is impossible. How can one make judgements at all? Yet, the very grounds of history require justification from within the historical sphere. The absolute platform contains the paradox of presence and absence, participation in and remoteness from the story. Self-consciousness and ecstasy are the secular rendering of the paradoxical relationship of historical distance and relation.

The genius involved in discovering or creating eternal or transhistorical time is embedded in post-European culture. We take it so much for granted that we fail to appreciate its significance. Our ability to be addressed and respond to past human expression, implicitly if not explicitly, is tied up with this insight. Historical time is qualitative, residing in the ideas of meaning and significance and not essentially in the measurability of cosmological conceptions of time.

The unique invention of biblical consciousness is the conception of historicity. It is an idea that transcends the logical problem of natural time. It provides a transhistorical or eternal notion of the temporal that binds past and future into the eternal now. But the biblical texts are no more historical than Thucydides. Let me reiterate the biblical texts give the world the structure of historicity that makes history possible without necessarily being history itself. Biblical consciousness understands a reverse order of the meaning of history than modern thinking. For modern consciousness the facts are immutable and the interpretation of the evidence is relative and subject to change. The biblical notion asserts that the interpretation is eternal and the facts bear minimum metaphysical value.

The analysis so far suggests that history is a discipline resting on quick sand. Neither the Greek nor the biblical model satisfies the demands of modern conceptions of knowledge. Since the biblical texts are inadequate as history why return to them for historical consciousness? The justification of a reversion to the biblical texts arises from a unique aspect of the culture of modernity. Modern culture is self-conscious about the human making of modernity. Uniquely, it recognizes the relationship between the made of the historical past and the human making of that past. This has been the source of modernity's glories and of the horrors of life in the twentieth century. The recognition of the association between the made and the making has encouraged the deification of humans as the exclusive makers. It has encouraged the confusion between the humility inherent in biblical freedom and the hubris of free will. The biblical commitment to partnership between God and humankind in worldmaking articulates the limits of human power in what can be made and the human cost of the making.

The historian is scarcely in possession of total knowledge. It is a truism that historians like the rest of us are conditioned by their inherited perspective. Studying history is an exercise in trying to peer around the corner of one's perspective. It is a way of trying to practice ecstasis. Ecstasy is the ability to metaphorically stand outside oneself and one's temporally-bound culture. The purpose of this act of self-consciousness is to come to understand and incorporate more universally the otherness that constitutes a fuller understanding of the human condition.

Two questions are appropriate in conclusion: does one need the biblical texts to practice a liberating history that demystifies the past in the name of liberation; and does a liberating, redemptive history enhance, strengthen, and redeem a postmodernist worldview? There is no simple answer to the first question. Further, the answer is not theoretical. It is practical. The response is grounded in the need for existential authenticity and commitment to biblical critique. A secular version of this is possible. Nietzsche and Benjamin provide examples of histories that are redemptive and liberating. But the lack of an explicit biblical platform can easily lead critique to despair and liberation into totalitarianism. The biblical conception of history is not proposed as a simple replacement for postmodernism. The cultural clock cannot be reversed. Nostalgia for a simpler intellectual worldview is just that, nostalgia. Resignation to and acceptance of the deconstructive impasse is nihilism. The insights of modernity and postmodernity are profound products of self-consciousness. They reveal the paradox of human existence. For Derrida and Jabes it is enough to understand the parable of the giving of the Instruction at Sinai. The tablets are smashed, making knowing the word of God a task of infinite interpretation. However, is that a sustainable position and to what end?

The intellectual task is to incorporate the reality of the power and strength of human culture-making and the humbling limitations of that power. But there are limitations to the postmodernist critique. Effectively, the task implies the discovery of alternatives to the canon of Greco-Western metaphysics. To that end a new-old conception of sacred history is required. It is only within a structure of historicity that the self-conscious modern and postmodern critique can be incorporated without becoming subject to the false canons of truth inherent in the Greco-Western tradition.

Every insight in the postmodernist worldview is already present in the framework of the Hebrew biblical texts. This fact is not coincidental. Modernism and postmodernism are grounded in an unacknowledged suppressed biblical structure. The differences between the modernist/postmodernist view and the biblical outlook relate to the interpretation of these insights and the intellectual aspirations of the competing worldviews.

Sacred historicity counters the postmodernist hermeneutical denial of the idea of God, history, and self. According to postmodernism the rejection of God implies the dismissal of the others. The repudiation of God rests on the Platonic definition of God as absolute Presence and self-identity. A denial of Presence, for structuralists and deconstruction, also implies the recession of an author and undecidable communication.

The deconstructionist God is not the same as the biblical God or the biblical conception of historicity. The biblical God defies the deconstructionist insistence that if the absolute Presence is not absolutely present then Presence dissolves into absolute absence. But the biblical God is infinitely near and infinitely remote, a presence that is neither wholly transparent nor undividedly opaque. In contrast to deconstruction's denial of the self, the biblical writers insist that God makes human beings, selves, in God's image. Hence they share some of God's attributes, albeit unequally. Biblically, the human being is not a solipsistic self but a person, with all of the characteristics implied etymologically, created in community and grounded in communion and communication.

Modernism and postmodernism are at war with themselves. The skepticism and irony central to their methods collide with the canons of knowledge and existence they presuppose. The war that modernism and postmodernism fights is against notions of certitude as the canon of truth and the hallmark of truth subsumed *sub species aeternae*. On the other hand the biblical texts reject the possibility of existential certitude and pose the issue of truth in terms of the question: to what extent can the truth be embodied? The alternative canons imply radically different conceptions of personhood, god, and the meaning of history and the function of biblical totality.

The failure of modernism and postmodernism to successfully integrate biblical insight into its critique leads to an intellectual and moral dead-end. What remains to be unmasked? How can the postmodern thinker justify thought, any thought or action? Nietzsche astutely warned his readers at the beginning of *Beyond Good and Evil* that an ungrounded dialectic leads inevitably to nihilism. The implied determinism in Nietzsche's admonition arises from his awareness that a challenge to the false but dominant definition of truth calls into question the grounds of Western culture. An unmasking of the inadequacy of the correspondence or identity canon of truth exposes the unbridgeable and irreconcilable dualism of conventional epistemology. The irony of the orthodox canon of truth is that it remains theoretical. It is inimical to the practical conception of truth revealed in the historical record of the history of ideas. Nietzsche's lacerating radical critique pits the Platonic theoretical conception of truth against the suppressed biblical version of truth as embodiment. The distinction is vital. The identity theory of truth is a flight from death into a false and illusory feeling of certainty. The biblical notion of truth as an embodiment creates the environment in which the dialectics of truth and error can be authentically expressed. It guards against totalitarian versions of existence but at the warranted price of anxiety. But such a version of truth, unless grounded, leaves us adrift in "the new infinity."

NOTES

1. This paper primarily addresses the issue of why history is worth studying. and not about how the historian works.

2. Henri Frankfort, *Before Philosophy* (New York: Penguin Books, 1949).

3. The most famous argument apparently decrying history is found in Friedrich Nietzsche's early essay "On the uses and disadvantages of history," in *Untimely Meditations* (Cambridge: Cambridge University Press, 1983). However, what is often ignored is that Nietzsche's attack on historical science revolves around the issue of values and not on historicity. See Bernard Zelechow, "The Redemption of Postmodernism: Nietzsche's Sacred Conception of Time" in ed. David Jasper, *Postmodernist Theology* (London: Macmillan, 1993).

4. For an a defense of Hegel vis-a-vis the historicity of philosophy, see E. L. Fackenheim, *The Jewish Bible after the Holocaust* (Bloomington: Indiana University Press, 1990).

5. It need not have turned out this way. Some versions of postmodernism are double-coded, incorporating the elitist canons of modernism in a new vernacular. See Margaret Rose, *The Post-modern & the Post-industrial* (Cambridge: Cambridge University Press, 1991). This version of postmodernism comes closest to reviving the romantic democratic elitism of the early nineteenth century. See Conrad L. Donakowski, *A Muse For the Masses: Ritual and Music in the Age of Democratic Revolution 1770-1870* (Chicago: University of Chicago Press, 1977).

6. I mean this in the same sense that Croce uses the term. We can never simply study the past as the past. Besides the logical impossibility of such an attempt it denies the reality that interest determines the choice of subject to be studied. On the relationship between interest and relational objectivity, see E. H. Carr, *What is History?* (New York: Penguin Books, n.d.).

7. Simon Schama, *Dead Certainties* (New York: Alfred A. Knopf, 1991).

8. The standard cliché in first year history courses is to tell students that Thucydides and Herodotus are the "fathers" of modern historiography. An alternate view, and in my estimation a correct interpretation, is that modern historiography finds its origins in biblical texts. See Page Smith, *Historians and History* (New York: Vintage Press, 1964).

9. This is appropriate if one means Nietzsche's conception of fiction. That is, that all knowing is fiction because it is based inevitably on a partial interpretation of totality. See Friedrich Nietzsche, *Joyful Wisdom* (New York: Schocken Books, n.d.). History, as Paul Ricoeur states, partakes of imaginative reasoning borrowed from literature. See Paul Ricoeur, *Time and Narrative*, 3 vols. (Chicago: University of Chicago Press,1990).

10. For an exposition of historical critique in the form of primary sources See ed., P. Gardiner *Theories of History* (New York: The Free Press, 1959). For a detailed philosophical analysis of the debate See Ricoeur, *Time and Narrative*, vol.3.

11. E. H. Gombrich, *Art and Illusion* (London: Phaidon Press, 1972).

12. The most famous essay on the problem of form and content is Irwin Panofsky's *Renaissance and Renascences* (Stockholm: Almquist and Wiksell, 1965). The notion of the relationship between distance and relation is expounded by Martin Buber in "Distance and Relation."

13. Jurgen Habermas, *The Philosophical Discourse of Modernity: Twelve Lectures* (Cambridge: M.I.T. Press, 1990).

14. Most cultures have eschewed historical consciousness. See Mircea Eliade, *The Myth of the Eternal Return, or Cosmos and History* (Princeton: Princeton University Press, 1954).

15. The agreement to agree is the definition of myth provided by Herbert Schneidau in *Sacred Discontent* (Berkeley: University of California Press, n.d.).

16. Brevard Childs, *Memory and Tradition in Israel* (London: SCM Press, 1962).

17. For an amplification of my position on the opening of the biblical texts, see Bernard Zelechow, "The Illusion of the Receding God, Biblical Speech and the Paradox of Freedom," *The Journal of Reform Judaism* 36/2 (Spring, 1989): 49-53 and Bernard Zelechow, "God's Presence and the Paradox of Freedom" in ed., Anne Loades and Michael McLain, *Hermeneutics, The Bible and Literary Criticism* (London: Macmillan, 1992).

18. Abraham J. Heschel, *The Sabbath: Its Meaning for Modern Man* (New York: Farrar, Straus & Giroux 1952).

19. I follow Everett Fox's translation of the name of God. See Everett Fox, *Now These Are the Names* (New York: Schocken, 1986).

THEOLOGY AND TEXTUAL TIMING

Robert Scharlemann

The title "Theology and Textual Timing" is intended to raise a question and suggest a proposal. It is intended to raise the question whether there is a textual ordering of time different from the ordering provided by the self and to suggest a way in which texts can institute their own time. We take it for granted, and rightly so, that the year 2000 is ahead of us and the year 1990 behind us. We think ahead to 2000; we think back to 1900. Both are brought together in the present because the self that each one of us is can anticipate the future and remember the past in the present. The future is what is present in consciousness through anticipation; the past is present through memory. We know from Kant, if not from our own reflections, that the pure intuition of time is connected with the self. If there were no human subject, no ego with its capacities to remember and anticipate, there would be no awareness of time. Time is not an ordering that is in things themselves; it originates in the self and is intuited as an order within which any object of experience must appear to human subjects. If there were no self to which objects appear, there would be no time. Not a property of things in themselves, not a property of objects, time is, rather, the pure form through which we intuit any objects whatsoever, the pure form in which objects appear in their objectivity. In some way, it is in the idea of the I that time has its origin and gets its structure. But is that the only origin of temporality? Or can the idea of God, perhaps in combination with the fact of textual reality, provide another source of timing, and does this other timing even invert the timing that originates in the subjectivity of a self in the world?

The question is not an idle one. It is provoked, if by nothing else, then by such biblical texts as those in which Paul addresses his hearers or readers as ones who have already died. For this is to suggest, if one thinks about it, that the ontological basis of everyday timing, located in the being of the self, is superseded by another timing with a theological basis and that the idea of God times things differently from the way in which the

119

idea of the ego does its timing. Ordinary temporality has its ontological basis—the basis of its being what it is as it is—in the qualitative distinction, within the phenomenon of nonbeing, made possible by the difference between the being-not that precedes birth and the being-not that follows death, a difference not discernible without reference to memory and anticipation. If Paul writes to the Colossians that they have already died and their life is hidden with Christ in God, are we to take this in a literal sense? Are we to take it as meaning that the phenomenon which otherwise defines the future inescapably as future is cast into the past? In the ordinary experience of time, existence is temporalized between two boundaries at which being is limited by nonbeing. Birth is one boundary at which nonbeing touches being; death is the other boundary. They are temporalized by the understanding of the one as the point that is always behind us and the other as always ahead of us. In the ordinary experience of time's passage, we are moving farther away from the nonbeing that preceded our birth and closer to the nonbeing that follows our death. The I, which is the I of this my own body and which uniquely localizes being by owning it in a time and space, is not derivative from another I; it comes from nothing. It emerges, in the ontological sense, not from another way of being but from nothing. Birth, in an ontological sense, is the boundary upon which the self can look back and prior to which there simply was nothing at all from which the ego might be derivative.

The being of the ego has nonbeing at its border. At one end is the nonbeing from which we came. At the other end is the nonbeing anticipated under the title of one's own death. This is not the phenomenon of passing away that is the common feature of any worldly thing in space and time. It is, rather, the anticipation of the nonbeing that is peculiarly manifested in the being of the I and the thou. Of the self of anything or anyone else it is possible to say, "It or he or she is no longer; it or he or she no longer exists." But of the self that is concretized in the thought of I or thou, it can never be said, "I am no longer, you are no longer; I no longer exist, you no longer exist." Nonexistence is, in short, a mode of being never predicable in the present tense of the subjectivity manifested in the self as I or as thou. It is predicable only in the past or the future tense *was* or were not and *shall* or will not be. The nonbeing by which being is limited is thus differentiated in itself by the way in which existence temporalizes it. Odd as it sounds, there is a difference between the one nothing and the other nothing.

Moreover, the distinction between the nonbeing before birth and the nonbeing after death does not have to do with the degree of negativity that each involves. With respect to the one as well as to the other, it is true that the nonbeing by which the I in its being as I is limited is a not-being-at-all. That we can distinguish, nonetheless, between the nonbeing that is prior to the I in a certain way and the nonbeing that is after the I in a certain way is the fact that makes possible a qualitative distinction within nonbeing. The qualitative distinction can be made by reference to a modality of being. As we know, Heidegger made a theme of the phenomenon of death by interpreting its ontological meaning as a *Sein zum Tode* (his ontological interpretation of Kierkegaard's "sickness unto death") with reference to its characteristic as the can-be, the *Seinkönnen*, which uniquely is a potentiality of being never convertible into an actuality by the I as I. The phenomenon of death is the appearance of a possibility of being which is always only possibility, never actuality, for the self as I because, unlike other ontological possibilities, it is one that can never in principle be converted into actuality. "Be dead" is what the I as I or the you as you always *can* do but never *do* do. It is what the I or the you can always possibly do but does never actually do. It is always real only as a potentiality and never as an actuality of being. Whatever may be referred to as the public phenomenon of our own death, yours or mine in contrast to his or hers or theirs, it is in any case something of which I am or you are no longer the *subject*. It can be an occurrence in the world for someone else, but it cannot be an event in the career of the self in the form of I or thou. It can befall us, and in that sense the self as I or you can be aware of its coming toward us, or our moving toward it. But it is not something actually done by the I as I or you as you. It remains the one possibility of being—namely, the possibility of being not—that never is turned into the actuality of being.

We have in this ontology of being finitely a characterization of the nonbeing by which the being of the self is defined or made finite. We also have an indication of the origin of the familiar kind of temporality. The temporality which can distinguish between the past and the future in the present is based upon the difference between the coming into being and the going out of being when referred to the subjectivity indicated and made real in the name and the meaning of the words "I" and "thou." It is true of the being of the I and thou that the can-be which is uniquely inconvertible to a do-be is indicated by the word death. The same is not true of a "he," a "she," or an "it." These are not peculiarities of the lexical value of the pronouns; they are attributes of the kind of being proper to the self and grasped in such ontological concepts as *Seinkönnen* and *Sein zum Tode*. Ontological concepts do not have to do with defining *what* something is; they have to do with grasping the being of what is named or defined. Here it is the *being* of the self-consciousness connected with the pronouns I and you.

An incidental consideration can be introduced briefly here. If being is related to nonbeing in a movement away from and toward the other, what is the subject of the motion? Is it we who, in being between beginning and end, move away from and toward nonbeing? Or is it nonbeing that moves away from and toward us? Or is it both? Are we, as the *Dasein* (or the being-there) tensed between nonbeing and nonbeing, moving away from and toward two fixed points? Or is it equally true that we perceive the movement as one of nonbeing's coming toward or going away from us? The German word for future, *Zukunft*, as well as one of the French words for future, *avenir*, both have the literal meaning of "coming to." The future is what is coming toward us. There may be an ontological concept in the etymology of such words for future if they suggest that nonbeing has a movement in it that can be called a coming toward us or a receding from us. The future, in that case, is not like the horizon that recedes as we approach it; it is like a horizon that approaches us as we move toward it. Although one's inclination would be to say that it is only with respect to the phenomenon of death, not that of birth, that we would speak of a movement toward or away from us, the question itself is not a matter of significance for our main theme, and it can be left with that brief mention.

What we have established so far is that there is a connection between the subjectivity of the self and temporality because this is the basis of making a real distinction in the formal sameness of nonbeing as nonbeing. What are the features of such temporality? How does the self's timing enter reflective experience? More briefly: what is time? The brevity adds to the difficulty of the question, as Augustine indicated. We know the answer if we do not raise the question. Once raised, the question is perplexingly difficult to answer. But four different points of reference offer guidelines. One is Augustine's meditation on time in book 9 of his *Confessions*; a second is Heidegger's analysis of time and *Dasein,* which puts Kant's account of the pure intuition of time into ontological concepts; the third is the phenomenon of monuments; and the last is one whose connection with time is seldom noted but highly illuminating—namely, the phenomenon which has come to be called kerygma.

Augustine's meditation on time is related to what occurs in the recitation of a memorized song. It shows how both the flux of time and one historical aspect of time are based upon the way in which the self in its present attention is distended between memory and expectation. The present attention of the self in its action is the intersection of what is remembered and what is expected. Before beginning the recitation, Augustine noted, the self's expectation is extended over the whole of the song. After the recitation has begun, memory extends over the part that has been transferred, by the action itself, from expectation into memory. The self's attention in the action, or the life of the activity, is stretched between the memory and the expectation. It extends into memory because of what action has already done and into expectation because of what action remains to be done. The present is always the attention through which what was future becomes past. As the action goes on, the portion belonging to memory is increased and the portion belonging to expectation is diminished until, at the end of the recitation, expectation has been fully consumed and everything has passed into memory. This process can be divided, in turn, into each of its parts—a whole song into its verses, its words, its syllables—just as it can be composed into the larger whole that is one human life and then the history that comprises all human lives. This is the sense in which the elasticity of the self makes it possible to experience time not only as a flow but as a movement toward completion.

Knowing the whole of the song while reciting it means being aware not only of the movement through the words of the text but also of the direction of the movement indicated by the passing of content from expectation into memory as well as of the proximity to the end. The flux itself is only the movement; it does not have the direction indicated by the terms "beginning" and "end"; it does not distinguish between the nonbeing that was before and the nonbeing that comes after. Only the difference between memory and expectation provides that basis and makes the flow historical. We know at any given point how much of the song has already lapsed and is behind us and how much is still to come. And we can, of course, begin again once the whole has been recited. But the recitation itself moves in one direction only, a direction in which the present is between what has gone and what is coming and in which the portion of the coming is decreased to nothing. The divine mind, in turn, is to the whole of time what the self is to the recitation of a single song. Without the capacity of the soul to hold together the memory and the expectation in the present, there would be no experience of time and no understanding of history. But without the idea of God, historical totality would not be possible. Noteworthy is that finitude, or the limitation of being by nonbeing, does not as such provide the basis for an understanding of temporality. Something can be finite without being temporal. Only the capacity of the self's attention to be distended between its own memory and its own anticipation in its grasp of the whole accounts for it. And only this capacity makes possible the distinction within nonbeing itself that is indicated by the "not yet" and the "no longer."

Augustine's meditation does also bring into view the difference between the being of the past and the being of the future, or the difference in the way in which the past is past and the future is future. But it does not use ontological concepts to do so; his is not an ontological interpretation of time. It does not interpret the temporal movement by the concepts of being and nonbeing, and it does not distinguish between the nonbeing at which the recitation begins and the nonbeing at which it ends. The meditation is, moreover, theological only to the extent that it projects upon God what appears in the reflection on the self's experience of its own temporal movement—God is, as it were, the one who knows the whole story and who, therefore, knows how much of the whole of history has already elapsed and how much is still left.

For an ontological interpretation one must turn from Augustine to Heidegger, but one must do so with the recognition that his main analysis of time, provided in *Being and Time,* is concerned with the difference between an unreal and a real temporal consciousness—in other words, with the difference between the unreal understanding of time that is expressed in everyday talk and the real understanding of time that belongs properly to human existence when *Dasein* is owned by the "I" or the "thou." Although *Being and Time* ends with the question whether it is even possible to move from an ascertainment of temporality as the meaning of *Dasein* to an ascertainment of the meaning of *Sein*, the analysis itself provides an ontological understanding of time that Augustine's meditation does not provide.

Heidegger's interpretation has to do with the way in which the proper understanding of time is hidden in the impropriety and unreality of everyday understanding. Everyday existence stands under the heading *verfallen*. *Verfallen* existence is a mode of existence in which the self has not come into its own as I. It is an existence which understands the self casually, as merely one case—the German word for case, *Fall*, is in the word *verfallen*, as the English word "case" is in "casual"—of what is always occurring. In such a casual understanding, birth and death are part of a process that is continually repeated. People are born, people live, people die; things come to be, they stay around, they pass away; any self is but one among many selves who come into being, are there for a time, and then pass on. It is the same process instantiated over and over. Casual understanding may recognize the direction of the temporal flow, but it has no conception of temporality as indicating a movement which happens only once. A real understanding knows that only once do I or you come into being; it happens only once.

Temporality singularizes absolutely the movement across the boundary between nonbeing and being and between being and nonbeing. The authentic—the real or the proper, the *eigentlich*—understanding of time is related to the self in the form of I or you. It understands time as the movement between the not-be that one always *has* done but never *does* and the not-be that one always *can* do but never *does*. The one is the nonbeing prior to being there; the other is the nonbeing after being there. The everyday, *uneigentlich* understanding is one which sees finite being as the cycle between birth and death that is always repeated. The real, or *eigentlich*, understanding, is the self's own as a self and sees the difference between the not-be that one always only can, but never does, do and the not-be that one always only did, but never does, do. The self as I or you never *does* not-be, but it always *has* not been and always *can* not-be.

Heidegger's analysis of the temporality of *Dasein*, when put in these terms, adds an ontological conceptualization to what Augustine describes in his self-reflection. In recitation we are both ahead of ourselves and behind ourselves in our present attention. Ontologically, this being ahead of oneself is conceived as the being that one always *can* but never *does* do, and this being behind oneself is the being that one always *has* done but never *does* do. The being that one always can but never does do is the nonbeing that limits finite being on one side; and the being that one always has done but never does do is the nonbeing that limits finite being on the other side. The negative as actuality is always the past of existence; the negative as potentiality is always the future of existence. Such concepts provide an ontological interpretation of what is commonly understood as the relation of existence to birth and death.

There is a third origin of the understanding of time. This one has to do not with the subjectivity of the self but with something that appears in the world. It is the phenomenon of monuments, including the written monuments we call documents. Monuments are there in the world. They differ from other worldly objects because a monument points temporally. It differs not only from things but also from signs and symbols. It is present as a *trace* of what is no longer there. It indicates something which is no longer there, can no longer be there, will never be there again, but was there once. It is true that even here time is related to subjectivity because monuments are reminders of the past *for* someone present. Nonetheless, they are not there simply in an objective givenness nor as symbols or signs of a meaning. They are vestiges, traces, left-overs of a past that is anterior to the self's own memory.

I shall pass over monuments with this brief mention and characterization in order to call attention to what is almost the opposite of a monument, namely, that which in twentieth-century theology, especially biblical theology, has come to be known as kerygma. Kerygma in this special sense is not just any message or announcement. It is the form in which the futurity, the adventivity, the coming-to-us of new being appears. It is the announcement of a reality which is simultaneously the presentation of that reality, but so structured as to be future: it "comes to" the auditor. Its character lies, as Bonhoeffer put it in *Act and Being*, in the *Zukünftigkeit der Verkündigung*, the adventivity of what is proclaimed.

The text of its presentation is the textual body of its existence, and the import of what it says as it says it is that of being there as the future of the one who is addressed by it.

Let us put aside for present purposes the way in which this conception is rooted in the Protestant notion of sermon and preaching. What is important is to see how kerygma is not only a message about something but also the very way in which the future reality is present in the linguistic body that is a text. Kerygma temporalizes as a reality that comes to— always comes to—those who are its auditors. It is in this sense the presence of the future named as the *basileia tou theou,* the kingdom of God. Being in the kingdom of God is being ahead of where *Dasein* is in its being in the world when that being is a *Sein zum Tode,* a being mortally. That aspect is contained in the very structure of advent and listening that is meant by the concept of kerygma—a message in which new being *comes to* those who dwell in it through the act of listening. That very act of listening to what is said is the participation in the reality meant. "Listening to" takes part in the "coming to" of the kerygma; it is, in this sense, a way of being in the reality present in it.

But there is more to this temporalizing of "coming to" and "listening to"; for the content of the New Testament kerygma has in it both the past, in the monumental time of the death of Jesus in the world it proclaims, and the future, in the adventivity of the proclaiming. The kerygma is, in other words, both the vestige of an event which antedates everything hearers can remember as their own activity or passivity and also the coming of a possibility of being lying beyond the extreme can-be of their own. Here the contrast with the timing illustrated by Augustine's example of the recitation of a memorized song is most emphatic. In that example it is the reciter who reaches the end of the recitation; in kerygma, the end comes to the hearer as an event put into the past. This inverts the temporal order of recitation and shows how the adventivity of kerygma is the temporality in which the hearer has, in Paul's words, already died.

The death of Jesus is present in the kerygma as coming from the monumental past, an event no hearer remembers but an event whose vestige is there; the death of the hearer is the event which the kerygma times as being past. In that sense it is true that Paul's writing to his readers, "You have already died," which rearranges the temporality of existence, is true not metaphorically but literally. It is literally true when the idea which times existence is not the idea of the ego but the idea of God. Under the idea of God, the death of the ego—that is, nonbeing with reference to the being of any entity as I—is true always and only as a future possibility; and the death of God—that is, nonbeing with reference to the being of God—is true always and only as the past that never was and the future that never can be.

With reference to the question of time, kerygma seems at first to be the opposite and the complement of a monument. The latter is a trace of the past in the present; the former is a presentation of the future in the present. But the parallel breaks down with reference to the way in which memory and expectation are brought in. The temporality of the structure that embraces the hearer and the message being proclaimed is oriented to the future by the futurity, the adventivity, of the message. Adventivity and vestigiality are both brought together when the content proclaimed involves the death of Jesus the Christ. For here it is the idea of God which temporalizes the whole structure of text, message, and hearer. Even of monuments it is clear that it is not the idea of the ego but the idea of the world that is the origin of monumental time. The world too can originate a timing. A monument is a trace of the past in the world; it has its vestigial quality not in the idea of the self, with its distention between memory and anticipation, but in the idea of the world as the idea of a time and place *in which* the I finds itself and which, as a spatiotemporal unity, is both a "situation" and a "horizon."[1]

Neither the idea of the world nor the idea of the ego, alone or in combination, accomplishes what is accomplished as a timing in kerygma under the idea of God. That is the idea which orders time in a way different from the ordering of it in the self or in the world.

The idea of the I, in being a self, differentiates within nonbeing by reference to its movement away from and toward being-not. The idea of the world, in being the world, differentiates among the things found in the world by reference to objects and monuments, things and traces. Each of these ideas has the effect of temporalizing being. It is only the idea of God, however, which reorders being and nonbeing so as to place nonbeing only in the past by reference to the new being that is future.[2]

This is, as it seems to me, what results from analyzing the four aspects of time that are made apparent in the recitation of a memorized text, in the analysis of authentic understanding of time, in a text when it is not just the present existence of the voice of a past author but a monument, and in the conception of kerygma which both has the form of future in its self-presentation and also abolishes the qualitative distinction in the nonbeing to which finite being is bound and by which it is defined. The abolition of that distinction reorders temporality. When text is kerygma, it is timed theologically.

NOTES

1. Paul Ricoeur, *Time and Narrative,* tr. Kathleen Blamey and David Pellauer (Chicago: University of Chicago Press, 1988), vol. 3, p. 220. "Here is the heart of the paradox [of the vestige or trace]. On the one hand, the trace is visible here and now, as a vestige, a mark. On the other hand, there is a trace (or track) because "earlier" a human being or an animal passed this way. Something did something. Even in language as we use it, the vestige or mark "indicates" the pastness of the passage, the earlier occurrence of the streak, the groove, without "showing" or bringing to appearance "what" passed this way," p. 119. Ricoeur's account misses, in part, the worldly origin of the phenomenon of a vestige (in contrast to an object) because it treats it in the context of three *historical* concepts: archives, documents, and traces. But the central point is the same: vestige indicates pastness.

2. To paraphrase a recurrent theme in Karl Barth's theology: nonbeing is that which God has always already put into the past.

THEOLOGY AND THE CRISIS OF REPRESENTATION

Graham Ward

"Whenever we claim to have round God in *this* world, we have found nothing but an idol; this happens more often than we think, since it is rarely noticed, when everyday terminology is used in naming it."[1] Thus the inability to be aware of our naming God turns God into an idol. Those familiar with the work of Jean-Luc Marion, whose book *God without Being* appeared last year in translation (though it was published in Paris ten years ago) might be forgiven for ascribing to him the quotation from which the issues of this essay emerge. It is not his, though it might well be, and that is part of the point. The quotation actually comes from an essay entitled "The Crisis of Culture" written in 1921 by the German theologian Friedrich Gogarten. The essay lies at the roots of dialectical theology. I might then have quoted from Karl Barth's second edition of *Romans*, finished in the same year and itself a classic account of crisis theology. But I wish at this point to stay with Gogarten in order to establish and clarify a certain cultural parallel between the theology issuing from the crises of post-World War I Germany and the theology issuing from our contemporary postmodern situation, specifically the theological investigations of Jean-Luc Marion. For Marion states that his work too "remains deeply marked by the spiritual and cultural crisis . . . which, in France, marked the years dominated by 1968."[2] By outlining and analyzing the character of his parallelism I wish to suggest three things. First, the cultural crisis in each case is a crisis of representation. Secondly, when cultures recognize their own crises, theology has its most profound insight into its own origins, procedures, and limitations; theology recognizes that it not only promotes the crisis of representation, but that the paradox of representation is the crisis which theology reads, by faith, as God's Word to us. And thirdly, what profoundly relates the theology issuing from these historical crises is its dialectical character. Theology, I suggest, looking towards the year 2000 and composed in view of the postmodern condition, needs to return to a deconstructed version of crisis or dialectical theology.

131

According to Fritz K. Ringer, Germany's cultural crisis began "[s]omewhere around 1890." It reached its "greatest intensity during the early years of the Weimar period" and by the 1920s "no German professor doubted that a profound 'crisis of culture' was at hand."[3] Metaphors of organic growth and development, the product of a center of *Lebensphilosophie*, are gradually displaced by metaphors of decay and decline. As Gogarten describes it: "when . . . the immanent strength dies out of that greater content of contingencies which we call culture, then this [liberal] religion— which is perhaps the closest, most direct, and most subtle expression of the immanent strength of culture—will die too" (291). He attempts to give a new theological expression for this condition in which belief in the self-regulating wholeness of the world and its history has collapsed. For Gogarten, like Marion, the crisis culture faces is a besetting nihilism and a consequent decline towards decadence. His theological response to "the hour of decline" (279) is to begin to develop a theology of the hour itself, a theology of time as *kairos*. This is a theology of the in-between for it is "the destiny of our generation to stand between the times" (278). The present *Zeitgeist* belongs neither a past cultural confidence now coming to an end nor can it offer a future restoration. What characterizes this in-between is an eclipse of transcendental meaning: "there is no longer any thought of ours which reaches [God]. None of our thoughts reach beyond the human sphere" (279). Linguistic expression has become inflationary and bankrupt. In this epochal hiatus, difference and otherness (grounds for the authentic) have disintegrated. And where, in the light of such a situation, Adorno and Horkheimer will call for "the negation of reification,"[4] Gogarten demands the destruction of the idols. Skepticism and iconoclasm lead to a negative dialectic. Theology now must "continually demonstrate the fact that thought about God and about his revelation can never have an object" (319). Only by theology performing this judgement upon itself can the yes or the Word of God be heard in this destructive No. "Here, and only here, in this annihilation, can creation become creative" (295). The in-between, then, is constituted by a double crisis—the crisis that all representation is merely human, and God cannot be presented within it; and the crisis that all representation must be destroyed if God is to speak from the profundity of His absence. The in-between is characterized *by* the crisis of representation, by the need to articulate and the impossibility of articulating an otherness in the human, the Word of God in the words of human beings. A theology of the in-between, then, is necessarily a theology of representation (in crisis) and a theology which proceeds both negatively and dialectically.

Minefields and craters often provide graphic metaphors of the crisis of post-1918 culture. Barth will read them as "the impress of revelation." But with Barth the crisis is located in subjectivity itself. "The insecurity of our whole existence, the vanity and utter questionableness of all that is and of what we are, lie as a text-book open before us."[5] The crisis without is a representation of the crisis within—for both are human representations: the void is manifested in both creation and the creature. The void for both Gogarten and Barth is the meaninglessness of the self-referential *Weltanschauung* of neo-Kantianism. "[H]uman logic always tends to arrange its propositions in a series and to leave out of account what is not pro-posed, which is in fact the pre-supposition of all pro-positions" (82). But by faith the void is read as plenitude. The Absence, what is always and inevitably left "out of account," circumscribes human finitude, judges the constructs of the transcendental I to be vanities[6] and becomes an "experience" of the Eternal working of grace. I will explain the quotation marks around the word "experience" in a moment. The *Weltanschauung* is ruptured by an absence that exceeds and cannot be explained or contained by the world of human representations. The crisis occurs, immanently, testifying to be a transcendence identified by faith as God. The dialectic opens up the space for the judgement of the idols, a metacritique, a theology which analyzes Kierkegaard's "infinite qualitative distinction" between what is temporal and what is eternal.

For Gogarten and Barth, the crisis of representation issues from the way we must necessarily construct the worlds we inhabit, leaving otherness outside. In his 1928 essay, "Protestantism and Reality," Gogarten affirms that "reality is not a unity, but a duality" (371). Their understanding of "dialectic" arises from their need to posit theologically an otherness which cannot be posited within systems of human representation without undermining them. By undermining them, they are undermining humanity itself as the legitimating Logos: God has no place in a world until man first utterly annihilates himself" (290). Thus two antagonistic Words are established which Barth describes as: society "now really ruled by its own logos," and the Word of God which is "the *dunamis*, the meaning and might of the living God who is building a new world."[7] In the Hegelian dialectic self and world are in continual negotiation, a negotiation which lies within the essential unity of the Spirit. But "dialectical" in "dialectical theology" is a radical critique, a metacritique, of the essential unity of self and world that issues from the positing of otherness, or heterogeneity. The dialectic cannot be closed; there can be no final synthesis because of the heterogeneity of origins—self and other. As one origin crosses through the other, the crisis occurs which bears witness to an external and constitutive alterity. The point of intersection is the incompleteness, the meaninglessness, the emptiness of the immanent process alone. This incompleteness of the self and its totalizing intentionality issues in Barth's "utter questionableness of all that is and of what we are" (46). The dialectic has, therefore, an existential consequence. There is, in human systems of representation, an inner questioning, an inner judging by this excluded and wholly other. The dialectic operates within representation itself, speaking of representation's own futility.

Theology, the discourse primarily concerned with the wholly other, magnifies the crisis of representation, making it more manifest. In fact, theology could be described as thematizing the crisis of representation. This is why Barth, in his preface to the second edition of *Romans*, speaks of the "perception of the 'inner dialectic of the matter' in the actual words of the text [a]s a necessary and prime requirement for their understanding and interpretation" (10). Therefore, dialectical theology is not simply a matter of method or style. It is not simply a technique to be applied to a particular subject nor, simply, the employment of paradox and oxymoron. Dialectical theology itself is anterior to method and style, and institutes both. It issues from recognition of the permanent crisis within which representation stands. It is a discourse that reflects upon the fractured state of discourse, and is, to that extent, a metadiscourse. By faith (at least in Barth), the fractured nature of discourse traces the judgement of God's Word upon the world.

> The appalling fact that no one can speak about God
> without speaking a great deal about himself is a parable of

> the Personality of God by whom all things are eternally upheld. The paradox of the final, despairing inadequacy of human speech as a medium for expressing the Truth is a parable of the absolute miracle of the Spirit. Our almost intolerably one-sided and narrow-minded presentation of the thought of eternity, which we can only avoid by talking about something else, is, nevertheless, a parable of the violent and direct claim eternity imposes upon us. (*Romans*, 333)

The "inner dialectic of the matter" is only manifested in "the actual words of the text." Textuality constitutes the dialectical in-between in which the Word crosses through human words. The crisis of representation is located only within representation.

Barth's theology of the Word is a theology of the crisis of representation, the unsynthesizable dialectic within discourse between presenting and representing. The language of God's immediate presence is recognized, dialectically, as also only rhetoric and parable: "we boldly employ this language, this language of romanticism, because it is impossible to describe the immediacy of divine forgiveness except by means of parables [*Gleichnis*] drawn from human immediacy . . . Broken men, we dare to use unbroken language. But we must remember [*Erinnerung*] that we speak in parables" (220-1, 202). The key word here, the dialectical turn that manifests the crisis and deconstructs what Barth later terms "direct language" (221), is the word *Erinnerung*.

There is no crisis of representation where there is a forgetting that language does not have immediate access to its object. Remembering installs the crisis, for what is remembered is exactly the temporal lapse, this aporia, which language attempts to dissemble, by focusing attention on what it portrays and enabling the forgetting of that which constitutes and organizes the portrayal. Language "presents" the world; the presentation is seen as immediate and so language seems to have captured the moment of the present, the *nunc*. The content appears to be given and this giving is the focus for more significance than the medium that allows the content to be given. The present (giving) masks the past (the giving that has already been given for there to be a representation of that giving) and masks the future too (the purpose in terms of the reason for the giving of this content). In this substantializing of the present time is a succession of instants which discourse mirrors. But in fact, what is forgotten is that there is no time without language. Furthermore the "presenting" is always a memory of what has already passed. Language has only "represented." Since this representation exists within the horizon of a total order of things and time (including the future), significance, the reason why this object rather than that object has been chosen as the subject to be represented, is determined by this overall scheme. Language, then, exhibits the tension of times which are never purely past, never purely present and never purely future—but always the negotiation of all three (or however many modes of verb any language is composed of). Language creates and portrays this zone of conflictual time that destabilizes any single, verbal pronouncement. Caught between mediation (of the past), immediacy (of the present), and prediction (of the future), meaning and reference slip and slide. Representation, which ceases to recall its own economy, slumbers in dogmatism and assumes the pretensions, in Lacan's phrase, "of a discourse of knowledge." Representation without remembrance freezes the relationship between subject and object, signifier and signified. In fact, it assumes that this relationship between a subject and object, a signified and signifier, *is* the relationship, the *only* relationship constituting representation. Realism, in both its philosophical and literary forms, could be seen as an expression of the highest confidence in (or the deepest self-deception concerning) the ability to represent. Modernity might be understood as an epoch in which the stability of Being and representation, the essential unity of Being and representation, went unquestioned—an epoch of forgetting. As Barth wrote in 1923: "we [dialectical theologians] wished and do wish with this really dialectical 'transcendence' nothing else than to warn against a forgetting of the crisis" (Robinson, 145-6).

Barth's theological method and discourse recall us to a thinking of heterogeneity and the complex relationship between time and representation. Only a discourse written in eternity can escape the crisis of time within representation, only the Word prior to words. And theology, just because it takes as its theme representing the unrepresentable (for God is not an object of our world), is not an extraordinary form of discourse in respect of this crisis of representation. Neither does theology simply "read" the crisis "down there" in its best condescending voice. Rather, theology, as a discourse, becomes the discourse which reveals to all other discourse the critical nature of discourse itself. In theological discourse, the judgement upon all discourses, the condition of all discourses, is writ large. The twisted logic of theology proclaims louder than any other discourse that there can be no access to a content outside language, since representation is always re-presentation, a coming after, a repetition, a doubling of presence. Theological discourse announces that representation cannot present. For God has always already passed and that passing is anterior to our beginning. Theological discourse lays bare, then, the roots, complexity, and irrepressible heterogeneity of all discourse. The crisis of representation is the very subject matter of its inquiry. "We know that human language can never break through the absolute . . . other sciences have attempted, more or less successfully, to arrange an understanding with [the greedy dialectic of time and eternity] in order that they may remain insecure; but theology menaces them all. According to its reckoning the impossible possibility of God appears as a position which cannot be a position. By this position all other reckonings are threatened with destruction at every moment" (*Romans*, 530). It is dialectical theology which both recognizes and thematizes the crisis of representation itself.

The crisis arises because Janus-faced, language does not offer itself as a *tertium quid* between reality and our knowledge of it. Language offers itself as the contradiction. It is both figure and presentation, *Gestalt* and *Darstellung*, idol and icon. Theological discourse provides such a clear portrayal of this crisis because the *a priori* of such discourse is revelation.

Throughout his work, Barth insisted upon the secondary nature of theological discourse. It is a discourse that always only comments on what has been given, an event that has passed. And yet it is also a discourse commanded to be by that past event. The secondary reflection is the response of faith binding upon the Word having already been spoken. Theological discourse must, then, communicate what it has received, must pass on the traditions, while also recognizing the inadequacy of all human language. It is not simply that theological discourse bears witness to the paradoxical doubleness of language; it is *the* discourse for the communication of the paradoxical doubleness of language. All recognition of the inadequacy of the double-bind of language is, therefore, a theological recognition. Hence, more recently, with Derrida and Lacoue

Labarthe, analysis of the economies of difference and deferral in language or the analysis of the economies of *Vorstellung* and *Darstellung* in representation, are conducted within a theological horizon. It is not that Derrida and Lacoue Labarthe are writing theology without knowing it. Rather, what they are saying are variants on what theological discourse (reflecting upon its own constitution and legitimacy) has always recognized. In fact, has not theology bequeathed the problem itself? If so, Derrida is involved in a secularized (insofar as it can ever be secularized) version of a problem tackled theologically by Pseudo-Dionysius, Augustine, and Aquinas. Of course, this can be reversed, and this reversibility requires much thought. For we could say that, in fact, the economies of discourse and representation championed by Derrida and Lacoue Labarthe are merely being "read" theologically. And thus theology is provided with a philosophical basis for its understanding of the Word in human words, rather than theology providing philosophy with a foundational insight. The struggle for the prioritizing of one discipline over the other has a long history, and the question is never going to be resolved. Resolution either way is an act of faith. It must remain a question if philosophy is going to remain consistent, and that means philosophy must always remain *this* side of nihilism. It must rest on an act of faith if theology is going to remain consistent.

The crisis of representation, portrayed clearly in theological discourse because both representation and theology concern the communication of what is other, installs the epistemological and ontological crisis that is now the domain of contemporary philosophical thinking. Dialectical theology, therefore, has close associations with postmodern thinking. Bultmann announces that there is "no position." Barth informs Tillich that "our 'science' has neither positive nor negative root, but no 'root' at all" (Robinson, 144), and that anyone who takes dialectical theology seriously can "hardly let so many *it is's* and *there are's* and *they stand's* flow from his pen" (149). Derrida writes that "undecidability is the *condition* of all deconstruction."[8] Lacoue Labarthe describes "mimeticism" as "that pure and disquieting *plasticity* which potentially authorizes the varying appropriation of all characters and function . . . without any other property than an infinite malleability."[9]

With crisis theology, then, we engage, prior to deconstruction and poststructuralism, in radical critique of the metaphysics of presence based upon a theological reflection upon representation itself. Furthermore, with its return to what Barth calls in his *Gottingen Dogmatics* "real dialectic" as opposed to Hegelian dialectic (77), we are engaged, prior to deconstruction and poststructuralism, in a radical critique of historicism, the idea of progress and the teleological movement towards a final enlightenment. If the postmodern condition can be described as "an experience of the end of metaphysics and the end of history," which is not confined to any specific historical era,[10] then in dialectical theology we already have a response to such a condition.

Postmodernism, like dialectical theology, is both a reflection upon and a promotion of crisis. Derrida writes "the classical crisis [which] developed from within the elementary tradition of the logos that has no opposite but carries within itself and says all determined contradictions."[11] Offering his own critique of historicism and ontology, he will recognize "crisis" as both "the danger menacing reason and meaning" and "decision," "choice," the "division between two ways . . . the way of logos and the non-way, the labyrinth" (62). Derrida describes the *crisis* of dialectic as the *dialectic* of crisis. Deconstruction itself issues from "Two texts, two hands, two visions, two ways of listening. Together simultaneously and separately."[12] The play of difference and deferral opens Hegel's dialectic, his "restricted economy," to a "general economy . . . related not to a basis, but to the non-basis of expenditure" (*Writing and Difference,* 271). What I am suggesting, then, is that there are grounds for a *rapprochement* between Derrida's deconstruction and Barth's (though not Gogarten's and Bultmann's) dialectic. In his 1985 "Letter to a Japanese Friend," Derrida writes: "The instance of the *krinein* or of *krisis* . . . is itself, as is moreover the entire apparatus of transcendental critique, one of the essential 'themes' or 'objects' of deconstruction."[13] Like Barth's dialectic, as a textual practice it opens up a double reading (Barth's "immanent dialectic") between intention and performance. It is always only a reading itself. It is not a method, it is not a style, it is not a critique from somewhere above the text. It always remains within the text, moving between the logos and its repetition, the Word and its words, and tracing the text's own critique or its crisis of representation. "The wholly other announces itself within the most rigorous repetition."[14]

What is it then that underlies the postmodern understanding of "crisis?" Vattimo, who has characterized postmodernism as an epoch of crisis, has the word reverberating throughout his book *The End of Modernity*. There is "the 'crisis of reason'" (23), "the crisis of humanism" related to the death of God and "the loss of human subjectivity in the mechanisms of scientific objectivity" (35), the "crisis of civilization" (35), the crisis" of metaphysics" (40), "the crisis of the future" (106), and the "crisis of value" or hermeneutics (104). All these inter-related forms of crisis circle for Vattimo about two important dialectics, both rooted in Heidegger's work: the dialectic of Being (arising from the ontological difference) and the dialectic (which later became Levinas's dialectic) between the Saying (*die Sage*) and the said. Both these dialectics are related in Heidegger through the notion of *Ereignis*. Both dialectics are involved in the crisis or instability of representation. For Saying "subverts both our usual referential way of understanding the word-thing relation and our own language to language itself" (68). A shattering takes place which "is not to be understood as a referential gesture which makes the sign disappear in the presence of the things signified, but rather as a peculiar relation between poetic language and mortality" (70). Vattimo's conclusion is that "truth is not a metaphysically stable structure" (76), but an event. The dialectic of the Saying and the said founds and ungrounds the notion of *Ereignis,* the "truth" in the crisis of representation.

Let us tease this out a little more, because it will become important for two reasons. First, it will open up dialectical theology to a deconstruction that I see is necessary if it is to assume any contemporary importance and provide a theology of the Word for the years to come. Secondly, it will lead us to see how a theologian like Jean-Luc Marion can proceed in writing his own postmodern theology. In the work of Philip Lacoue Labarthe, we find an explicit analysis of the crisis of representation. Once more readings of Heidegger are paramount. Lacoue Labarthe's analysis deepens our understanding of the mechanism of the crisis for postmodernity.

In Labarthe's essays, collected and translated in the volume *Typography: Mimesis, Philosophy, Politics*, representation is understood as fundamentally agnostic.[15] It is agnostic because it performs and perpetuates in performing a certain doubling. The mirror expresses the doubling and redoubling that is the "'constitutive undecidability' of mimesis" (97). Mimesis flickers between two functions—*Darstellung and Vorstellung.* There is, therefore, a "thought of representation in which the *re-* of *representation* would govern—and carry away—any presentational value" (112). He concludes his essay "Typography" by stating that "There is always, whether it is referred to or not, whether or not it is 'shown,' a mirror in a text" (138).

The presentation of the mirror, or as Labarthe's argument develops, the "trick of the mirror," is axiomatic for his understanding of the permanent crisis in which representation stands. The "trick" consists in the fact that the mirror allows for a forgetting of the one who points the mirror in the economy of representation. This forgetting is inevitable and constitutive. There is representation only because we are blinded by what we see. For the product of representation (what we are "shown") displaces any attention we might turn upon the producer of the representation (both in terms of the subject who "sees" and the language employed by that subject). The question "who" is deflected by the question "what," and it is this deflection that allows for the possibility of a naive realism. The mirror opens the space for speculation, for reflection, for theory, for the metaphysics of presence. It masks the fact that it too is a surface by concentrating upon, by filling its field with what can be seen. The mirror provides representation with the tool it needs to organize and present the visible as a stability. Without the tool where would we be? This is the crucial question. It is, I believe, the most pressing of theological questions. And it cannot be solved; it must always remain a matter of question, of quest. For, given the hypothesis of being unable to represent, would there be plenitude or void? Would we confront the mystical self-presence of the One or would we confront the nihilistic anarchy of the Manifold? The history of metaphysics and philosophical theology has revolved around this question: the privileging of plenitude and the resolving of the question by the dissolving of representation itself. (Although even asking the question presupposes some sort of condition 'beyond' representation). For Labarthe, there would be nothing, or rather there would be the chaos of the perceived, what he terms *dementia.* The mirror then, Labarthe argues, is a *pharmakon*, a necessary poison required to keep the fever of possibilities, the madness of mimesis, at bay. The mirror permits the constitution of what Derrida, in his essay on

Labarthe, calls, "a truth determined as homoiosis, adequation, similitude" (25). The mirror allows for the suggestion of the immediate truth of things.

Labarthe argues that this mirror is a "trick," or rather only a trope. It substitutes, it counterfeits; and the recognition that "it is all done with mirrors" also belongs to the economy of representation. "[T]he structure of representation, whatever it is, (*Vor* or *Darstellung*), necessarily occasions the uncontrollable proliferation of doubles (of doubles that do not know themselves to be such, caught up as they are, in effect, in the representative mechanism)" (105). It is the doubling (and redoubling) as the mirror reflects back upon its own surface, that opens up the *mise-en-abime* which racks and rakes what is made visible by the mirror. Immediacy stares into the starless depths of its own endless mediation. This means that, despite appearances, there is no closure of representation (and therefore no closure of the question of representation, of the question too of a 'beyond' representation). There is only the prolonged substitution—Derrida's "supplementation"—issuing from the immanent violence of representation itself. It is a substitution always attempting to usurp the throne and seize power for itself, repressing the difference in discourse. Representation becomes, then, a war-ravaged no-man's-land—that is its crisis, its tragedy, and ours. But it is only in and as crisis that the question of a "beyond" representation can again be heard. It is only in and as crisis that the suggestion of what is unrepresentable crosses through the repressive power of representation. It is only in the rupturing of representation that the wholly other announces itself. And it is with this "revelation" of the wholly other that theology begins.

The "revelation" must remain in quotation marks. For theology too can become blind to its own metaphors (and this indeed is what happens in the dialectical theology of Gogarten and Bultmann, as we shall see). In theology's own dependence upon the language, it can deceive itself that with words like "gap" and "aporia" an opening for otherness is marked off from what is otherwise textuality. But this is not so. There is only what Jean-Luc Marion terms *"mediation immediate."* Revelation is not a moment outside discourse and outside meditation. If all knowledge, identity and understanding is represented, is a form of representation, then the "gap" or "aporia" announce themselves as questions or instabilities installed within textuality itself. This is very important for understanding the nature of dialectical theology in Barth and Marion, and in particular their emphasis on the *a priori* of faith. The crisis of representation frees us from the enchantment of the mirror and releases us into an undecidability that opens the space for the operation of faith. For the condition of instability requires, for any form of stabilizing, an *a priori* choice, an *a priori* hermeneutic. The immanent dialectic of language is constituted and dissolved by an ongoing logic of paradox, a paralogic which is both within and yet also outside noetic reasoning and presents the possibility of alternative reasonings, more original reasoning, the reasoning the other. And so the reasoning of faith, the *ratio fidei* of Barth's analysis of Anselm's dialectic of existence, can pitch its tent here. It is by recognizing this that Barth, in his more mature dialectical theology, and Marion, in his mediations upon the "gift" and the Eucharist, can turn negativity and absence into a more positive theology. It is not a certain theology—"*intellectus* . . . cannot establish the object of faith as such"[16]—but it is a theology which names that which is other and older than representation. Both of them see in the mediation of all "revelation" the requirement of faith which allows for a *theological* realism.

With Lacoue Labarthe's work on the economy of representation we have a deeper grasp of what Barth termed "the 'immanent dialectic of the matter' in the actual words of the text," that is, how language *both* presents truth and counterfeits it, how representation reveals and yet is "the interdiction of revelation" (118). The logos is also always lexis. It is not that nothing is *present*, but that *nothing* is also present. This is fundamental and relates to Heidegger's work on ontological difference (and Barth's work on Anselm's dialectic of existence). For representation is an economy within this difference, operating both with and beyond ontology. That is why Derrida calls Labarthe's project *desistance*. For "*desistance* does not modify "estance," and does not belong to it as one of its determinations, but rather marks a rupture, a departure, or a heterogeneity with respect to 'estance' or 'Wesen'" (28). The site of this unsynthesizable dialectic, this paralogic, is the body of the text. Barth, in his subtle analysis of language and dialectic in *Die christlich Dogmatik in Entwurf*, describes this liminal zone as "the way from word to counterword and back again, and returning once more. . . . We either forget or do not know that our theology is a *theologia viatorum* and necessarily so. Or we imagine instead being able to take shelter from this movement of speech (*Rede*) and counterspeech (*Gengenrede*) in the certain harbor of the ONE Word."[17] In representation there is always more than ONE word. There is always "the confrontation or conflict between two interpretations of the truth " (119) for Labarthe, two antithetical speeches for Barth, the idol *and* the icon for Jean-Luc Marion.

Marion's theology is a response to postmodernism. It is a theology born from a negotiation with the work of Nietzsche and Heidegger, Levinas and Derrida. It is attempt to read the crisis of representation theologically. In his first, and still I think his best book, *L'Idol et La Distance* (1975),[18] his major preoccupation is describing theological discourse as the crucial reversal of "the wisdom of the world by 'the folly which we preach'" (45). This crisis or crucifixion of representation is constituted by a dialectic between the logos of onto-theology and "a logos foreign to onto-theology, the logos of the Cross" (37). Marion writes that "On the Cross, the Word is killed, but in his way it manifests, in all its paradoxical light, *another* discourse" (37). This book argues for, traces, and develops a theology upon the basis of "[T]he conversation between Him who speaks (the metalanguage) and what is said [*l'enonce*]" (236). The conversation issues from the recognition that "[t]he proposition exceeds the condition of the object, the usage of signification, its verification" (240). This excess, the play between what is stated and what is in excess of that statement, reveals a distance, and it is distance (or *di-stance*) which both joins and separates the divine and the human enabling "recognition [and] communion" (256). The dialectic which fosters the permanent crisis of representation is constituted by this distance which is asymmetrical. The asymmetry is fundamental, for although distance "concerns two poles, or rather creates and guarantees two poles . . . this definition [of distance] only comes to expression through one of the two poles—ours. It is humanly [de]fined" (257). Furthermore, "Distance does not let itself be represented . . . Di-stance cannot display any representation," (257) even though it issues from representation. It hovers then on the edge of absence and void, and it may be nothing more than a human construct. But by faith absence is read theologically, read by the light of "the folly which we preach," as "a kind of negative theophany" (26). "Distance must exceed absence, or rather, it occurs in its own rigor to the extent that 'believing without having seen' (John 20:29) absence, fundamentally, presents the paternal figure of God" (261).

This presentation of a figure results in Marion's major preoccupation with the dialectic between the idol and the icon. This is a dialectic within representation itself, much in the same way as Barth talks about the "'inner dialectic of the matter' in the actual words of the text." The idol and the icon are understood as two conflicting moments within, as well as forms of, representation. But the icon's form of representation issues from placing the act of representation itself into crisis. "[I]n the art of the icon, the codified colors (gold, red, blue, yellow, etc.) bear no resemblance to anything . . . their relevance asserts itself on purely semiotic grounds" (26). Nevertheless, and this is the paradox of the icon, these colors "express eternity, divinity, glory, humanity, etc." (26).

It is in his book *God Without Being* (1982) that Marion most succinctly outlines his phenomenological account of the idol and the icon and the dialectic within representation that they institute (or which institutes them). The dialectical character of Marion's theology in this book, as elsewhere, is complex and sophisticated. In attempting to argue for a God outside textuality (*hors texte* is the title of an essay appended to this book) he suggests a relationship between the idol and the God of onto-theology, the God of the philosophers. All representation is caught within the nets of onto-theology and so is potentially idolatrous. "When a philosophical thought expresses a concept of what it then names "God," this concept functions exactly as an idol" (16). It is representation itself that must be outwitted, then, if a God with being is to be understood as coherent. It is the outwitting or representation that presents itself in the dialectic between the two antithetical modes of apprehending "the divine in visibility" (9)—the idol and the icon. For when a concept allows itself "to be measured by the excessiveness of the invisible," (23) then it can serve as an intelligible medium for the icon. The idol is a constituted visibility— what is seen is seen by someone as something. Marion talks here along similar (but not identical) lines to Labarthe about the invisible mirror which constitutes the idol as idol. The mirror is invisible because what the idol appears to present "fills the gaze, saturates it with visibility, hence dazzles it" (12). Because of this excessive visibility, because (in Labarthe's terms) the one who gazes cannot behold the "trick of the mirror," then "the idolatrous gaze exercises no criticism of its idol" (13). There is no seeing beyond the idol (beyond one's own constitutive gaze) and so the "idol allows no invisible" (13). The deity it presents, then, is all too visible, its significance is consumed by its visibility, and "the idol consigns the divine to the measure of the human gaze" (14). Human beings create and can only create God in their own image. On the other hand, the icon is exactly that form of visibility or representation which allows the invisible to appear. It signals, beyond itself, the other who can never appear. It allows the intention of the other to enter the field of what is seen, drawing the gaze beyond what is seen towards the infinite and into veneration. In fact, and here comes the dialectical twist, it is the intention of the other which constitutes this mode of visibility, inverting the idolatrous gaze. And rather than enabling us only to see ourselves (as in the idolatrous mirror), we are enabled to recognize that we are seen. It is able to perform this—and here is the pivot upon which the dialectical twist turns—by rendering the mirror in the idol visible. "[W]e become the visible mirror of an invisible gaze that subverts us to the measure of its glory" (22). The icon reveals, in negating the visible (by drawing attention to what constitutes its visibility as such), the abyss, the infinite. The icon announces the advent of a gift. This gift is incarnate in Jesus Christ.

In *L'idol et la distance* Marion clarifies the economy of the atonement in relation to the gift of the infinite, or the infinity of giving. He asks whether "The incarnation and the resurrection of Christ do not affect ontological destiny or whether they remain as a purely ontic occurrence" (272). He answers, by way of Levinas's critique of Heidegger's ontological difference and an exposition of divine kenosis, that Christ's givenness, which figures the infinite givenness of God, manifests a "relation with another person (*Autrui*) . . . prior to all ontology" (278). While then "the ontological difference will remain, [it is] transgressed" (280). Theologically, and quoting St. Paul, as Marion also does, "Christ is the icon of the invisible God" (Col. 1:15).

Beneath its specific ontological idom, Marion's dialectic of the idol and the icon differs little from the dialectic between the logos of this world and the Word of God found in Gogarten, Barth, and Bultmann. That is not to devalue Marion's critical engagement with the ontological difference, but to draw that engagement into a comparison with those earlier forms of dialectical theology. For it is exactly the lack of any awareness of ontological difference in Gogarten and Bultmann's dialectics (though not, as we shall see in Barth's) which causes them to stumble into uncritical thinking about the immediacy of revelation. Without any sense of the ontological difference, the crisis of representation dissolves as representation itself dissolves. Without any sense of the ontological difference, theology merely walks into ways of the gnostics.

In a long and complex section of *L'idol et la distance,* Marion outlines his understanding of "immediate mediation" (*mediation immediate*). For there *is* an immediacy of reception. "To receive the gift from God, as gift, demands that the man himself receives the gift into his essence immediately" (212). But this immediacy is qualified by the "transmission" itself. "Each one becomes the interpreter (not the deliverer) of the gift, transmitting it to the extent that he receives it" (213). Revelation is transmitted by and through interpretation. So, there is no "immediate transparency. On the contrary, mediation and immediacy cross each other radically. The moment of meditation . . . does not mask immediacy, but plainly (*sans fard*) surrenders the gift . . . in something concrete (*dans une actualite*). . . . Mediation alone constitutes the given that merits immediacy because it produces it. Mediation alone produces immediacy" (216). Marion then develops this in terms of "the trinitarian play" which he calls the *"thearchie"* and the role of Christ as the icon of the invisible. Christ alone is the analogy of immediate mediation. When Marion, in *God Without Being,* describes how "the invisible is made visible through a hermeneutic that can read in the visible the intention of the invisible" (21), that hermeneutic is Jesus Christ. A prior acceptance of Jesus Christ is necessary in order "to receive the world as an icon from God," (225) and therefore, "[t]he final iconic gift which renders the immediate mediation possible . . . will be Revelation contained in the words of Scripture" (227).

To engage in the concerns of the ontological difference, to posit a God beyond Being as the condition for the ontological difference (which is Marion's position), is to engage in the crisis of representation. On the basis of faith in Jesus Christ this crisis can then be read theologically—as the gift, as the revelation of the Word of God. Immediacy has to be mediated, that is the paradox: the icon is always also an idol. This is the crux of the crisis of representation as it issues from the dialectic of ontological difference. Without ontological difference there can be no dialectical theology in the radical way Gogarten, Barth and Bultmann conceived it, because the dialectic returns to the Hegelian movement of the Same-in-the-other, where the moment of negation is dissolved into a higher affirmation. It is the ontological difference that maintains the otherness of the other, enabling it to remain wholly other. The dialectic expresses the radical difference (*l'autre differant*). This radical difference issues both from and in the crisis of representation where "the unthinkable enters into the field of our thought only by rendering itself unthinkable there by excess, that is, by criticizing our thought" (*God Without Being*, 46).

There is, then, no radical difference without the crisis of representation when the other "enters" the same and allows itself to be thought as other than idolatrous. To depict the coherence of this "entrance," to outline how the unthinkable can be thought, how the other can enter the same without being domesticated by it, an economy of the crisis of representation needs to be sketched. Theologically, the theologian must present us with an account of the entrance of the Word into words, the icon into the idol, the invisible into the visible, It is this economy which is lacking from Bultmann's work, as Paul Ricoeur points out in his important essay "Preface to Bultmann." "A complete meditation on the word, on the claim of the word by being, and hence a complete ontology of language is essential here if the expression "Word of God" is to be meaningful, or, in Bultmann's terms, if this statement is to have nonmythological signification. But in Bultmann's work this remains to be thought."[19] The collapse of difference into immediacy, the dissolution of mediation, occurs in Bultmann because he fails to provide an adequate account of the Word in words. Or, to reverse this, we might say, he fails to provide an account of the Word in words because he fails to mediate upon the ontological difference between the Word and words. The dialectic collapses because beings and Being are understood synecdochally. His dialectical theology presupposes an *analogia entis* which facilitates direct revelation. His is a negative natural theology. His theological existentialism fails to take note of its own dependence on language, that the recognition itself (and hence the revelation) is mediated.

In his 1920 essay "The Crisis of Culture," Gogarten understands the crisis as providing a means for "really living the moment." The phrase echoes throughout the essay, where he explains that "really living the moment means that . . . the immediate moment requires nothing but to be immediately lived; it means . . . an encounter with God in moment, brought to its final perfection" (284). In this present the crisis is felt no more; it has been made sublimely meaningful and the dialectic has disappeared into the rhetorical mists of that sublimity. But it is precisely the rhetoric of immediacy that needs to be "deconstructed" in negative theology. This is what I suggested must happen, at the beginning of this essay, if we are going to recover the tradition of dialectical theology and see its relevance for postmodern theologies. The crisis of representation remains *in crisis*. There are no grounded guarantees of the meaningful, no evasion of the slipperiness of "human nature." There is no immediacy without mediation. The dialectic continues. A dialectical theology which remains tracing this instability, and does not attempt to resolve the process (either by collapsing theology into cultural anthropology, as with Feuerbach, or by assuming theology into some romantic apotheosis, as with Gogarten) remains true to itself. Gogarten's theological discourse forgets its own tropes are tropes and falls into existential dogmatism. A true dialectical theology, on the other hand, must always remain dangerous and in danger—because it must always keep in play, alongside its commitment to a doctrine of the knowability of God, a consideration of the rhetoric (and therefore the limits) of that knowability. A certain agnosticism remains. It must be alert to "the idolatrous presupposition of every conceptual discourse on God" (*God Without Being*, 33). A deconstructed dialectical theology must be a theology suspicious of the language of presence. It must be a theology suspicious too of ontologies of language (such as Ricoeur demands) in which the Word and words are correlated. A deconstructed dialectic theology must operate within the horizon of Heidegger's ontological difference.

Barth understood this (and prior to Heidegger). He understood it through his analysis of Anselm. Earlier, in his second edition of *Romans* he had recognized the importance of the epistemological difference, fundamentally Kantian, for theology: the difference between our constructed knowing and "knowing" God. But in his book *Anselm: Fides Quaerens Intellectum*, he came to see the relationship between the ontological difference, dialectical theology, and faith. It is in that book that he works out the distinction between *analogia entis* and *analogia fidei*—though neither of the terms feature in the book. For Anselm, as Barth reads him, what is axiomatic is that the being of objects in the world and the existence of God are not of the same order. Neither is one quantitatively different from the other—along the lines of Aquinas's being/Being correlation. These two forms of existence are radically different. "God does not exist as other things exist. . . . But God exists—and He alone—in such a way that it is impossible to conceive the possibility of his nonexistence" (134-5). God's existence "is therefore independent of the antithesis between knowledge and object" (141). This form of existence is caught up in the processes of verification and adequation between the intramental and the extramental, between what is known and the independent reality of the object "in itself." But "[i]f God were to exist merely generally, in the manner of all other beings, then not only would he not exist as God, but according to Anselm . . . he would not exist at all" (154). It is on the basis of this ontological distinction—a God who is totally other than beings as we conceive them, a God beyond or other than a correlation between beings and Being—that Barth restates the epistemological difference he recognized earlier: "[t]he identification of two possible *modi* of thinking (of existence) of an object" (163). It is the role of dialectical theology to examine the conflict between these two modes as they adhere to and are constituted by representation.

For Barth the dialectic of being, the ontological difference, reinforces the dialectic of knowing, the epistemological difference. There is no ontological participation in this other being, except by faith. As such the *analogia fidei* operates within both this ontological and epistemological difference, and is therefore anterior to *analogia entis*. In fact, it creates the condition for the *analogia entis* which can only function within and return us to an onto-theology, a metaphysics of presence and immediacy. The *analogia fidei* is a recognition that there is only what Marion calls "immediate mediation."

Marion has consistently written theology within the horizon of ontological difference. "Ontological difference . . . presents itself thus as a *negative* propaedeutic of the unthinkable thought of God" (45). The word "propaedeutic" is significant. For Marion emphasizes what Heidegger was well aware of, that the Being of ontological difference is not, in itself, a name for God. The God of theology is otherwise than this Being, and so the aim of Marion's work is to move beyond ontological difference to what he calls *l'Autre differant*. This is not easily translated because Marion is utilizing Derrida's concept of *la differance* and turning it into the name of an object. It is, at least, questionable whether this is possible—in Derridean terms—for *differance* names a process, a movement rather than an object. But Marion employs this notion to go one step beyond Heideggerian *die Differenz* and *der Unterschied*.[20] Whether, as he claims, Heidegger does "subordinate the rapport with the Other to ontology" (275)—which is Marion's major criticism of Heidegger—is also questionable. Particularly because, having made much of this criticism, Marion ends *L'Idol et la distance* by appropriating Heidegger's notion of *Ereignis*: "in *Ereignis*, the very conversion of the idol into the icon is at stake" (313). He does this seemingly oblivious to intimate the relationship between *Ereignis* and *Unterschied*. *Ereignis* is the experience of di-fference as di-fference for Heidegger.[21] But if we lay aside these questions for the moment, what remains evident is the dialectical crossing the idol by the icon. It is a dialectic of which "we can only glimpse G-d" (*God Without Being*, 108), a dialectic founded upon the distinction between G-d and God as an object like other existing objects. There is "Revelation (I say icon) . . . [and] 'God' as being (I say idol)" (52); there is, to use Heidegger's distinction, "theology" and "theiology." The latter is thought as, and must adhere to, onto-theology. But the former is a matter of faith (as Heidegger writes and Marion quotes): "for faith does not need the thought of Being" (61). By faith, then, we move beyond existence, existants, and the idol of god as *ens, realissimum,* or *causa*. With Marion postmodern theology returns (though he has not noticed it, as far as I am aware) to Barth's *analogia fidei*, faith which is still a thinking, but a mode of thinking (of existence) based upon a radical ontological difference.

For Marion, the critical moment in the judgement or crossing of the "wisdom of this world" is a kenotic act. He owes much to Levinas here. The kenotic act institutes the crisis (as judgement) in ontology. For the being of the world is now seen not as the possession of the world, but as a gift to the world. He analyzes this more clearly in *la Croisee du Visible*: "Every portrayal is a Eurydice, saved (rather than lost) because she has been seen . . . [And so] All representations (*tout tableau*) participate in a resurrection, every painter imitates Christ, in bringing the unseen to light."[22] Every object is presented as unique, as a gift, the gift of being. The negative side of this, which *God Without Being* emphasizes, is that "the 'world' under the light of God is revealed as a foger," (94) as a purveyor of vanities, a realm of simulacra. In his more recent work, it is the positive side, gained by "maintaining faith in the visibility to come, the salvation of the unseen" (54) that gains the upper hands. The world does not own what it believes it owns. It has frozen Being into a collection of objects, establishing a fabulous shrine for an idolatrous host. But by maintaining the faith in a revelation to come (again), Being is recognized as a gift, and in the giveness of Being remains a trace of the given, the anonymous one, who has withdrawn. That which sets the game of giving in play is love. The unseen, the infinite, manifest in the icon is the trace of this withdrawal. The withdrawal manifests the kenotic act of love—love that gives without appropriating. The withdrawal, the trace, the distance make necessary, and institute, the dialectic. The dialectic announces that "difference does not at all seem to be an appearance, but a reality, *the* reality" (122).

Marion's dialectical theology is a theology which retraces the cross or the crossing of what is visible. The crisis of representation, which guards faith, is read as a gift, and to accept the gift is to abandon all desire to possess (all desire to know and identify and "see"). One has to suffer the giving, bear the crisis, as love. The call to God is abandonment and so the crisis of representation is inseparable from kenosis. Kenosis installs, and perpetuates, the crisis and kenosis is the Christian response to the crisis. Kenosis names theologically the moment of *de-construction*.[23] It names the ethical nature of *de-construction*. "[T]his KENOSIS of the Son of God, this *form of a servant* . . . is not accidental but essential. It is imperative . . . that it should move on to final self-surrender and self-abandonment; imperative that we . . . should be scandalized" (*Romans*, 281).

For Barth and Marion, being scandalized is a result of the historical incarnation which "criss-crosses every form of rationality" (*Romans*, 276). The incarnation is the paradigmatic moment of crisis and kenosis; dialectic, as Barth understood when writing his *Gottingen dogmatics*, is the tracing of this Word in the all too human flesh of language. The dialectical tracing becomes the problem dogmatics sets out to tackle, the problem that "the audible and visible Word, are still a human word, with the implied concealment of the divinely posited reality" (*Gottingen Dogmatics*, 24).

What distinguishes Barth's dialectical theology from Marion's is the privileging of the Eucharist, by Marion, as the site of theology. For insofar as *[t]he theologian must go beyond the text to the Word, interpreting it from the point of view of the Word"* (*God Without Being*, 149), Marion claims "[t]he Eucharist alone completes the hermeneutic; the hermeneutic culminates in the Eucharist" (150). It is because this culminating hermeneutic has been located that Marion can then append to *God Without Being* his *Hors-Text*. This title is plainly an allusion to, and critique of, Derrida's axial statement in *Of Grammatology*, that "there is nothing outside of the text," (163) or "there is no outside-text [*Il n'y a pas de hors-texte*]" (158). Barth, too recognizes a connection between the Word in human words, the task of theology, and the Eucharist. But where their thinking differs is in Marion's insistence upon the logic of transubstantiation and Barth's Lutheran emphasis upon consubstantiation. Echoing consubstantiation's doctrinal formula, Barth can speak of God meeting us "in, with and under the sign and veil of . . . other objects" (III, 16). The "sign and veil" are never transparencies through which God is visible; Barth draws attention to the opacity that will always remain by employing three conflicting prepositions. The very scandal of the Eucharist, and the crisis of representation that it installs, exists in the tension between "signifying in, signifying with," and signifying under." Consubstantiation, then, instances and perpetuates the crisis and the dialectic of representation that theology bears witness to. Theology outlines the logic of this scandal and crisis. In naming the otherness that crosses the surface of the text, theology allows the otherness to speak in, with, and under the crisis of representation. In fact, it is the crisis which legitimates theology as a discourse. As Marion puts it, "theology must be conceived as a *logos* of the *Logos*" (*God Without Being*, 143). But the paradoxical nature of that "of" must never be forgotten. We return to Barth's insistence upon remembering. The "of" is both a subjective genitive (the word belonging to the Word) and an objective genitive (the word about the Word). It is always both, and that is why there is a crisis. The theological economy of consubstantiation belongs, then, to the thinking of the crisis of representation. But what about transubstantiation?

In *God Without Being* Marion outlines four sites in which the Word crosses through the word, or the invisible through the visible: the Bible, theology, the incarnation, and the Eucharist. We have access to only three of these, but all three are testimonies to the historical incarnation. Two of the three we have access to are texts—the Bible and theology—and, as Marion reminds us , "the text *does not* make an event" (145). It is the hermeneutic that releases the event from the text. Because of the emphasis upon the equiprimordiality of the sign and the referent in consubstantiation, the Eucharist for Barth remains caught in the nets of textuality. There is not, there cannot be (as Derrida said) anything outside textuality, there can only be *nothing* or absence. There remains, then, for Barth a skepticism about any theological knowledge, for "[a]ll we have are conceptions of objects, none of which is identical to God" (*Anselm*, 29). The skepticism keeps the dialectic open and all theological statements provisional. For Marion, on the other hand, the transubstantial Eucharist is a site that is nontextual, the site in which the Bible and theology *as* textual are stabilized. The Eucharist opens up a way beyond the textual to the referent: *"theology cannot aim at any other progress than its own conversion to the Word* . . . in the common Eucharist" (*God Without Being*, 158). The Eucharist is explicitly defined as "the nontextual Word of the words" (150). And so the rhetoric of presence, at this point, forgets itself: "[t]he Word intervenes in person in the Eucharist" (150) and in "the Eucharistic moment" there is assimilation (151). In this site an analogy is forged between the priest (theologian *par excellence* for Marion) and Christ. The priest is *icon* or *persona Christi* in "an authentically Eucharistic—eschatological—site" (157). The Eucharist provides for the possibility, which Barth (and Derrida) would deny, for a *hors-text*.

Marion is aware the Eucharist comes dangerously close to being the ultimate idol (171). Some extremely sophisticated thinking argues that this does not happen—that the Eucharistic gift is not the consummation of the present, but rather the present is the result of the emphasis in the Eucharist upon the past (as memorial) and the future (as eschatological announcement). What is immediate is a product, then, of mediation.

Marion certainly does not forget the problem of time and the constitution of the crisis of representation by difference and distance.

From the point of view of this essay, it does not matter whether Marion's thesis is logically cohesive or not. I raise the question because in postmodernity there can be no return to a natural theology and the *analogia entis*. Faith remains paramount for Marion, and faith is no longer faith when it begins to make unconditional assertions. Marion certainly has a tendency to make such assertions (and to endorse the authority of bishops in the Catholic Church). He has a tendency also to mention the importance of faith in odd folds of his discourse—a discourse fundamentally trying to locate, upon a philosophical basis (phenomenology), a place beyond and other. I question whether he succeeds, but it still remains true that the problematic he is working with, the crisis of representation and his dialectical analysis, are similar to those employed by dialectical theologians in Germany in the 1920s and 30s. His postmodern theology remains a dialectical theology.

The substance of this essay has been arguing for the need to reappropriate (by re-reading) and to deconstruct the legacy of dialectical theology, and to appreciate the relevance of its theological procedures as we look to the future composition of theology. Put boldly, what I am claiming is that dialectical theology is the only coherent theological response to the postmodern debate. Any other theological response, which must be a variation of correlational theology, merely falls victim to the debate. Dialectical theology does not fall victim because the major themes of postmodernism—ontological difference, the crisis of representation, the end of historicism—are the very themes it is attempting to think through theologically. Other forms of theology must either avoid the postmodern debate or pass through it tangentially. Dialectical theology *is* the postmodern debate. It places the debate itself in an area anterior to philosophies of discourse and representation, an area also beyond humanism and the rationality of the Enlightenment subject. It presents theological discourse as a palimpsest upon which the nature of discourse and representation itself is inscribed. For what is axiomatic in dialectical theology is the possibility of the wholly other, the unrepresentable. And it pursues the thoughts of the wholly other not by a process of ascesis (as with negative theology), but by plunging into the agonistics of representation itself. The agonistics of discourse is the "in, with, and under" whereby the passing of wholly other is traced. When representation faces itself, recognizes its ground is a trick with mirrors, then what is opened for us is a hither side of representation, and alternative mode of reasoning and the call for faith. Between God as Creator and human beings as epistemologically and ontologically fallen, there proceeds the grace that saves. The soteriological operation of the Trinity becomes the condition for this crisis of representation. Or is it that the soteriological operation of the Trinity is a reading of the "older" crisis of representation? By faith, dialectical theology privileges the truth of the former description. (By faith?) postmodern thinking privileges the truth of the latter. But both dialectical theology and postmodern thinking raise and keep the other in place and maintain the heterogeneity of origins. As such, dialectical theology must always submit is claims to a further deconstructive process; deconstruction is a repeated moment in its economy. But if, as Vattimo claims, ours is an epoch at the end of modernity, and if, as Vattimo also claims, that epoch is characterized by thinking at the end of metaphysics and history and humanism, then it is with dialectical theology, and only dialectical theology, that theological thinking can confidently enter the twenty-first century.

NOTES

1. The Gogarten essays referred to in this essay, and the page numbers following quotations from these essays, are found in ed. James M. Robinson, *The Beginnings of Dialectical Theology*, (Atlanta: John Knox Press, 1968). Hereafter cited parenthetically. The book is an almost complete translation of a book published in Germany in two volumes in 1962-63 by Jurgen Moltmann, *Anfange der dialektischen Theologie*.

2. Jean-Luc Marion, *God Without Being*, tr. Thomas A. Carlson (Chicago: The University of Chicago Press, 1991), xix. Hereafter cited parenthetically.

3. *The Decline of the German Mandarines* (Cambridge, Mass.: Harvard University Press, 1969), pp. 253-4.

4. *Dialectic of Enlightenment* (London: Verso, 1979), xii.

5. Karl Barth, *The Epistle to the Romans*, 2nd ed., tr. Edwyn C. Hoskyns (Oxford: Oxford University Press, 1968), p. 46. Hereafter cited parenthetically.

6. "Vanity" is another term developed in Marion's work. See chapter four of *God Without Being*.

7. Karl Barth, *The Word of God and the Word of Man* (London: Oxford University Press, 1928), p. 280.

8. Jacques Derrida, *Memories for Paul de Man* (New York: Columbia University Press, 1989), p. 135.

9. Philip Lacoue Labarthe, tr. and ed. Christopher Fynsk, *Typography: Mimesis, Philosophy, Politics* (Cambridge, Mass.: Harvard University Press, 1989), p. 115.

10. See Jon R. Synder's introduction to his translation of Gianni Vattimo's *The End of Modernity*, tr. Jon R. Synder, (Oxford; Polity, 1988), xviii. Hereafter cited parenthetically.

11. Jacques Derrida, *Writing and Difference*, tr. Alan Bass (Chicago: University of Chicago Press, 1978), p. 42. Hereafter cited parenthetically.

12. Jacques Derrida, *Margins of Philosophy*, tr. Alan Bass (Chicago: University of Chicago Press, 1982), p. 65.

13. Jacques Derrida, "Lettre a un ami japonais," *Psyche* (Paris: Galilee, 1987), p. 390.

14. Jacques Derrida, *Of Spirit*, tr. Geoffrey Bennington and Rachel Bowlby (Chicago: University of Chicago Press, 1989), p. 113.

15. Lacoue Labarthe, *Typography: Mimesis, Philosophy, Politics*.

16. Karl Barth, *Anselm: Fides Quaerens Intellectum* (London: SCM, 1960), p. 39.

17. Karl Barth, *Die christliche Dogmatik in Entwurf*, Gesamtausgabe, Bd. 14 (Zurich: Theologischer Verlag, 1982), p. 582.

18. Jean-Luc Marion, *L'Idol et La Distance* (Paris: Bernard Grasset, 1977).

19. Ed. Lewis S. Mudge, *Essays on Biblical Interpretation* (London: S.P.C.K., 1981), p. 70.

20. I doubt the validity of Marion's understanding of the ontological difference in Heidegger's work. In particular, he sees that there is a relation for Heidegger between being and Being. He speaks of the inversion of the wisdom of the world by the judgement of God as that which "undoes the jointing or being/Being" (*God Without Being*, 101). In *L'Idol et la distance*, where he first formulates the distinction between Heidegger's "di-fference" and his own *l'autre differant*, he

states that: "Difference does not mark such an antagonism between Being and being. It only deepens definitively their irreducible fold (*Zweifalt*) in order to reconcile them in a manner more intimate" (258-9). This is a highly Hegelian reading of Heidegger (the kind of reading found time and again in Levinas's work). It brings the ontological difference much closer to Aquinas's thinking. In *God Without Being*, Marion actually says that "Heidegger takes a position, in a debate that can be historically situated, in favor of the *ens* as the first divine name" (72). He goes on to relate this thinking specifically to Aquinas. Marion, despite quoting texts such as Heidegger's *Anaximander Fragment, Time and Being* and the essays in *Identity and Difference* does not read the provisional nature of any naming of Being. Being is not related to being; the fold (*le pli*) is *Zwiefalt* (double-fold), not *Falte*. Being is unthinkable because it is of an entirely different order to beings. It is not *ens* in the sense of onto-theology's *ens realissimus*. "Being can only be thoughts from Appropriation as the gift[s] of Appropriation" ("Time and Being," 23). Being is the gift of *Ereignis*, for Heidegger—and that returns us directly to Marion's own thinking. Heidegger, who is not ever naming God, is in fact far closer to Marion (as he is closer to Levinas) than Marion accepts.

21. See Heidegger's essay "Time and Being" in *Identity and Difference* tr. J. Stamburgh (New York: Harper & Row, 1969).

22. Jean-Luc Marion, *La Croisee du Visible* (Paris: La Difference, 1991), pp. 53-4.

23. I employ the French word here because the English translation "deconstruction" retains none of the ambiguity of the French *de*. In Derrida's article "Lettre a un ami japonais," *Psyche* (Paris: Galilee, 1987), pp. 387-93, Derrida refers to several dictionary definitions of the term and then proceeds to outline his own understanding. For him, "deconstruction" is both negative ("*une geste antistructuraliste*") and positive ("*une geste structuraliste*") (389).

"THE POET'S TRUE COMMITMENT"

Geoffrey Hill, the Computer, and Original Sin

Avril Horner

In 1980, during an interview with Blake Morrison, Geoffrey Hill made the following statement:

> The poet's true commitment must always be to the vertical richness of language. The poet's gift is to make history and politics and religion speak for themselves through the strata of language.[1]

This statement might seem immediately problematic. After all, in what sense can "history and politics and religion *speak for themselves*" (my italics) when a poem is a series of linguistic choices made by the poet? One aim of this essay is to shed some light on this conundrum; to show how Hill's choice of words in certain poems involves a highly self-conscious awareness of a culture's coercive forces; to explain how, for Hill, the good poem is an act of resistance. My linking of Geoffrey Hill with the computer and original sin owes its provenance to Hill's review of the Second Edition of the *Oxford English Dictionary* which appeared in *The Times Literary Supplement* in April, 1989. In that review, Hill took issue with the editors of the *O.E.D.* for omitting unusual and conflicting uses of certain words in favor of their more common usage, or indeed, in favor of more common words. The idiosyncratic use of the word "private" by both John Bunyan and Milton, for example, Hill sees as an omission from the dictionary; Hopkins's coinage of "unchancelling" is another omission he regrets; he notes, however, that the word "tofu" carries a full and comprehensive entry. This leads Hill to ask: "Is the the name of an easily analyzable substance that has appeared on a million menus more *real* than a word, peculiarly resistant to analysis, which had lodged itself in a few thousands of minds?"[2] (my italics). The review article concludes with the statement:

> Most of what one wants to know, including much that it hurts to know, about the English language is held within

159

these twenty volumes. To brood over them and in them is to be finally persuaded that sematology is a theological dimension: the use of language is inseparable from that "terrible aboriginal calamity" in which, according to Newman, the human race is implicated. Murray, in 1984, missed that use of "aboriginal"; it would have added a distinctly separate signification to the recorded examples. In 1989 it remains unacknowledged. In what sense or senses is the computer acquainted with original sin?[3]

The implication here is that human use of language constitutes an act of moral intelligence of which the computer, constrained as it is by the parameters of technology and able to reflect only certain elements of the working consciousness, is not yet capable. However, the poet, as someone who has a special sensitivity to the nuances and lost meanings of words and, above all, to their changing value within different historical and social contexts, is inevitably committed to guarding a language, the resonances of which bespeak the politics, history and religion of a culture. This implication in the cultural genealogy of words makes the poet, then, a "speaker" of "history and politics and religion." Thus in Hill's work, acute sensitivity to the nuances of words combines with a scholar's interest in etymology;[4] he is sternly critical of those who do not meet his own scrupulous and exacting standards. So the editors of the *O.E.D.* are further castigated for their entry on the word "dexterity," "one of the rhetorical janus-words of seventeenth-century politics" as Hill describes it. Noting that Clarendon's use of the word in his *History of the Rebellion* carries conflicting meanings according to context and that Clarendon contrives his own exceptional use of the word against "the usage of the time," Hill suggests that such a desire to resist "the current" of common usage not only confirms Clarendon's own verbal dexterity, but also speaks of the historical, political and religious conflicts of that time. In omitting Clarendon's use of the word, the editors of the *O.E.D.* omit a thread of English history and reduce the properties of the English language:

> They edit less authoritatively those cases, equally characteristic of the seventeenth century, in which distinct, even opposed, senses of a word alternate in the work of a single author, changing that "long and sometimes intricate series of significations" into a stylistic field where the compounding of language with political

or religious commitment may be either a matter of
deliberate display or a case of unwitting revelation.[5]

The point is not simply that the *Oxford English Dictionary* is not as
inclusive as it should be; rather, there are other issues involved, such as
attitudes toward language, poetry, and knowledge. Both Murray and
Bradley, as past editors of the dictionary, are berated for their attitudes
toward literature; in both cases there is, Hill suggests, a "sharp
discrepancy between the remarkable accuracy of philological knowledge
and the postprandial murmurings of literary 'taste.'" This discrepancy
indicates a superficial and complacent attitude to literature and literary
use of language; both Murray and Bradley, it is implied, all too readily
succumbed to a vague blandness encapsulated in phrases such as "the
sentiments of their authors," "true insight" (and) "rich poetry." This
"condescending tattle,"[6] as Hill describes it, into which both men slipped
when discussing the merits of literary works, still infects, in his view, the
discussion of literature in our own time:

> I'm frequently most impressed by the tenacity and acumen
> with which current affairs commentators on television
> and radio approach the task of attempting to elicit facts
> and truths from quick-talking politicians. When they
> move, on the same program, from that world of politics
> and finance to matters of art or literature, as they
> occasionally do, there is a distinct loss of pressure and
> interest. It is as if they feel they're moving from the
> centrally significant to the trivial and the marginal, and
> are therefore willing to accept assertions and rumors that
> they would resist and refute in a more "serious" area of
> discussion.[7]

Such intellectual slackness is sharply at odds with the critical and
creative practice of the poets whom Hill most admires: Pound's theoretical
insistence on verbal economy and precision has clearly marked Hill's
poetry, as has Hopkins's argument which, like Hill's own, was concerned
"both in theory and practice . . . to guard the essential against the
inessential, the redundant, the merely decorative."[8] The poetic uses of
certain words omitted from the *O.E.D.* are, for Hill, examples of
"ordinary words raised to an extraordinary pitch of signification" in which
they carry both "physical and metaphysical significations."[9] (It is,

however, worth remembering here Hill's caveat in *The Lords of Limit* in relation to J. L. Austin's style: "By 'poetic' in this context one means no more than that the richness and subtlety of 'ordinary language' have been amply realized."[10] To neglect these usages is to neglect a vital dimension of cultural intelligence and to reduce the "protean energy" and "genius"[11] of language to its common usage, thereby succumbing to what Hill has described as the "inertial drag of speech" (*LL*, 87). The *Oxford English Dictionary*, by giving preference to the common use of a word over a rare and possibly esoteric, but more intellectually complex and morally challenging use of the same word, thus lays itself open to the charge of what Hill defines (via Hobbes) in *The Enemy's Country*, as "compleasance," that is to say *"That every man strive to accommodate himselfe to the rest."*[12]

Undoubtedly, then, for Hill, the poet's prime task is one of regulating meaning within what he has described as the "fecund recalcitrance" (*EC*, 9) of language, in which the word, like a coin, has a value relative always to its social and political context: he has recently stated that "the writer's judgement of word-values both affects and is affected by his understanding of, or his failure to comprehend, the current reckonings of value in the society of his day" (*EC*, 5). The fact that, in the words of Hobbes, "there is scarce any word that is not made *equivocal* by divers contextures of speech, or by diversity of pronunciation and gesture" (*EC*, 22) is part of the perplexity of the poet's craft. It is perhaps worth noting here how Hill refuses to use a poststructuralist vocabulary when referring to what others might call the slippage of the signifier, but instead returns to the words of a seventeenth-century philosopher to express the same idea. Much of Hill's poetry can be read in a postmodern spirit (*The Mystery of the Charity of Charles Péguy* in particular lends itself to such a reading), and remarks made in conversation suggest that he is well aware of its deconstructive impulse,[13] yet he resolutely avoids the critical vocabulary of poststructuralism. Such avoidance is probably grounded in several profound reservations which make him "out of key with his time,"[14] despite what some have seen as Foucauldian tendencies in his work.[15] Further, Hill's emphasis on poetry as a responsible act accords with the spirit of modernism more than that of postmodernism:

> Poetry is responsible. It's a form of responsible behaviour,
> not a directive. It is an exemplary exercise. Ezra Pound
> said in his *Letters* that "The Poet's job is to define and yet
> again define, till the detail of surface is in accord with the
> root in justice."[16]

Hill, however, is not simply a late twentieth-century version of Pound or Eliot; although tradition is an important concept for Hill—as it was for Eliot—his deep engagement with history never simply mimics the rather conservative "quest for stability"[17] that informs the earlier poet's work. In Hill's writings, any sense of nostalgia and loss is historically situated and is subjected to skeptical enquiry. Moreover, what some critics see as Hill's problematic relationship with Christianity neither derives from the modernist nostalgia for faith nor endorses postmodernism's skepticism which defines itself through the death of such metanarratives. Various readers have commented on what they see as a disturbing tendency in Hill's early poetry to dwell on the strange sweetness of agony and martyrdom which Christianity offers its followers.[18] Such readings, it seems to me, ignore Hill's constant quizzing of the metanarrative offered by Christianity and mistake his deconstruction of the iconography of the Christian faith for a salacious dwelling on the deeds perpetuated in its name. What we have in Hill's work is not his own nostalgia for an unproblematic Christianity but a delineation of society's nostalgia for simple faith; what his poetry often expounds—particularly in the volume *Tenebrae* published in 1978—is not the certainty of God, but the secular and sublunary nature of the language in which God is "realized." His work thus exhibits what Patricia Waugh has described as "a fall from an original state of harmony into a fragmentation" or a state of "postmodern apocalypticism,"[19] but this is an entirely self-conscious enquiry. Any consequent sense of loss concerning the transcendent is, however, offset by the attempt to reintegrate some of the tenets of Christianity within a philosophy of language and theology particularly tuned to poetry. In this sense, if he is a Christian poet (and he is equivocal about this[20]), Hill must be described as a postmodern one, although he clearly rejects the state of cynicism and moral neutrality embraced by so many postmodernist thinkers and, presumably, fears what Bernard Zelechow has described as the "counterproductive" agenda of postmodernism which might simply result in the exchange of one set of cultural coercions for another.[21]

How, then, does Hill's claim that "poetry is responsible" translate itself into poetic practice? In his first collection of essays, *The Lords of Limit*, Hill noted that "The question 'how the moral intelligence gets into poetry' is of course quite distinct from the question 'how morality gets into poetry' or 'how moral is poetry?'" (*LL*, 115). Hill's concern with "how the moral intelligence gets into poetry" links him with modernist poets such as T. S. Eliot, Allen Tate, and, of course, Ezra Pound. These writers were also concerned—often in what now seems a rather paternalistic and reactionary manner—with the relationship between poetry, ethics, and society. Hill has clearly adopted their use of technical strategies such as ellipsis, allusion, and ambiguity yet he has moved the subjects of their debate into a late twentieth-century arena which encompasses the concerns of a postmodern theology. His technical strategies result in difficult and challenging poetry, yet for Hill such difficulty is one of poetry's attractions; he has quoted, with approval, Coleridge's notion of the reader as a "fellow laborer" (*LL*, 119) and has praised, in a review of *Tyndale's New Testament* and *The Revised English Bible*, former editors of the Everyman Library for showing "respect for the intelligence of "ordinary" people by occasionally making demands on it."[22] In 1958, when he was only 26, Hill quoted with approval Allen Tate's pronouncement that "The artist as man invariably has the same relation to the society of his time as everybody has: his misfortune and his great value is his superior awareness of that relation."[23]

For Hill, this insight translates itself into a self-conscious awareness of how linguistic choices reflect and constitute a moral position in so far as they negotiate a path between the "inertial drag of speech" that encodes coercive cultural forces and a sense of individual autonomy. Rather than colluding with the postmodern notion that the "self" is a vanishing dot within the matrices of intersecting discourses and ideologies, Hill allows for a certain amount of autonomy within those forces and thereby restores to us the notion of "a dignified being bearing responsibility for action in the world."[24] For Hill, as for Blake, the imagination enables the poet to probe the social and ethical implications of linguistic choices and thereby to examine the morality which underlies the "clichés and equivocations of propaganda or of 'public relations' (which) are . . . part of the living speech of a society" (*LL*, 39). This frequently involves an imaginative identification with the victims and/or perpetrators of tyrannical systems in a manner which, as Christopher Ricks pointed out in a highly perceptive early review of Hill's work, "achieves truthfulness by not eschewing cliché."[25] Hill's best known poem, "September Song," from the volume *King Log* published in 1968, is a fine example of this strategy.[26] Since this poem has received so much praise and critical analysis already, I do not wish to dwell on it at length here.[27] However, it is worth re-emphasizing that Hill struggles to avoid an unseemly appropriation of Jewish suffering by making explicit in the poem both the moral dilemma facing the poet who wishes to use such material as subject matter and the manner in which "the living speech of society" can foster collusion with acts that are morally appalling. Thus, clichés and phrases such as "Undesirable," "untouchable," "As estimated," and "Things marched" (evoking the fatalistic "Things happened" as well as the inhumanity of the marching Nazis) are placed in contexts in which punning ambiguities intellectually tease the alert reader into a state of moral discomfort. The words "Undesirable" and "untouchable," for example, recall both the caste system of Hindu society and the unstated caste system of the Western world which often enshrines itself in religious difference and which distinguishes certain individuals as "undesirable aliens." The phrases "As estimated" and "Things marched" not only evoke the bureaucratic efficiency of the Nazi régime which morally seduced thousands of ordinary German citizens, but also suggest how language can be used to evade moral responsibility: the "clichés and equivocations" of a society, which include, of course, the veiling of cruelty under a cloak of pseudo-scientific or commercial vocabulary, provide a semantic shelter for those who find it in their interest to remain morally undiscerning.

The poem is, in fact, an act of atonement in so far as any poem can "atone" for such atrocity;[28] whilst implicitly condemning Nazi policy, it nevertheless makes painfully clear how a certain use of language can "normalize" within a society acts which, in retrospect, appear barbaric. Indeed, in exposing the moral danger posited by such use of cliché and equivocation it charts the subtle and pervasive menace of the "inertial drag of speech." Moreover, it seeks to commemorate a child who, exterminated at the age of ten, was denied both justice and epitaph on this earth.[29] In a lapidary and elegiac manner, "September Song" construes an epitaph for this dead child and, by implication, for all victims of racist policies. The language of the gravestone hovers beneath that of a poem which commemorates a victim who had no gravestone: "deported" resonates with the phrase "departed this life"; the sentence "Not forgotten/ or passed over at the proper time" evokes not only the Passover but also the graveyard euphemism "Passed over to the other side." Similarly, the phrase "Not forgotten"not only draws attention to the ruthless efficiency with which the Nazis tracked down the Jews, but also evokes the common tombstone inscription "Not forgotten, but gone before." Thus the common language of death which allows the most ordinary mortals an earthly commemoration hovers, in ironic juxtaposition, with the bleakly terse language of the first stanza, whilst the clichés used to cover and veil acts of barbarity are revealed as part of the the "inertial drag of speech" which trundles a terrible ideology in its wake. Our recognition of what Hill has described (when discussing Hopkins's choice of words) as "the metamorphic power of . . . context"[30] is a crucial element in learning to read Hill's own work.

Poetry then, for Hill, must expose the coercive force of language. For this reason Hill, like Ezra Pound, sees the poet's prime duty as one of resistance:

> a poet's words and rhythms are not his utterance so much
> as his resistance. His "choice of *Words*, and Harmony of
> Numbers" as Dryden would say, his "technic" as Yeats and
> Pound called it, must resist the pressure of circumstances
> or be inundated by the tide of "compleasance." (*EC*, 5)

Consequently, Hill admires those like Coleridge "constitutionally against the 'set' of the age, whose style, in prose argument is characterized by phrases descriptive of resisting the current;"[31] in our own time, he notes with approval what he has described as C. H. Sisson's "resistant intelligence."[32] Such writers, it would seem, harbor a "superior awareness" of the coercions of contemporary culture and the language in which they are expressed. In similar spirit, his own work seeks to resist "the attraction of terminology itself, a power at once supportive and coercive" and to offer "some resistance to the reductionist tendency of modern science" (*LL*, 1, 6). In this respect Hill fully meets Raymond Williams's demand that "a commitment to examining our most settled commitments might be the most literate thing we could attempt."[33] The way such resistance is expressed through poetic technique is of the utmost importance to Hill. Throughout his writing career, Hill has followed Jonson's definition, referred to in *The Lords of Limit,* that language which is "literary in the best sense of the term" scrutinizes the "unquestioned connotations" to which "certain words and phrases, by constant repetition in popular literary modes, shall have been reduced . . . " (*LL*, 46). In this way, Hill makes manifest the liaison between "moral exactitude and technical precision"[34] which constitutes the burden of poetic responsibility.

But to return to the question of "how the moral intelligence gets into poetry": we have seen how, in "September Song," technical precision can embody moral intelligence in so far as the poet's choice of words can both represent and resist the moral climate of a society through quizzing the language in which that climate is encoded. But use of rhythm can also be indicative of moral intelligence in Hill's poetry. He has noted in his essay on C. H. Sisson, that Charles Maurras's statement, "Reason may convince, but it is rhythm that persuades," is "potentially dangerous," presumably because rhythm might, according to this definition, arouse an aural, emotional response and work against reason and ethical discernment.[35] If rhythm holds such powers of persuasion, then *ipso facto*, the poet holds a power which he or she can use for good or ill. *Mercian Hymns*, published in 1971, is an exciting experiment in poetic rhythm, and is rich in aural diversity. The "distinctive irregularity of ordinary speech" which Derek Attridge has noticed in Hymn VII, for example, produces a rhythm quite different from the alliterated, accentual rhythm of Hymn XXVI.[36] Certain rhythms and poetic forms present themselves as aural memories of verbal patterns; although the hymns appear visually homogeneous, rhythmically and linguistically they in fact chart a variety of poetic choices. Hymn XXVI, for example, opens with alliterated words that are heavily stressed; it therefore evokes the aural impact of Anglo-Saxon verse. Since this hymn irreverently conflates modern Christmas celebrations with more brutal eighth-century festivities, the use of Anglo-Saxon meter is here particularly appropriate. In contrast, Hymn IV gradually slips into the rhythm of blank verse. It can easily be so rearranged and indeed, as such, the last two lines form perfect iambic pentameters: "where dry-dust badgers thronged the Roman flues,/the long-unlooked-for mansions of our tribe."

Hill's choice of rhythms in *Mercian Hymns* evokes the poetry and the visions of the past, and these complement his fascination with etymology—"the crypt of roots and endings." But in *Mercian Hymns* rhythm also functions as an instrument of moral intelligence. Take, for example, the rhythmical contrast between the first and second "hymns" which "celebrate" an eighth-century king, Offa of Mercia (an area encompassing Worcestershire where Hill was raised as a child). The first hymn presents us with some of Offa's attributes, woven into what sounds like a public celebration, in bardic praise-song, of the Anglo-Saxon king's versatility.[37] Of the ten phrases, seven open with a strong beat: the absence of articles dispenses with the off beat which usually accompanies the use of definite and indefinite articles. These strong beats are separated by single or double off beats so that a distinct rhythm emerges. The result is a heightened use of language; what is essentially a list is metamorphosed, through rhythm, into public and authoritative proclamation, although of course there is a comic tension between this and the ironic "updating" of Offa's skills. This rhythmic, rhetorical effect is, however, completely subverted by the next hymn which, in concentrating punningly on the *sound* of the king's name, not only conjures up Offa in a contrastingly ludic and irreverent manner, but also inverts the rhythm which preceded it. Here, the use of liberally sprinkled indefinite articles produces a very different rhetorical effect. Eight out of the eleven very short phrases begin with an off beat: the list structure is more evident and the rhythm, far from being incantatory, bears the stress-patterns of inconsequential remarks or private musings. The second hymn therefore deflates the first hymn not only *semantically* but also *rhythmically*. The rhythm itself functions as an antiphonal voice, challenging and subverting the rhetorical effects of the previous hymn.[38]

For Hill, then, the poem is not only artifact but also speech act; as his quarrel with J. L. Austin in "Our Word is Our Bond" suggests, for this poet "utterance" and "act" are not distinct entities" (*LL*, 11). Hill's belief in the moral and social importance of poetry stands or falls by his claim that the good poem constitutes a moral action within the social fabric. The theological dimension of this equation is made manifest in Hill's affirmation of MacKinnon's statement that "the language of repentance is not a kind of bubble on the surface of things" (*LL*, 6) and his more recent assertion that "Language . . . *is* a doctrinal solution."[39] Indeed, Hill's poetry can profitably be read in conjunction with both the negative aesthetics of Adorno's work and the radical theology of Don Cupitt. Cupitt's description of art as a "counter-culture" which eschews the transcendental and affirms language as the basis for faith—since "every aspect of what we call "reality" is established in and by language"— accords well with Hill's manifesto for poetry.[40] As in Adorno's essays, contradiction in Hill's work frequently resolves itself as style, in writing which is a "crabbed, rebarbative practice"[41] but one which allows the writer to negotiate resistant and conflicting meanings. Both men endorse the aesthetic project "even if its terms of reference have been permanently tainted by fascism and 'mass' society"[42] and both see art as an act of commitment. Their sense of commitment has, however, nothing to do with the notion of being *engagé*: Adorno's comment, "But what gives commitment its aesthetic advantage over tendentiousness also renders the content to which the artist commits himself inherently ambiguous" both illuminates the notion of commitment to which Hill is wedded and focuses on its problematic nature.[43]

For Hill, then, "rhetoric" is a part of the ontology of moral action" (*LL*, 158) despite J. L. Austin's claim to the contrary. Indeed, his challenge to Austin in "Our Word is Our Bond" embraces "the importance of Nettleship's perception" which "does not seal off the moral action from the linguistic action" (*LL*, 118). For Hill the poem is not governed merely by aesthetic criteria but must be tuned in relation to matters of ethics as they surface within the language of the poem. Hence the scrupulous care with which, like Donne, he sifts or "cribrates" (*EC*, 32-3) language; like Ben Jonson, another writer he admires, Hill is "prepared to risk appearing over-scrupulous in the attempt to define true goodness" (*LL*, 52). Increasingly in his work this concern with language and moral integrity coalesces with theological debate; in his recent review of a book by Isabel Rivers he stated:

> Against the odds and a good deal of evidence, I still regard
> the effort to bring secular scholarship (and poetics and the

"fine arts") into the field of theological judgement as
something other than a search for the philosopher's
stone.[44]

Having moved away from the circumscribed dynamic of atonement
and redemption and its validity as a paradigm for literature which marked
his early essays, Hill now engages in a more catholic manner with the
theological dimension of language and has recently coined the term
"meta-poetry" to describe the manner in which the good poem
acknowledges its nature as the most "immersed" of crafts or
"knowledges":

> in the *Essayes in Divinity*, Donne had coined the term
> "meta-theology" to denote "a profounder theology than
> that recognized by divines." The analogy here is palpable;
> self-evidently affecting the metaphysics, conscious that it
> is "misinterpretable; since to some palates it may taste of
> Ostentation." The knotty riddling of Donne's verse and
> prose moves from, and through, rhetorical bravado and
> "alarums" (he himself enters that caveat) to an
> engagement with meta-poetics, a profounder poetry than
> that recognized by conventional instructors in rhetoric
> and conduct . . . . "Meta-poetry," as I labor to define it,
> challenges Bacon's "Policie" as the most "immersed" of
> crafts or "knowledges" while resisting the cynical fatalism
> that may accompany the "logical" liberation of the mind.
> Meta-poetry is immersed in the knowledge that it is so
> immersed. (*EC*, 59-60)

Although Hill's own poetry may smack to some of "Ostentation," its
"knotty riddling" derives, like that of Donne's verse and prose, from an
engagement with language which is both profoundly philosophical and
deeply unfashionable in its emphasis on sematology as a theological
dimension of experience. Resisting both the inert use of language offered
by the computer and the "cynical fatalism" offered by much contemporary
linguistic and literary theory, Hill's poetry strives to keep words "living
and accurate"[45] as an act of moral intelligence. Reluctant to admit or state
openly the nature of his faith, Hill might nevertheless be regarded as a
religious poet whose concept of "meta-poetry" not only restores the notion
of moral intelligence to the act of writing, but also revives, Lazarus-like,

the author from the state of "death" and unaccountability created by the rhetoric of postmodernism.

NOTES

1. Geoffrey Hill in conversation with Blake Morrison, "Under Judgment," *New Statesman* (February 8, 1980): 212.

2. Geoffrey Hill, "Common weal, common woe," *Times Literary Supplement* (April 21-27, 1989): 412.

3. "Common weal, common woe": 414.

4. See his remark "etymology is history" in conversation with ed. John Haffenden, *Viewpoints: Poets in Conversation* (London and Boston: Faber & Faber, 1981), p. 88.

5. This and the previous quotations from Geoffrey Hill, "Common weal, common woe": 412, 411.

6. "Common weal, common woe": 412.

7. "Interview: David Sexton talks to Geoffrey Hill," *The Literary Review*, 92 (February, 1986): 28.

8. "Common weal, common woe": 412.

9. "Common weal, common woe": 414.

10. Geoffrey Hill, *The Lords of Limit: Essays on Literature and Ideas* (London: André Deutsch, 1985), p. 148. Hereafter it will be referred to in abbreviated form as *LL*.

11. "Common weal, common woe": 414.

12. Geoffrey Hill, *The Enemy's Country: Words, Contexture, and other Circumstances of Language* (Oxford: Oxford University Press, 1991), p. 1. Hereafter it is referred to in abbreviated form as *EC*.

13. See, for example, Hill's conversation with Blake Morrison in "Under Judgment": 212-14.

14. The phrase is from Ezra Pound's *Hugh Selwyn Mauberley, Ezra Pound: Selected Poems 1908-1959* (London and Boston: Faber & Faber, 1975), p. 98.

15. Compare Andrew Roberts in a review of Hill's *The Enemy's Country*:

> Hill, in examining a range of seventeenth-century writers, together with some earlier writers such as Wyatt, and a single twentieth-century poet in the shape of Ezra Pound, is concerned with the pressure exerted upon their use of language by political and social discourse, and the ways in which their language resists and responds to that pressure. Foucault has articulated the manner in which language represents and transmits the power-structures of society. Hill shares something of that vision of language as permeated by power and is preoccupied with the way in which this constrains but also gives life to the more metaphorical "power" of literary art . . . "Circumstantial Evidence," *English* 41/171 (Autumn, 1992): 261.

16. Haffenden, *Viewpoints*, p. 99.

17. The phrase is Michael Schmidt's and is taken from his essay on Eliot in *An Introduction to 50 Modern British Poets* (London: Pan, 1979), p. 126.

18. See, for example, Harold Bloom on Hill as a "martyrologist" and Neil Corcoran on the "eroticism" in Hill's work which is "apparently fascinated by sexual estrangement and by the postures of bodily pain" in Bloom's introduction to Hill's *Somewhere is Such a Kingdom: Poems 1952-1971* (Boston: Houghton, 1975) and Neil Corcoran's review article "Postures of Pain," *Times Literary Supplement* (March 4-10, 1988): 253, respectively.

19. Patricia Waugh, *Practising Postmodernism, Reading Modernism* (London: Edward Arnold, 1992), pp. 13-14.

20. Such equivocation is expressed in Hill's reply to John Haffenden's enquiry as to whether he would class himself as an agnostic or describe himself in Harold Bloom's phrase as a "desperate humanist":

I would not wish to describe myself as an agnostic. There's a phrase by Joseph Cary in his book *Three Modern Italian Poets*—I forget which poet he's referring to—that, if it were applied to my own poetry, might seem to be not wholly irrelevant, "a heretic's dream of salvation expressed in the images of the orthodoxy from which he is excommunicate." That seems to me an apt phrase to describe the area in which my poetry moves." John Haffenden, *Viewpoints*, p. 98.

21. See Bernard Zelechow, "Nietzsche's Theology of History and the Redemption of Postmodernism" in ed. David Jasper, *Postmodernism, Literature and the Future of Theology* (London: Macmillan, 1993), p. 122.

22. Geoffrey Hill, "Of Diligence and Jeopardy," *Times Literary Supplement* (November 17-23, 1989): 1275.

23. Geoffrey Hill, "The Poetry of Allen Tate," *Geste* (Leeds) 3/3 (November 1958): 8. The passage is taken from Allen Tate, *The Man of Letters in the Modern World* (London: Thames, 1955), p. 315.

24. Zelechow, *Postmodernism, Literature and the Future of Theology*, p. 123.

25. Christopher Ricks, "Cliché as 'Responsible Speech': Geoffrey Hill," *The London Magazine* 1/8 (November, 1964): 97.

26. The poem "September Song" appears in Geoffrey Hill, *King Log* (London: André Deutsch, 1968), p. 19 and *Geoffrey Hill: Collected Poems* (Harmondsworth: Penguin, 1985), p. 67.

27. See, for example, Christopher Ricks, *The Force of Poetry* (Oxford: Oxford University Press, 1984), p. 296 ff.; ed. Peter Robinson, *Geoffrey Hill: Essays on his Work* (Oxford: Oxford University Press, 1985), pp. 120-2; and Stephen T. Glynn, "Biting Nothings to the Bone: The Exemplary Failure of Geoffrey Hill," *English* XXXVI/156 (Autumn, 1987): 236-240.

28. See Hill's essay "Poetry as 'Menace' and 'Atonement'" in *The Lords of Limit*, pp. 1-18.

29. It is of interest to note that Hill's birth date is June 18, 1932, one day before that of the nameless victim commemorated in "September Song."

30. "Common weal, common woe": 411.

31. "Common weal, common woe": 414.

32. Geoffrey Hill, "C .H. Sisson," *P. N. Review* 39: 11/1 (1984): 14.

33. Raymond Williams, "Commitment," *Stand* 20/3 (1979): 11.

34. See Geoffrey Hill:
"One would agree that it is generally taken for granted that to talk about success in poetry is to assume that one has precluded an artificial distinction between moral exactitude and technical precision: that the one is embodied in the other." "The Dream of Reason" [*The Review* 5, 6 (June, 1963) *Special Number—William Empson*], *Essays in Criticism* 14/1 January 1964, p. 96.

35. Geoffrey Hill, "C. H. Sisson": 14.

36. Derek Attridge, *The Rhythms of English Poetry* (London: Longman, 1982), p. 317.

37. *Mercian Hymns* (London: André Deutsch, 1971), reprinted in *Geoffrey Hill: Collected Poems* (Harmondsworth: Penguin, 1985), pp. 105-34.

38. One can, of course, also see this rhythmical exercise as a quarrel with Pound's glamorization of the "factive" hero. For more on Hill's debts to, and quarrels with, Pound see my "The 'Intelligence at Bay': Ezra Pound and Geoffrey Hill," *Paideuma* 22 (Spring and Fall, 1993): 243-54.

39. Geoffrey Hill, "Style and Faith," review of Isabel Rivers's *Reason, Grace and Sentiment, Times Literary Supplement* (December 27, 1991): 5.

40. Don Cupitt, *The Long-Legged Fly: A Theology of Language and Desire* (London: SCM, 1987), p. 18.

41. Terry Eagleton, *The Ideology of the Aesthetic* (Oxford: Blackwell, 1990), p. 341.

42. Eagleton, *The Ideology of the Aesthetic*, p. 344.

43. Theodor Adorno, extracts from *Aesthetics and Politics,* in ed. Dennis Walder, *Literature in the Modern World* (Oxford: Oxford University Press, 1990), p. 91.

44. Geoffrey Hill, "Style and Faith": 6.

45. The phrase is Ezra Pound's: "The *mot juste* is of public utility . . . . We are governed by words, the laws are graven in words, and literature is the sole means of keeping these words living and accurate." Ed. T. S. Eliot, *Literary Essays of Ezra Pound* (London: Faber & Faber, 1954; 1968), p. 409.

THROUGH THE EYES OF A CHILD

Looking for Victims in Toni Morrison's *The Bluest Eye*

Mark Ledbetter

. . .
And then last night, I tiptoed up
To my daughter's room and heard her
Talking to someone, and when I opened
The door, there was no one there . . .
Only she on her knees, peeking into

Her own clasped hands

Imamu Amiri Baraka (LeRoi Jones)[1]

Introduction

Desperation characterizes the victim. The victim will do most anything to avoid his fated end, which is disappearance. Victims are a lost people; they are victims because they are neither heard nor seen. To posture any sense of "real" presence is to no longer be a victim.

"Otherness" characterizes desperation.[2] A tremendous mystery—awe inspiring, even religious—embodies acts of desperation. The desperate act is always described by the voyeur with the phrase, "Why did she do that?" The irony, here, is that the voyeur, too, is desperate to see and, therefore, to know and to experience the mystery, however horrible, of the observed "other." As a result, she becomes victim, too, of the unanswered question, "Why?"

Violence characterizes otherness. Victims in an ethic of reading and writing are those persons desperate to be heard and seen (note the passive voice) and whose alternative to a literal disappearance from the human story, is to commit desperate acts of violence to themselves, even to those whom they love, in order to create a world that, while not of their choosing, is at least of their making. In this world, the victims are seen and heard. The voyeur is implicated into the lives of the victims, for the

177

violence violates the sensibilities of the observer, who knows, because of this violation, that he has encountered otherness, a moment beyond human control and definition and so physically and emotionally scarring, that he must embody this moment in order to define his existence.

The voyeur is characterized by need, the need to control a situation by surreptitiously looking at and into the world around him. The voyeur is not simply the "peeping-Tom" variety, but also the reader of newspapers and the follower of fire engines. And yet perhaps the most persistent voyeur is the reader of literature. This voyeur, the reader of literature, experiences an ethical moment when she is blinded, at least temporarily, when the object of her sight, the text, looks back at her. With this "returned gaze" comes the moment of implication. Narrative's victim(s) is discovered when the text "looks back," and the reader (voyeur), in turn, blinks.

At this moment, the text's ethical dimensions reveal themselves, and the victim is named. Writer and reader, as well as characters in the text, must choose from a discourse inherently ethical and one which encourages responsible reflections, if not actions. What are my connections with narrative's victims, particularly the violence they experience and the violence they cause me? In response to such a question, I suggest that personal violation, beyond our control and as a result of our observing the body violence to narrative's victims, is a claim of human community. Personal violation is the moment of silence, where writer and reader become victims themselves, and is a silence out of which come questions of, Complicity? Empathy? Naivete? Ignorance?, questions which Levinas might call "the rumbling within silence,[3] questions which make reader and writer profoundly aware that no one is immune from the disease of victimization. There are only pained victims and anesthetized victims, but there are only victims.

I   The Desperate Victim

Thus, I begin the application of theory to practice with a brief essay on discovering and naming the victim. I believe that this exercise is critical to any argument concerning the ethical dimensions of writing and reading, particularly the suggestion that such an ethical enterprise involves making heard and hearing silenced voices. I turn, now, to a novella by Toni Morrison, *The Bluest Eye,* and ask, "Who are society's victims?"

Desperate acts of violence by text, character, and reader provide intimately profound moments of ethical reflection in Morrison's *The Bluest Eye*. Remember, desperation characterizes the victim. Characters are desperate for love and will choose freely to violate society's most strictly-held moral codes, as well as to inflict violence on their own bodies, in order to be loved. The text itself reveals a language of desperation, fragmented by the nature of the story it tells and violently interrupting any attempt, on the part of reader or writer, to create a neat or romantic closure to the narrative. The reader is desperate to avoid the pain that comes from seeing the world through an abused child's eyes, and to avoid the moral impotence that comes with knowing that another victim has vanished from the human story, violently lost to a world dark and silent, "right before our [your] very eyes".[4]

The Bluest Eye is the story of black America in the South during 1941, pre-civil rights legislation. African Americans were shunned and denied opportunities by the powerful white community. This disease of prejudice and hatred infected the African American community itself, where a disenfranchised people, struggling to "make ends meet" economically, as well as create a stable social community, find little time to develop a family life that gives love and nurture to the individual members. Through physical and emotional violence, family members forge a world of love, however seemingly perverted and mutated, given the one thing they possess: their bodies.

The painfully constant theme in *The Bluest Eye* is that desperation forces the victim to victimize others and even the self. Victimization has a vicious circuity in the community of the hopeless and the helpless, and more often than not requires not merely the unpredictable act or event, by the narrative and/or characters, to break free from the victim's cycle but more so a horrifyingly indecipherable, if not shockingly inhuman, act or event by the narrative or characters. These acts or events are the moments in narrative where the text confronts the voyeur, the reader, the "me" of the narrative, and forces "me" to blink. Roles are reversed; I am being read, and ethical reading begins.

The Bluest Eye has many such moments. Cholly, the father, rapes his daughter, an act that horrifies and excites him and is his last and only claim on/to love. Mrs. Breedlove rejects her own child—a violence to maternity—yet calls the daughter in the white family for whom she works, "baby," in a vain attempt to construct a family life that she will never know. Pecola, the daughter, longs for blue eyes, a sign of acceptance in the white person's world. Everyone loves a blue-eyed child. When her wish is not granted by God, she blinds herself—physically?—certainly mentally, turning inward to the dark world of the victim where she can define love on her own terms and leaving the blue glaze of her mutilated or crazed eyes to look upon her victimizing world.

II   The Desperate Text

The text, at first glance, attempts to gloss the world of the victims. *The Bluest Eye* is not about victims, suggest the epigrams of the early chapters; rather, the world is victim-less. Each chapter begins with the world of the Dick and Jane primer, indeed, an Edenic life where all the people "are very happy" (7). But the Dick and Jane story has nothing to do with the African Americans' story of victimization, and language becomes desperate. The narrative tries three times to construct the story of the friends and the nice house, of Dick, Jane, their parents, and the dog.

> Here is the house. It is green and white. It has a red door.
> Here is the family. Mother, Father, Dick, and Jane live in
> the green-and-white house. They are happy . . . See the
> dog run. Run, dog, run. Look, look. Here comes a friend.

> Here is the house. It is green and white. It has a red door. Here is the
> family. Mother, Father, Dick, and Jane live in the green-and-white
> house. They are happy . . . See the dog run. Run, dog, run. Look, look.
> Here comes a friend.

> HereisthehouseItisgreenandwhiteIthasareddoorHereisthefamilyMotherFather
> DickandJaneliveinthegreenandwhitehouseTheyarehappySeethe dogrun
> RundogrunLooklookHerecomesafriend

Each time, the story refuses to be told in its entirety, until the language of the story crumbles in on itself, violated by an inability to approximate the harsh realities of a world, a world of victims, that will never live with such security or happiness.

The narrative is divided into chapters by the names of the four seasons, beginning with Autumn, an odd beginning for most of us, a sort of "in-the-middle" existence, but which seems appropriate for the life of the victim. The victim-less text would end or begin with Spring, a time of rebirth and new beginnings. The language within each chapter of the text violates the season which names it. Autumn is not a season with leaves of beautiful colors, as one might expect, but rather a season of a child's sickness, coughed-up on her bed, and the colors of fall are used to describe her vomit. "The puke swaddles down the pillow onto the sheets—green-gray, with flecks of orange" (13).

"Winter," says the young narrator, "tightened our heads with a band of cold and melted our eyes" (52). The winter should be expectant and should not hold you tightly in its moribund grip. The child's winter should be playful, and the primary emotion should be anticipation. Yet the only "epiphany" the young children have in *The Bluest Eye*'s winter is to discover a reason to hate someone "better-off" than they are: "we discovered that she had a dog tooth" (53).

Spring echoes autumn and winter with references to death. The text violates itself. Desperate to name lives that will change, like the seasons, naturally and for the good, the language reminds us that there are no seasons in the lives of victims. Pecola is raped by her father. Ironically, his last name is Breedlove; she carries his child. Spring is incestuous for the victim; it breeds on the familiar, violating her purity and offering only the false hope of birth.

Summer is "the season of storms" (146). Summer is the most frightening because it represents the "*Moirai* of our small lives" (146). Pecola is summer's child and is fated to be victim. In the summer, Pecola's child by her father dies before the pregnancy completes term. The victim has no sense of completion to her life. Acquiescing to the world's claim that "the victim had no right to live" (160), Pecola disappears into a world, violent and silent and sadly alone.

Seasonal change is seductive; its newness offers hope to those of us at liberty to define ourselves in its beauty and predictability. Yet for the victim, the seasons serve as metaphor for the old adage, "what goes around, comes around." Indeed, in *The Bluest Eye*, the seasons represent lack of change, a violation of nature's narrative, which should suggest that with each season something other than the status quo awaits us. The victim discovers that there are no seasons in her life, only *a* season of silence, which is characterized by frustration, pain, and a lack of control over her life.

Thus, the language of the text violently turns on itself, refusing to allow the victim to go unnoticed. Dick and Jane stories, as well as the pleasant and sensual changes of the season, are seductive, and they appeal to the person who neither knows desperation nor runs the risk of disappearing from the human story. But these master plots fail to tell the story of language's victims. Yet Morrison's language, like all language, has the power to invoke the other. In *The Bluest Eye*, this language of "otherness" is the language of victim. The victims in an ethic of reading and writing stand as an other against the master plot. When the master plot encounters the story of victim, an other, the victim-less and romantic story, like the tale of Dick and Jane, crumbles. The victim is revealed.

III   *The Desperate Character*

The wish of the victim often reflects the depth of her desperation. Victims wish not only for those things they are denied but also for those things which they can never have, much like a one-armed person wishing to grow another arm. The inability to fulfil that wish, regardless of its impossible nature, leads to the desperate act that is often violent and serves, at a level of distortion, if not perversion, to meet the requirements of the wish and to horrify the seemingly "normal" observer of the desperate act.

I suggest that the "wish" is Levinas's notion of "obsession," which is "irreducible to consciousness, even if it overwhelms it." This wish or obsession is, in Levinas's terms (which I think reflects Morrison's text's intentions), the victim's last grasp at "freedom," an almost pre-reflective wish or obsession to be other than she is.[5] In this obsession exists the desperate act, which culminates all previously "failed" acts to free oneself from being the victim. The desperate act, in an attempt to be other, creates an otherness that violates all traditional or normal expectations of what those of us who control narrative's master plots consider to be human and humane and challenges our definitions.

The Breedlove family has wishes. Pauline Breedlove wishes for a house and a family like the one for whom she is a servant. "Power, praise, and luxury were hers in this household" (101). Life here is ordered and neat. Finding satisfaction in this white family's household, "she stopped trying to keep her own house" (101). She establishes an intimate connection with the family. They give her "what she had never had—a nickname—Polly" (101). "She is the ideal servant" (101). Yet Mrs. Breedlove's wish can never have fulfillment. She is the "ideal servant." Her wish is to be the "ideal" mistress of her own house, yet she is neither white nor monied and her wish is bound to fail.

We are not aware of the desperate nature of her wish until she denies the maternity of her own child to act as the mother of the white child for whom she is a servant. By laying claim to the white family's daughter, she attempts to lay claim to their lives. The irony is that in the same motion with which she dismisses her daughter, she is valuing the role of daughter in the family life.

Pecola spills a blueberry pie on the white family's floor, or as Mrs. Breedlove says, "my floor" (87). Pecola is slapped to the floor and abused verbally. The family's little girl, "in pink," starts crying. Sending her own child out the door, she begins to call the white child "baby," and when asked who the other child was, she will not say that Pecola is her daughter, only "don't worry none" (87).

While I may not condone physical violence as the appropriate punishment for children, I am not horrified by the violent act of mother striking daughter. I am moved to reflect on a moment of violence in which mother denies the identity of her daughter. This desperate act, a result of what Langston Hughes calls, "a dream deferred," reveals a moment of ethical reflection that names Mrs. Breedlove not a bad mother, but rather a victim of racial prejudice certainly, but perhaps more so of a world that has lied to her, the "ideal servant," and told her that she could ever be other than a victim, an otherness she exposes to us—the violence of a mother dis-owning her daughter—causing further, more profound, ethical reflection about the lies we tell to those whom we control and in turn encourage the victim to tell herself.

Cholly Breedlove's wish is less easy to define but is as poignant as Mrs. Breedlove's, and the wish's denial leads to a violent act even more horrifying than familial rejection. Cholly wants to be wanted by a family.

There was a time, before the whiskey, when Mrs. Breedlove wanted him to take her away from her poverty, and she wanted him sexually. "But it ain't like that anymore. Most times he's thrashing away inside me before I'm woke, and through when I am" (104). Their love for each other is equalled only by their hate. "She needed Cholly's sins desperately" (37), and for Cholly, she was one of the few things abhorrent to him that he could touch and therefore hurt (37). In desperation, the victim hurts the one whom he loves the most. Loved ones are the most convenient, and ironically, because victims are drawn to a community of pained others, they make themselves available to one another.

Cholly's life is a series of failed communities. "Abandoned in a junk heap by his mother, rejected for a crap game by his father, there was nothing more to lose. He was alone with his own perceptions and appetites, and they alone interested him" (126). What the world will not give, Cholly is prepared to take. He will be impotent no longer, the male victim's final words before an act of desperation.

Cholly rapes his daughter. The voyeur is repulsed by the violence. Cholly is overwhelmed with ambiguity. "He wanted to break her neck—but tenderly . . . What could he do for her—ever? What give her? What say to her" (127)? The language is that of the poor boy proposing to the rich girl; then, he reminds us that she is "his eleven-year-old daughter" (127). Suddenly remembering the first time he saw his wife, Cholly takes his daughter. Now he wants "to fuck her—tenderly" (128). Pecola becomes the victim's victim.

Cholly disappears from the text, the ever possible, even probable, fate of the victim. The crime of incest, one of Freud's original taboo's, demands serious judgement. And I make no apologies for a society where "our manhood was defined by acquisitions. Our womanhood by acquiescence" (140). And yet I am moved by the narrator's argument for sympathy. "Cholly loved her. I'm sure he did. He, at any rate, was the one who loved her enough to touch her, envelop her, give something of himself to her. But his touch was fatal" (159). The victim is left without choice, no romantic option between loss of integrity with life or maintained integrity with death. Loss of integrity and death go hand and hand for the victim. Cholly, emasculated by society, asserts his manhood on a girl-child, losing his integrity and a place in the narrative. The victim disappears.

Pecola Breedlove's wish is the most desperate of all wishes. She, a young black girl, wishes to have blue eyes. To have blue eyes, "Pretty blue eyes . . . Morning-glory-blue-eyes" (40), will make her world, now torn and violent, whole and peaceful. "Cholly would be different, and Mrs. Breedlove too. Maybe they'd say, 'Why, look at pretty-eyed Pecola. We mustn't do bad things in front of those pretty eyes'" (40). Unlike Claudia, a young girl her age, who can distinguish between the possible and the impossible and who "destroyed white baby dolls" (22), quite aware that she did not have access to their privilege, Pecola wishes for the blue eyes of the young white girls. Seduced by her obsession, she is seemingly ignorant of the fact that such a change cannot happen.

"Each night, without fail, she prayed for blue eyes" (40). To be seen is the victim's most profound desire and is why Pecola wants blue eyes. She sees the world clearly with the eyes she has, and what she sees with crystal clear sight is that the world ignores a young black girl. The storekeeper, "does not see her, because for him there is nothing to see . . . . Nothing in his life even suggested that the feat was possible, not to say desirable or necessary" (42). The face of the victim is blank and indistinguishable.

Of course the world reminds her, all the time, that blue eyes are favorites. Shirley Temple has blue eyes. Even the "Mary Jane" candy she buys has a a young girl, "blond hair in gentle disarray, blue eyes looking at her out of a world of clean comfort" (43), and depicts a life denied her. The sky, where the white families live, is "always blue" (84).

When a "Reader, Adviser, and Interpreter of Dreams" (130) arrives in town, Pecola comes to him. After all, his card reads, "If you are overcome with trouble and conditions that are not natural, I can remove them" (137). The dilemma is interesting. Pecola believes that her dark eyes are unnatural; she is a victim of society's rhetoric that describes beautiful and powerful people. Rhetoric, to be successful, need not be true, only persuasive, which is rhetoric's own inherent perniciousness. Though Pecola's eyes are very natural, the white world's rhetoric has won; rhetoric's best audience is desperate people.

This false prophet convinces Pecola that her eyes will turn blue; he convinces himself that her request is "logical" (137), "an ugly little girl asking for beauty . . . . A little black girl who wanted to rise up out of the pit of her blackness and see the world with blue eyes" (137). The promise is a lie, and the lie is devastating. "To rise up out of the pit of her blackness," may be the most evil statement in Morrison's text. The phrase's horror is that it embodies both truth and lie. Pecola's blackness is a "pit," not of her own making but no less depthful and restraining. And yet, what world would ask her to rise out of her blackness? For the victim, the right, true, and beautiful world is always other, and leaves the victim no choice but to become like the world or to vanish, silently.

Pecola's eyes turn blue. "A little black girl yearns for the blue eyes of a little white girl, and the horror at the heart of her yearning is exceeded only by the evil of fulfillment" (158). Does she blind herself or does she go crazy? The text says that, "She . . . stepped over into madness" (159). Whether Pecola's eyes become blue from the blue-like glaze of the physically blind or whether she simply turns inward, creating a world of her own in which her eyes are blue, I think, does not matter. From either perspective, the violation of this young girl's mind/body, her eyes, is both painful and unsettling.

Pecola spends her time now in conversation with herself, creating a fictitious friend who confirms that her blue eyes are beautiful. "What will we talk about? *Why, Your eyes.* Oh, yes. My eyes, My blue eyes. Let me look again. *See how pretty they are.* Yes. They get prettier each time I look at them. *They are the prettiest I've ever seen*" (156).

The victim may either disappear, like Cholly, or create a world frightening and other, if she is to continue to exist. Pecola creates the world of other. This new world violates the sensibilities of those persons who chose to look upon it or who fall under Pecola's gaze. Those persons of her world, other victims, are "frightened" when they see her (158). Their world may, by necessity, become like hers. Others, who see her "blue eyes" know that they have "failed" her (158). Victims exist because there are those who victimize. Pecola's life, "among the garbage and the sunflowers" (160), where she "flailed her arms like a bird in an eternal grotesquely futile effort to fly" (158), indicts her observer, calling us either to be a participant in her world or the cause of it.

IV   The Desperate Reader

The frightening implication of the rhetoric that describes a victim is the loss of freedom. The victim is not free to be other than victim. In fact, to be other than victim is to lose one's power of mystery and awe, is to lose otherness. The empathetic observer of society's victims is not free to free the victim from her bondage, whether economic, religious, racial, sexual, or otherwise. The reader of texts, who sees and hears the victims of those texts, is violated by a moral powerlessness, discovering, as in *The Bluest Eye*, that "it's too late. . . it's much, much, much too late" (160) for Mrs. Breedlove, Cholly, and Pecola.

The admission of powerlessness is the reader's desperate act, a moment of confession, when he reveals a personal victimization and, therefore, a oneness with the text's victims. Perhaps, this moment is narrative's ethic, for if we all become victims, then there are no victims.

Such an idealistic moment does not deny difference, in race, gender, or economic status, the differences between us which produce victims. I am looking only for a moment of complicity and community, where distinctions are erased. Differences will/should remain, as a cause for celebration and, more important, perhaps, as the revealer of victim. For as long as there is difference, there will be victims. So, what is left for the desperate reader? I think that an ethic of reading and writing reminds the reader that he should take a turn as victim.

To choose to be victim is the one powerful freedom that the reader, privileged, even omniscient, has. But readers only make such a choice out of desperation, and readers only reach such desperate moments when they are violated by the violence of the text, by moments shocking to and discordant with our everydayness: a father wants love, a wholesome desire, and so he rapes his daughter; a child wants blue eyes, and (because?) she's black, so she steps "over into madness" (159) to gain them.

The victim's world, through a child's eyes, is a violent and horrifying moment, a moment that should so awaken our anesthetized existences, as readers, that narrative as an ethical event is one of many givens in the critical process called reading. In fact, I think that narrative is the one certain and predictable event in which an ethic is implied because reader and writer, by their very actions, *choose* to participate in a community, a narrative community, where society's victims are most profoundly and uncomfortably presented back to the very society which creates them.

Narrative has the power to hear the voices of the young Pecolas say, "Please God, . . . make me disappear" (39), and to describe her disappearance: "she squeezed her eyes shut. Little parts of her body faded away . . . . Only her tight, tight eyes were left. They were always left" (39). Perhaps most important, narrative has the power to force our gaze upon her gaze, those blue eyes, and know who the victim is.

NOTES

1. Imamu Amiri Baraka, "Preface to a Twenty Volume Suicide Note," ed. Arna Bontemps, *American Negro Poetry* (New York: Hill & Wang, 1974), pp. 178-9.

2. I would describe my use of "Otherness" here, if not in agreement with, certainly influenced by Emmanuel Levinas in an essay called "Time and the Other." He describes the other by saying: "its hold over my existing is mysterious. It is not unknown but unknowable, refractory to all light. But this precisely indicates that the other is in no way another myself, participating with me in a common existence. . . . We recognize the other as resembling us, but exterior to us; the relationship with the other is a relationship with a Mystery." Ed. Sean Hand, *The Levinas Reader*, (Oxford: Blackwell, 1989), p. 43.

3. See Levinas's "There is: Existence without Existents," in Hand, *A Levinas Reader*, p. 28.

4. Toni Morrison, *The Bluest Eye* (New York: Washington Square Press, 1970), p. 58. All future references are to this text and are parenthetically referenced in the essay.

5. See Levinas's "Substitution" in Hand, *A Levinas Reader*, pp. 88-92.

TRINITARIAN RHETORIC IN MURDOCH,

MORRISON, AND DOSTOEVSKY

David Cunningham[1]

Dr. Terry Wright has noted that literature and theology often appear to employ two different ways of thinking—one dramatic, the other systematic.[2] But he has also indicated that he believes theology to be a very literary endeavor—and I would agree. Yet if theology is indeed replete with literary categories, why is it so often assumed to be a logical, propositional system? If Christian theology was literary from the start, why is it so often *contrasted* with literature?

To answer this question, one might point to the scientific Enlightenment, the rise of historical consciousness, the impact of the disciplines of sociology and anthropology, and the progress made by empirical procedures which employ tests of verification and falsification. But these explanations seem to suggest that theology has merely been led down the garden path by the social and natural sciences, as though by some irresistible power of temptation. As far as I can see, theologians have always been perfectly capable of losing their way *all by themselves*.[3]

If Christian theology is literary, yet is typically *contrasted* with literature, perhaps some shifts in theological *doctrine* helped to bring about this perceived opposition. Consider, for instance, the Enlightenment's modification of the Christian doctrine of God—from Trinitarianism to radical monotheism. We know that, during the seventeenth century, philosophical discourse on God moved away from a grounding in revelation to a grounding in reason alone. This much has been thoroughly documented.[4] Less frequently observed is that this change swept away, in its wake, nearly all vestiges of Trinitarian doctrine. All that remained was a radically monotheistic, even monistic, concept of God. Thus, a thinker such as Descartes could find room in his system only for a generic "god of the philosophers"—not for the Christian Trinity, which was known through revelation, rather than by unaided human reason

189

alone. And even Schleiermacher, whose interests were more avowedly theological, relegated Trinitarian discourse to the status of an appendix to *The Christian Faith*.[5]

This shift to a monistic monotheism tempted theology to emphasize—in Dr. Wright's words—"unity and coherence," and thus to set itself in opposition to literature's "anarchic celebration of the creative possibilities of language."[6] This supposed opposition, I believe, can be further challenged by reading some literature through *Trinitarian* categories. By doing so, we can begin to question modern monistic assumptions, and perhaps thereby even retrieve a Christian critique of the isolated self. For each of the three writers whose work I examine, a gulf opens up between a Trinitarian reading of the work and a monistic one. My concern is not whether one reading or the other was intended by the writer; neither am I concerned about whether the writer believes in one God, in the Triune God, or in no God at all. Rather, I want to demonstrate how the text changes, depending on the reader's theological and metaphysical assumptions. But before tackling the texts, a brief methodological segue.

I

The word *rhetoric* in my title is carefully chosen. I use it here not in the generic sense of "writing" or "discourse," but in its classical sense: according to Aristotle, rhetoric is "the faculty of discovering the available means of persuasion."[7] Rhetoric in this sense fell out of vogue after the Renaissance, but has recently experienced a significant revival—especially in U.S. universities, where departments of speech or speech-communication are flourishing. The classical rhetorical tradition urges us to take account of the entire rhetorical context—speaker, audience, and argument—when analyzing a text.[8]

In this essay, I am interested in one particular aspect of the rhetorical perspective—namely, persuasion by means of the audience (Aristotle's term is *pathos*). Literally, this term refers to the text's effect on the audience's emotions. But the term should not be understood in its most restrictive sense, for Aristotle also uses it to refer to the audience's state or condition—that is, everything that the audience brings to the context of the rhetorical event.

How might this rhetorical approach to the question of audience be distinguished from other literary-theoretical accounts of the role of the reader? Many literary theorists speak of "the reader" as a structure of the text itself (think, for example, of Iser's *Implied Reader* or of Eco's *Role of the Reader*[9]). A rhetorical analysis would seek to expand the investigation to include the whole process of a text's creation, with an emphasis on the role of the *writer*. It would focus on the ways in which a writer *assumes* certain attitudes (and seeks to *create* other attitudes) in the mind of the reader. One must take account not merely of writer, or reader, but of their relationships to one another and to the wider social context. As Terry Eagleton notes,

> Rhetoric, which was the received form of critical analysis all the way from ancient society to the eighteenth century, examined the way discourses are constructed in order to achieve certain effects. . . . It saw speaking and writing not merely as textual objects, to be aesthetically contemplated or endlessly deconstructed, but as forms of *activity* inseparable from the wider social relationships between writers and readers, orators and audiences, and as largely unintelligible outside the social purposes and conditions in which they were embedded.[10]

The question we are asking is this: What are some of the "wider social relationships" operative in the writing and reading of texts?

I am not here interested in discovering an author's intentions, whether conscious or otherwise. Nevertheless, as the rhetorical tradition emphasizes, all writing and speech have a source, and whatever knowledge we may have (or suppose that we have) about that source will frequently influence our interpretations. I am interested not so much in the author-as-subject, but rather in the "whence" of the text—what Calvin Schrag has called its "space of subjectivity."[11] This "space," in which the play of various forces intersect and bring a text into being, is (in Schrag's view) a postmodern attempt to capture some of what Enlightenment thinkers were attempting to describe when referring to the "subject." This space of subjectivity reminds us that the source of a text is pluriform and contingent, not the isolated self of Romantic hermeneutics.[12] Every text is constructed (by its writers *and* by its readers) within a complex, multifaceted, highly structured "space" which is "always already" determined by a variety of beliefs and practices. These assumptions are at work in the space within which an author writes a text, and within the space in which a reader reads—even if author and reader do not consider them their "own" assumptions. They can be brought to light with the help of a rhetorical analysis of the text. In other words, we can take some clues from the dialogical milieu from which a writer writes, in order to discover new, fruitful ways for readers to read.

My claim in this paper is that Trinitarian assumptions help to structure the "space of subjectivity" within which each of these three writers writes. However, such assumptions are almost completely absent from the present-day culture of readers—both Christian and non-Christian. This absence accounts, in part, for the apparent resistance of some texts to a theological reading, and also for the apparent incompatibility (to which I alluded at the outset) of theology and literature. These barriers might be breached if we move against the grain, choosing to read from a Trinitarian perspective.

And now to the texts.

II

The icon in this novel is not just any icon. Not just any icon would do. It is a very specific icon: a copy of Rublev's fifteenth-century masterpiece, "The Holy Trinity." It depicts the three messengers of God, visiting Abraham and enjoying a bit of lunch by the oaks of Mamre, who, through an odd editorial crevice in the text, are identified as "the Lord" and thus, by Christian theologians, as the Trinity. In Iris Murdoch's *The Time of the Angels,* the icon comes into contact with almost everyone in the story, and in doing so, reveals the character of each.

But the icon remained opaque to most reviewers; one completely flummoxed critic could only manage to describe the plot of this novel as one in which "Marcus loves Leo, who loves Muriel, who loves Eugene, who loves Pattie, who loves Carel, who loves Elizabeth."[13] In other words, the subjectivity of the human characters was taken to be the primary focus. But what if we were to examine the narrative from the point of view of the icon itself?

The icon is owned by Eugene Peshkov, the porter at a rectory in a badly bombed-out area of London. Early in the story, the icon is stolen and pawned by Eugene's son, Leo, who seeks tirelessly (but quite unsuccessfully) to fashion himself into a great anarchist and a great lover. The icon is of such value to Eugene that Muriel, the rector's daughter, tries to convince Leo that he should recover it. It is purchased from the pawn shop by Marcus, the rector's brother, whose fondness for Leo makes him especially susceptible to the latter's insipid, lying apologies. The icon provides Marcus with an excuse to enter the often-barricaded rectory. But before it can reach its intended recipient, both the icon and its bearer are intercepted by Carel Fisher, the enigmatic rector, whose atheistic speculations on existentialist philosophy have led to his assignment to this rectory-without-a-church (everything except the tower having been destroyed in the war). The icon is thus present during the novel's most sustained discussion of the nature and existence of God. At the end of the discussion, the icon's paper cover is stripped away, and its presence seems to confirm the outcome of the conversation. The icon is held firmly in Carel's grasp; and, because Marcus is too mesmerized to retrieve it, the icon remains in the rector's darkened study.

But it leaves the study soon afterwards, when Muriel is called in to speak with Carel. The icon attracts her because its owner, Eugene, has been the object of her naïve affection. But it doesn't reach him yet, because Muriel is intercepted by Leo, who announces that he is in love with her. The icon is placed on a side-table, while Muriel dispatches Leo. There it is discovered by the rector's long-time housekeeper and sometimes mistress, Pattie. Through her intervention, it finally makes its way back to its owner.

Of course, *The Time of the Angels* is not told from the point of view of the icon. Again, to most critics, the novel appeared to be a somewhat too-typical example of Murdoch's fiction: a rectory novel about an unrealistically eccentric priest, with a cast of characters too diverse to allow the plot to cohere. The novel is easily read in these terms, because the icon is thought to be simply an archaic item of religious devotion—the equivalent of an unused rosary, or a relic which is known to be false. The critics, like the iconoclasts of Christian history, failed to treat the icon *as an icon*: they saw its surface, but were unable to look "through" it to the reality beyond. I suspect that Murdoch was amused at the critical reception of this book, which often betrayed a phenomenal lack of theological sophistication on the part of its readers. She set them up for it, of course, by having a character describe the icon as "three angels confabulating around a table." Its role thus seemed primarily illustrative—of the book's title and of the rector's cosmology, in which "the death of God has set the angels free. And they are terrible" (173).

About the best the critics managed was to see the icon as a symbol for God, both graphically and metaphorically, and thus see its haphazard sojourn as an indicator of God's low cultural status. But this assumes that the icon simply represents God *in the abstract,* rather than God in the concrete specificity of God's threeness-in-unity. For the reader who reads with Trinitarian convictions, the icon becomes the central focus of the story: not simply a scrap of wood being casually tossed about, but rather the only fixed point of reference in the story. It reveals the nature of the characters by the ways in which they treat it, describe it, and relate to it.

For example, the icon highlights Carel Fisher's inner conflict about the nature of God. He has come to believe that the philosophers were wrong in affirming that the Good is "one, single, and unitary" (172). In conversation with his brother, he argues that "There is only power and the marvel of power, there is only chance and the terror of chance. And if there is only this there is no God, and the single Good of the philosophers is an illusion and a fake" (172). But his only alternative to unity is chaotic multiplicity, which he recognizes as the essence of evil.

> There are principalities and powers. Angels are the thoughts of God. Now he has been dissolved into his thoughts which are beyond our conceptions in their nature and their multiplicity and their power. God was at least the name of something we thought was good. Now even the name has gone and the spiritual world is scattered. There is nothing any more to prevent the magnetism of many spirits. (173)

These are the only choices for Carel: the unity of the Good, which seems impossible in the light of the evil of the world; or the multiplicity of many spirits, the terrible angels who pull us into the void. But when he sees the icon, Carel is stopped for a moment by its power. He recites a single word which has been used throughout the novel to emphasize power: the word *tall.* "They would be so tall," Carel says. When Marcus points out that the icon represents the Trinity, Carel is yanked back into his version of reality.

He quickly dismisses the Trinity with the assurance of a logician: "How can those three be one? As I told you. Please go now, Marcus" (176).

Throughout the novel, the icon points to the quiet desperation of the characters, because it embodies what they all lack: peaceful, mutual relationality. Many art historians and theologians have commented on the success of Rublev's effort. One sample: "Similarity and difference, rest and movement, youth and maturity, joy and compassion, restraint and pity, eternity and history, these all come together. There is no separation or confusion or subordination of the Persons."[14]

But the icon of the Trinity is not simply a glimpse of the inner life of God. If we are to take seriously the Christian doctrine of the *imago dei,* then this icon must also be a portrait of humanity, or at least, its *telos.* Rublev's

> image of the divine Trinity rules out all egotism— whether individual or collective—all life-destroying separation, any subordination or levelling of persons. It invites all humanity to make this world a permanent eucharist of love, a feast of life. Created in God's image (Gen. 1:26), humanity is called to live in the image of the divine life and to share its daily bread together.[15]

And this, of course, is precisely what most of the characters in *The Time of the Angels* are so desperately unable to do. They all live in separate rooms somewhere in the darkened rectory; the walls that divide them become a towering symbol of isolation, as often in Murdoch's novels.[16]

But even when the walls are breached, the individuals remain alone: Muriel sits idly with Elizabeth; Eugene's thoughts constantly drift to his native Russia; Leo pursues material self-satisfaction. A quick glance through a crack in the wall into Elizabeth's bedroom brings further estrangement between Muriel and Carel, and a suddenly-opened linen-closet door further divides Leo from Muriel and Marcus from them both. Finally, every character who comes into contact with Carel suffers some form of violence—whether sexual, emotional, or psychological.

The characters of the story are all monads: no windows, no relationships, no contact with an "other." Such is life in the modern world, and most critics have read *The Time of the Angels* as symptomatic of post-Enlightenment individualism. But the icon offers another direction: a heightened appreciation for relationality and community which is inherent in a fully-actualized understanding of the Christian doctrine of the Trinity.

When we read the novel from this angle, we are reminded that Murdoch writes from the great tradition of philosophy—one which felt the pressing need, at various times in its history, to grapple with Trinitarian doctrine. As Hans-Georg Gadamer noted, "the Doctrine of the Trinity . . . has constantly stimulated the course of thought in the West as a challenge and invitation to try and think that which continually transcends the limits of human understanding."[17] Murdoch is an avid participant in the "course of thought" which Gadamer here describes, and her writing—when read from this perspective—illuminates both the doctrine itself and the nature of relationality which it seeks to describe. Again, I do not claim for the author any particular views about Trinitarian dogma; indeed, she occasionally denies even believing in God. But I do want to argue that the "space" from which she writes is a space which has, for many centuries, served as the abode of a sophisticated concept of the Triune God. Indeed, Murdoch's own philosophical treatises have emphasized that the intellectual movements of the seventeenth and eighteenth century have led us down the wrong path. She knows that the struggle for the unity and sovereignty of the good is constantly challenged by contingency and flux. As Murdoch has noted, these two forces are difficult to hold in tension:

> Form is the temptation of love and its peril, whether in art or life: to round off a situation, to sum up a character. But the difference is that art has *got* to have form, whereas life need not. . . . To combine form with a respect for reality with all its odd contingent ways is the highest art of prose.[18]

Murdoch's recognition of this contingency, even in the midst of a search for unity, helps us to read her work through Trinitarian categories.

III

Toni Morrison's writing shows a clear provenance in the biblically-rooted traditions of African-American spirituality. But Morrison's *Beloved* is a difficult novel for North American whites to read, because the overpowering evil of racist slavery, in which U.S. whites are so widely and recently implicated, quickly eclipses the abundant biblical imagery which Morrison so deftly employs. In other words, as white readers, we spend all our time trying, without much success, to defend ourselves against Morrison's implicit accusation that our country was, and continues to be, built on the backs of black slaves. Consequently, we are too preoccupied to see that this novel speaks to us straight out of the profound convictions of African-American Christianity.

That faith, I would suggest, is a profoundly Trinitarian faith—much more so than mainstream Protestantism or Catholicism in the U.S. or British contexts. Admittedly, my knowledge of African-American Christianity is that of an outsider, and I stand in need of correction by those who can speak from experience. But to me, American black religion is more profoundly Trinitarian because it is Trinitarian in *praxis,* rather than simply in theory. The white Church may perhaps speak the systematic Trinitarian name of God more frequently, and has more frequently dissected and analyzed it. But it is primarily in black churches that a Trinitarian faith is lived.

The Trinity implies community in the purest sense: not the isolation of one, not the competitive dualism of two, but the altered sense of relationality and difference which immediately come into play whenever the number of participants rises to three. While a community can obviously include more than three, the number *three* is the smallest number in which a multiplicity of relations is implied. And by means of the *imago dei,* the multiplicity of relations in God implies that true humanity should bear a similar multiplicity.

Within black Church communities, people are much more likely to understand their lives in these relational terms: as a shared experience with others, rather than a journey of isolation. The Church is a community center: where people gather to worship together, to live in fellowship with one another, to exist in communion with God and with the community which God has called into being. And that community extends beyond the precincts of the church building; it is not limited to a brief period of time in a particular place on one day of the week. This profound nature of community does exist in some white communities and white churches in the U.S.; but it is much more prevalent in black churches.

But it would be misleading to label African-American Christianity as Trinitarian *in practice only,* as though no one had given serious thought to the theoretical implications of the doctrine. Indeed, African-American theology emphasizes the significance of oppression, liberation, and solidarity, thus providing an excellent framework for Trinitarian thinking. James Cone comments:

> Taking seriously the Trinitarian view of the Godhead, black theology says that as Creator, God identified with oppressed Israel, participating in the bringing into being of this people; as Redeemer, God became the Oppressed one in order that all may be free from oppression; as Holy Spirit God continues the work of liberation. The Holy Spirit is the Spirit of the Creator and the Redeemer at work in the forces of human liberation in our society today.[19]

Elsewhere, Cone has shown how black worship is highly Trinitarian, especially in its stress on the significant role played by all three persons of the Trinity in the event of liberation.[20] One could also note the importance, in black worship, of give-and-take among the participants.

This is the relational environment in which Toni Morrison was nurtured. We are told that she thinks of her community in Lorain, Ohio as a *neighborhood*:

> . . . a life-giving and sustaining compound, a village in the traditional African sense, where myth—a "concept of truth or reality a whole people has arrived at over years of observation"—abounds. Like the community in which Pecola of *The Bluest Eye* finds herself, it was a place that cared if someone was "put out" or "put outdoors." Morrison tells Robert Stepto: "And legal responsibilities, all responsibilities that agencies now have, were the responsibility of the neighborhood. So people were taken care of."[21]

The relationship of such a community to traditional African communities, as well as to Latin American based communities, has been well documented.[22]

But again, my purpose is not to demonstrate that Morrison herself writes necessarily or intentionally from this point of view. Rather, I want to argue that this world provides *the space out of which* she writes, and that it may have implications for the way in which her readers read. As

Morrison herself has put it, "I have a family of people who were highly religious—that was part of their language. Their sources were biblical. They expressed themselves in that fashion. They took it all very, very seriously, so it would be very difficult for me not to."[23] If Morrison writes from a world which is deeply involved in "practical Trinitarianism," then we should not be surprised to discover that a Trinitarian reading of her fiction can bear much fruit.

"124 was spiteful. 124 was loud. 124 was quiet." These are the initial sentences of the major divisions of Toni Morrison's *Beloved,* and those who have not yet read this masterpiece of fiction might be surprised to learn that "124" is a *house.* 124 Bluestone Road is inhabited by Sethe, a woman who sought some respite from the violence of slavery by travelling the underground railroad to southern Ohio. It is inhabited by Denver, her daughter—the only one of Sethe's children willing to reside in this very mysterious house. And it is inhabited by Baby Suggs, Sethe's mother-in-law, whose power as a leader in the community prompts everyone to tack on, to the end of her name, a sanctifying epithet: like "Yahweh, blessed be he," she is "Baby Suggs, holy."

But the house, 124, is not content with this triad of women; it is always inviting others in, or kicking some of its inhabitants out. It is haunted by the ghost of the child, Sethe's own child, the child whose grave is marked only with the word *Beloved*: the child who, Sethe once decided, would be better off dead than enslaved. The house is visited by Paul D, one of Sethe's friends from the plantation, who temporarily exorcises the house of its spirit; but the spirit returns—this time, incarnate. Paul D leaves; Baby Suggs dies; Denver sometimes enjoys the visitor, sometimes cannot abide her and must leave. The harmony of the inhabitants of 124 Bluestone Road is always being disrupted—always threatening to dissolve into undifferentiated chaos, or to merge into a destructive dualism or monism. Given the pain and conflict that takes place within its walls, the house is very aptly numbered: 1-2-4. The "three" is missing.

In this novel, Trinitarian categories operate not through a particular event or material object, but through the familial relationships which shift and redesign themselves at every turn. Morrison's novels make frequent use of "intergenerational trinities"[24]—in which threeness and unity are both clearly present: one family, three generations. But I am not suggesting a simplistic treatment in which the three persons of the Trinity are identified, respectively, with Sethe, Beloved, and Denver (or Baby Suggs or Paul D). In fact, a number of elements in the novel resist such an interpretation. I am more interested in the triangulations of various characters in the novel—how they always interrupt things and thereby prevent us from "taking sides" with either of the two extremes.

One such triad is that of Baby Suggs, Sethe, and Denver, whose shifting alliances and relationships keep the whole household in a state of non- authoritarian flux. In some senses, Sethe is clearly "in charge" in this household; Denver is her child, and Baby Suggs is in Sethe's care. But Baby Suggs maintains some clear seniority by means of her age and her sanctity; and Denver, who is learning to read, points us toward the authority of the future. Sometimes the characters change, but the non-linear structure of authority remains. When the baby's spirit returns as the incarnate Beloved, a new triad forms with her mother and her sister, and all enter into a new experience of the pleasure and pain of communion—most beautifully reflected by three poetic soliloquies (in which each woman reflects upon her relationship with Beloved), and by the section that follows them, in which the three voices are woven together into a tapestry of relationality and difference.

This novel wrestles with the dilemma of existential freedom: freedom for one person necessarily implies subjugation of others. Morrison is seeking a way of breaking out of this dilemma, and what she hits upon is something quite similar to classic Christian Trinitarian doctrine. As in the Trinitarian doctrine of appropriations, each person appears to have a special region of authority (e.g., the first person of the Trinity is primarily responsible for creation); yet that authority is constantly being mitigated, tempered, or supplemented by the other persons (e.g., Christ and the Spirit are also held to be at work in creation). By allowing some of her characters to "participate" in the authority of other characters, Morrison calls into question the typical assumptions of authority—not only of masters over slaves and men over women, but of property-owners over interlopers, parents over children, and adults over their aging parents. These authoritarian dualisms are always being broken up by the intervention of an "other"—a third force which disturbs the false equilibrium, and unmasks the creeping tyranny. As Denver realizes late in the novel, "Whatever was happening, it only worked with three—not two" (298).

Essential to this portrait of human relationality is a sense of participation in the life of the other: call and response, interchange of properties. The divine equivalent, in the Christian doctrine of God, is the idea of *perichoresis*: the "divine dance" in which the three persons participate in one another, rather than one person being subordinate to another. This image is marvelously mirrored in *Beloved*, with Baby Suggs preparing the crowd for her preaching at the Clearing:

> After situating herself on a huge flat-sided rock, Baby Suggs bowed her head and prayed silently. The company watched her from the trees. They knew she was ready when she put her stick down. Then she shouted, "Let the children come!" and they ran from the trees toward her.
>
> "Let your mothers hear you laugh," she told them, and the woods rang. The adults looked on and could not help smiling.
>
> Then "Let the grown men come." she shouted. They stepped out one by one from among the ringing trees.
>
> "Let your wives and children see you dance," she told them, and ground life shuddered under their feet.
>
> Finally she called the women to her. "Cry," she told them. "For the living and the dead. Just cry." And without covering their eyes the women let loose.
>
> It started that way: laughing children, dancing men, crying women and then it got mixed up. Women stopped crying and danced; men sat down and cried; children danced, women laughed, children cried until, exhausted and riven, all and each lay about the Clearing damp and gasping for breath. In the silence that followed, Baby Suggs, holy, offered up to them her great big heart. (107)

The categories do not remain precise and distinct; they blur together, interpenetrate one another, until each has so informed and altered the others that their separatedness cannot be maintained.

Because the characters of the novel move about one another in this way, we as readers are invited to do the same. We are invited to participate, not just in the plot, but in the characters themselves: to allow their memories to become our own. In an interview essay with the author, Sandi Russell describes the process clearly:

> The key to these forms of expression is participation:
> "There were spaces and places in which a single person
> could enter and behave as an individual within the
> context of the community. A small remnant of that you
> can see sometimes in black churches where people shout.
> It is a very personal grief and a personal statement done
> among people you trust. Done within the context of the
> community, therefore safe." Just as the black preacher or
> the blues singer leaves room for the hearer's response, so
> Toni Morrison argues, "I have to provide places and
> spaces so that the reader can participate."[25]

In the lives of the characters, as in the lives of the readers, nothing is more
antithetical to true humanity than separatedness, aloneness.

There is yet another Trinitarian theme operative in *Beloved*, and for
this I must retrieve the work of St. Augustine, whose triad of "memory,
understanding, and will" provided an imperfect but, in his view,
appropriate analogy for the Trinity. Unfortunately, the course of Western
thought has led to the assumption that these three faculties operate within
a single center of consciousness: the isolated human mind. This made it
relatively easy for modern theologians to draw a straight line from
Augustine to modern anti-Trinitarian monotheism: one God who does
three things.

But Morrison's writings explode the modern myth of the individual,
and do so along lines which, I believe, Augustine would have appreciated.
For Morrison, memory, understanding, and will are not isolated
individual activities, but communal activities which cross the barriers of
time, space, and consciousness. Memory is always rememory: it is a
recalling to mind of something out of the past, something which we have
willfully forgotten, something which can only be made present through an
active moment of un-forgetting.[26] Likewise, will is not something
performed by an isolated center of consciousness, but always a communal
activity: a product of so many external influences, a conjunction of various
traces which maps only the faintest outlines of a distinct "self." If we could
learn to read Augustine's Trinitarian categories, not through the dominant
Enlightenment culture in which we have been schooled, but through the
communal, participative categories operative in Morrison's fiction, we
might begin to understand why Augustine considered the communally-

shaped human mind—which, by the way, never exists except in relation to others—to be an appropriate *vestigium trinitatis*.

The last triad which I will address is a triad of brothers.

IV

The God of whom Ivan Karamazov speaks in the chapter called "Rebellion"—the God of whom he says, "I just most respectfully return him the ticket" (245)[27]—is a radically monotheistic God. Ivan admits as much when Alyosha protests his verdict. In concluding his descriptions of the tormentors of children, Ivan asks, "Is there in the whole world a being who could and would have the right to forgive?" (245). Alyosha eventually responds that "there is such a being, and he can forgive everything, forgive all *and for all,* because he himself gave his innocent blood for all and for everything" (246). Alyosha invokes Christ, understood in an orthodox and traditional sense—the son of God, God incarnate, the Lamb of God who takes away the sin of the world. But Ivan had anticipated this response, and was ready with "The Grand Inquisitor." This chapter is the true anti-Trinitarian polemic: the claim that Christ's mission, Christ's sacrifice, even Christ's humble character—noble though these elements may appear—are failures, in that they leave millions of ordinary people unable to undertake the way of life to which he calls them. Even the suffering God cannot pacify Ivan, for the suffering God has an unfair advantage: the strength to endure what no mere mortal can endure—the strength to persevere beyond the tempter's power, and to live without miracle, mystery, or authority.

In creating the story of the Grand Inquisitor, Dostoevsky believed that he had created an argument so powerful and so persuasive that even he, its author, would have a difficult time responding to it.[28] It is powerful precisely because it is not an argument for atheism *tout court,* in the sense of a-theism, the denial of God. Rather, it is the denial of a very specific God, the Triune God of Christian revelation. Until this point, most Enlightenment atheism had contented itself with a refutation of the God of the philosophers, and had not ventured to deny the truth of revelation—though some certainly seemed willing to do so, had their political and intellectual contexts allowed it. Dostoevsky's Ivan takes that step; he denies not only rational theism but Christian revelation, as did his Western contemporary (some would say, his real-life incarnation), Friedrich Nietzsche. For both, God is dead; but more to the point, Christ is dead. The "god" who suffers and dies does not rise again.

Dostoevsky's response to the story of the Grand Inquisitor is contained primarily in the section which follows it—the life of a saint, the life of the Elder Zosima. But there is also a sense in which Dostoevsky's entire novel is a response to Ivan's "poem-in-prose." As Nathan Rosen has argued,[29] the life of each of the three brothers provides a response to this story. All three are forced to choose between an apparently rational, justifiable course of action, and a very different path—one which seems motivated by something larger, something which pervades the whole of their being. Alyosha is tempted by the "rational" conclusion that his faith is a sham (because of the corruption of Zosima's body), yet he holds fast to that faith; self-interested calculation tells Dmitri to kill his father, yet he does not; Ivan proves to himself, by means of logic, that he is not to blame for the murder—yet he confesses to it. Each brother, as Rosen suggests, in some way turns against the Inquisitor's calculative reasoning.

To Rosen's perceptive comments I would simply add that this overcoming occurs within a Trinitarian framework. Surely it is no accident that there are three Karamazov brothers. Even Smerdyakov's status as a possible fourth brother emphasizes the importance of the number *three*: like the thirteenth guest at the banquet, the ill-intentioned intruder spoils the perfection of the number. In a sense, the three brothers function as an icon of the Trinity—they are the *imago dei*, the triunity of God recreated in humanity. No single one of the brothers—not even Alyosha—is, by himself, created in the image of God. But the three of them, together in relationship, are.

For the purposes of my argument, each brother need not represent a person of the Trinity. More significant is the perichoretic way in which the three brothers relate to one another: the way in which their various characteristics interpenetrate one another as do the characteristics of the three Trinitarian persons. Ivan's anarchism is embraced by Dmitri and even, in various moments of crisis, by Alyosha himself (after the "stink of corruption" following Zosima's death, or the climax of Ivan's account of the tormentors of children in "Rebellion"). Dmitri's quarrelsome and confrontational nature occasionally comes to life in Alyosha, and more obviously in Ivan (especially at the trial). And of course, Alyosha's gentle faithfulness is recognizable both in Ivan, whose passion for justice leads him finally to confess his own "involvement" in the crime, and in Dmitri, who endures the humiliation of the accusation and trial with uncharacteristic calm.

On one level, the relationships among the three brothers simply constitute one instance of the polyphonic character of Dostoevsky's work, so thoroughly documented by Mikhail Bakhtin. But something more is at work here, since the "plurality of independent and unmerged voices and consciousnesses"[30] of which Bakhtin writes is, in the case of this particular novel at least, not as "unmerged" as one might expect. Indeed, the tendency among critics has been to read Bakhtin as emphasizing only animosity and opposition among the "voices" of Dostoevsky's text. But this cannot be the whole story; had Bakhtin believed that the diverse voices of the novel were completely unrelated or opposed to one another, he would have described the result as "chaos" or "anarchy" rather than "polyphony." A true polyphony demands some semblance of mutually productive relationship, as well as a guarantee of diversity and difference.

The symphonic power of the three voices of this novel is secured by the fact that all three brothers are Karamazovs. Each brother provides us with a slightly different reading of what it means to be a Karamazov, but the family as a whole tells us more than does the sum of its members. As Boyce Gibson has pointed out, Dostoevsky's novel "can be read as the story of Dmitri, or of Ivan, or of Alyosha: it has in fact been read in all these ways, naturally with different results." He then goes on to argue for a reading which keeps "the whole of the family in perspective the whole of the time."[31] And if we follow him in this reading, we cannot elevate Alyosha to the status of an angel, nor simply dismiss Ivan as a devil. To be a Karamazov is to be angelic, and demonic, and many others things as well: indeed, to be possessed of all these elements—to differing degrees, to be sure—but possessed all the same.

These observations would seem to have some rather profound theological implications, especially concerning the Christian doctrines of the Trinity and the Incarnation. These implications have been given some initial shaping by Janine Langan. She focuses on the novel's closing lines, in which an answer to its most basic question is proposed by Alyosha's disciples, in a statement not judging but eucharistic, beyond the closure of normative language: "Hurrah for Karamazov." This choral extolling of Alyosha under his family name—black smeared— brings to an end all deflated attempts at mythical egoism. Calling for joyful response to their common mirror-image, it demands of all present the ritual acceptance of their iconic vocation, the incarnation of God in fallen flesh, if only for an instant.[32]

But here we must pause, for we have already noted how Dostoevsky anticipated the appeal to Christ as a response to the atheist's argument. Ivan's poem claims that "the incarnation of God in fallen flesh" cannot fully answer the questions he is raising, for we are not graced—at least not as fully as was he—to follow the course to which he calls us. This is why Ivan's complaint must be answered by the novel as a whole; his protest cannot be quieted merely by Alyosha's claim that Christ "can forgive everything, forgive all *and for all.*" This answer is insufficient because most people will understand the incarnate Christ in purely historical terms—as an ethical role model that we will emulate only with considerable difficulty. This is Ivan's view, and that of his Inquisitor; his concern is with "the *historical* Christ, who had come and gone," in contrast to "the *spiritual, or essential, Christ,* who has always been present in human souls and had become man in order than he might manifest the fullness of the Godhead bodily."[33]

So if Ivan's protest is to be answered, it must be answered not by purely historical references to the man Jesus, but in cosmic terms—with reference to Christ, the one person of the Holy Trinity who becomes incarnate and suffers in the flesh, who takes up all of history into his act and transcends it. This is not to deny the materiality of the Incarnation, as abstract and mystical interpretations of Dostoevsky have tried to do.[34] It is rather simply to emphasize that the importance of the Incarnation is not to provide a role model for the ethically-minded. Christ is of *cosmic* significance precisely because of the intersection of the material and the divine which is part and parcel of Christian theology, and which requires us to recognize the larger Trinitarian context which surrounds the doctrine of the Incarnation. The Inquisitor, on the other hand, is concerned only with the *visible* aspects of the Church: the externalities of material necessity and rational analyses of faith, and he symbolizes the great gulf that exists between the visible and the invisible Church, since he cannot and will not accept the concept of the Holy Spirit and Christ Himself dwelling in both the visible (earthly) and invisible (eternal) Church, effecting a perfect harmony of the earthly and the heavenly, the human and the divine.[35]

Dostoevsky responds to Ivan's Inquisitor by demanding that Christ be seen not just as a historical figure who comes on stage to save the day and then exits with a kiss. This portrait too easily distills into a romantic individualism in which Christ is the hero. Such isolationism—so much a part of the intellectual furniture for those of us in the West—leads only to alienation and violence. In Dostoevsky's view, "the ultimate source of all social ills is the spiritual disintegration and dissociation of human life, the decay or decrease of brotherhood among men."[36]

How is this alienation to be avoided? Dostoevsky believes that it requires us to participate *in* and *with* the lives of others—not only in the ultimate sense countenanced by Zosima in the novel ("responsibility to all and for all"), but also in our perichoretic relationships. According to N. A. Zabolotski, Dostoevsky insists that the human being must learn to be,

if we may use Christian terminology (whether understood theologically or in a secular fashion), a "conciliar person," a member of the Body of Christ. . . . In the dialectics of living relationships this . . . implies a movement from the personal, always somewhat egoistic, to the social, in other words, from "I" to "we."[37]

Of course, one could read all this as nothing more than a lesson in social psychology, an invitation to break free from loneliness and ennui and to join the human race. But something else may be at stake here, as Zabolotski goes on to suggest:

This also implies movement through the "social," with a certain suppression of the personal . . . to the harmony of the personal and the social in the process of growing perfection, whose marker beacon always is and always will be "God, all in all." The Trinitarian nature of God as recognized in Christianity implies the ideal harmony of

> the personal attributes of God in the Father, Son and Holy
> Spirit within the *koinonia* and the dynamics of
> *symphonia* for the "unity of all in all."[38]

Thus, once again, the Christian doctrine of God provides a rhetorical framework within which we can begin to make better sense of the unity and pluriformity of the Karamazov family. It is not only one of the characters, nor *any* one of them, who can, alone, bear God's image. For the image of God belongs not to one human being, but—according to Genesis 1:27—to human *beings*. At the end of the novel, the gathered children do not shout "Hurrah for Alyosha"—as many commentators seem to have done—but "Hurrah for Karamazov." Only when we recognize how all three brothers define the essence of this name do we fully realize the novel's profound Trinitarian implications.

> Any one of the three brothers, from a particular point of
> view, is the center of the story. Dmitri commands the plot;
> Ivan is the ideological center; Alyosha is the spiritual
> climax. As the novel has a plot, an ideology, and a
> destination, none of them can be neglected and all must
> be held together at every turn of the road.[39]

Perhaps no other novel is so supremely successful at holding together the elements of oneness and threeness as is this story of the three very different brothers, all of whom are still Karamazovs.

The Brothers Karamazov has never, to my knowledge, been studied as a work of Trinitarian theology, even though it is shot through with Trinitarian signifiers: from the number of (legitimate) brothers, to the constant recurrence of triads in the novel (three "confessions of an ardent heart," three temptations of Christ, three meetings with Smerdyakov, three "torments of the soul"), to Herzenstube's brief catechism which accompanied his gift of a pound of nuts (Gott der Vater, Gott der Sohn, Gott der heilige Geist"). Still more important than all of this, perhaps, is the novel's constant reminder that God dwells in the mundane aspects of the created order as well as its most glorious aspects. This is why the shout "Hurrah for Karamazov" at the end of the novel is so important.

> Beyond all Romantic judgmental aggression, it is a pledge
> of solidarity with all the Karamazov adolescents
> encountered in the book, not only Alyosha but his father

> and brothers as well. For they, too, are icons. However
> crippled, however involved in myth, they testify through
> their growing pains and twisted faces to the irresistible
> presence in them of an ineradicable seed: God's image and
> likeness.[40]

The Karamazov family as the image of God: this is the true scandal. It is comparatively easy to believe that God might be manifest in one particular, historical, ultimately good human being. And the notion that people might kill God's incarnate image is comprehensible, even if something of a *skandalon*. But that God might be manifest in the *Karamazov* family, with all its faults and failings: this is the true scandal of the Trinity, and that which Dostoevsky most thoroughly underscores in his work.

Dostoevsky's rhetoric is Trinitarian in this sense, at least: it provides an account of the nature of belief in God which not only prescinds from the standard theistic justifications which had been called into question by the Enlightenment, but also notes the insufficiency of proofs based on the "historical Jesus" (as did Strauss's *Life*, Nietzsche's *Antichrist*, and many more works which would follow in their wake). Dostoevsky seems to recognize that claims about the moral perfection of Jesus will soon be subject to a devastating critique. He thus decides to pre-empt that attack by writing it himself, and then showing that we are not banished from participation in the divine life simply because we cannot perfectly imitate Jesus's rejection of miracle, mystery, and authority. The means of our salvation is more cosmic, more divine; it is not dependent only upon our own privatized, isolated selves. In Dostoevsky's economy, it is only by the grace of the Triune God that human beings—together in relation with others who communally bear the same image—can learn to reject the superstitious use of miracle, the hegemonic use of mystery, and the tyrannical use of authority.

V

To return to my original thesis: the "space of subjectivity" from which these novels are written is structured, in part, by the categories of Trinitarian thought. By reading a novel with these categories in mind, we prevent ourselves from forgetting the degree to which the doctrine of the

Trinity has pervaded the world from which the novelist writes. And in doing so, we are reminded that Christian doctrine is not the perfectly coherent, propositional system that it is sometimes imagined to be. Indeed, any faith with the doctrine of the Trinity at its center must necessarily be destabilizing, irruptive, creative, polyphonic. This is why Christian theology can be compatible with literary analysis, and is why the interdisciplinary conversations such as those taking place within this volume of essays are so essential to the work of both the literary critic and the theologian. For the opportunity to participate in this discussion, I am very grateful.

NOTES

1. My thanks to Andrew Adam, Margaret Adam, Greg Jones, Philip Kenneson, and David Penchansky for their helpful comments on an earlier draft of this essay, and to the participants at the Sixth Conference on Literature and Theology, Glasgow, where an earlier, abbreviated version of this paper was originally presented.

2. T. R. Wright, *Theology and Literature,* Signposts in Theology (Oxford: Basil Blackwell, 1988), vii.

3. This seems the obvious conclusion of the historical sections of John Milbank's profound study, *Theology and Social Theory: Beyond Secular Reason,* Signposts in Theology (Oxford: Basil Blackwell, 1990).

4. See, Richard J. Bernstein, *Beyond Objectivism and Relativism* (Oxford: Basil Blackwell, 1983); Michael J. Buckley, S.J., *At the Origins of Modern Atheism* (New Haven: Yale University Press, 1987); Eberhard Jüngel, *God as the Mystery of the World,* tr. Darrell L. Guder (Grand Rapids, Mich.: William B. Eerdmans, 1983).

5. Friedrich E. D. Schleiermacher, *The Christian Faith,* tr. H. R. Mackintosh (Edinburgh: T. & T. Clark, 1928), pp. 738-51.

6. Wright, *Theology and Literature,* p. 1, referring to a statement of Ezra Pound.

7. *Rhet.* 1355b26.

8. I have elsewhere attempted to explain, in some detail, the usefulness of rhetoric as a methodological tool for theology in particular. See *Faithful Persuasion: In Aid of a Rhetoric of Christian Theology* (Notre Dame, Ind.: University of Notre Dame Press, 1991). A briefer exposition of this argument may be found in "Theology as Rhetoric," *Theological Studies* 52/3 (September 1991): 407-30.

9. Wolfgang Iser, *The Implied Reader: Patterns of Communication in Prose Fiction from Bunyan to Beckett* (Baltimore: Johns Hopkins University Press, 1974); Umberto Eco, *The Role of the Reader: Explorations in the Semiotics of Texts*, Advances in Semiotics (Bloomington: Indiana University Press, 1979).

10. Terry Eagleton, *Literary Theory: An Introduction* (Minneapolis: University of Minnesota Press, 1983), pp. 205-6.

11. Calvin O. Schrag, *Communicative Praxis and the Space of Subjectivity* (Bloomington: Indiana University Press, 1986).

12. See the helpful comments by Joseph C. Flay, review of *Communicative Praxis and the Space of Subjectivity*, by Calvin O. Schrag, in *Philosophy and Rhetoric* 21/4 (1988): 294-304.

13. Anastasia Leech, review of *The Time of the Angels*, in *The Tablet* (September 24, 1966): 1074.

14. Dan-Ilie Ciobotea and William H. Lazareth, "The Triune God: The Supreme Source of Life. Thoughts Inspired by Rublev's Icon of the Trinity," in ed. Gennadios Limouris, *Icons: Windows on Eternity: Theology and Spirituality in Colour*, (Geneva: WWC Publications, 1990), pp. 202-3.

15. Ciobotea and Lazareth, "The Triune God," p. 203.

16. For example, Charles of *The Sea, The Sea*, whose "vaguely sinister house with its windowless inner rooms reflects his lack of self-understanding." Sally Cunneen, "What Iris Murdoch Doesn't Know," *Commonweal* (November 9, 1979): 623.

17. Hans-Georg Gadamer, "The Relevance of the Beautiful: Art as Symbol, Play, and Festival," in ed. Robert Bernasconi, *The Relevance of the Beautiful and Other Essays*, tr. Nicholas Walker (Cambridge: Cambridge University Press, 1986), p. 5.

18. Quoted by Granville Hicks, *Saturday Review* (October 29, 1966): 26.

19. James H. Cone, *A Black Theology of Liberation*, with a Foreword by Paulo Freire, 2nd ed. (Maryknoll, N.Y.: Orbis Books, 1986), p. 64.

20. James H. Cone, "Sanctification and Liberation in the Black Religious Tradition, with Special Reference to Black Worship," in *Speaking the Truth: Ecumenism, Liberation, and Black Theology* (Grand Rapids, Mich.: William B. Eerdmans, 1986), pp. 17-34.

21. Wilfred D. Samuels and Clenora Hudson-Weems, *Toni Morrison* (Boston: Twayne Publishers, 1990), pp. 4-5.

22. See, for example, Clodovis Boff, *Feet-on-the-Ground Theology: A Brazilian Journey*, tr. Phillip Berryman (Maryknoll, N.Y.: Orbis Books, 1987).

23. Bessie W. Jones and Audrey L. Vinson, *The World of Toni Morrison: Explorations in Literary Criticism* (Dubuque, Iowa: Kendall/Hunt Publishing Co., 1985), p. 137.

24. Linda Susan Beard, Seminar, University of St. Thomas, August 23, 1991.

25. Sandi Russell, "'It's OK to say OK'" (1986), in ed. Nellie Y. McKay, *Critical Essays on Toni Morrison*, Critical Essays on American Literature (Boston: G. K. Hall and Co., 1988), pp. 43-7.

26. For further helpful reflections on this issue, see Marilyn Sanders Mobley, "Memory, History and Meaning in Toni Morrison's *Beloved*," in ed. with an Introduction by Harold Bloom, *Toni Morrison*, Modern Critical Views (New York: Chelsea House Publishers, 1990), pp. 189-99, esp. pp. 191-5.

27. Fyodor Dostoevsky, *The Brothers Karamazov*, tr. Richard Pevear and Larissa Volokhonsky (New York: Random House, Vintage Books, 1990). All quotations of the text are from this translation; page numbers are cited parenthetically.

28. Fyodor Dostoevsky, Letter to K. P. Pobedonostsev, August 24, 1879, in ed. Ralph E. Matlaw, *The Brothers Karamazov*, tr. Constance Garnett, Norton Critical Edition (New York: W. W. Norton and Company, 1976), pp. 761-2.

29. Nathan Rosen, "Style and Structure in *The Brothers Karamazov*" (1971), in Matlaw, ed., *The Brothers Karamazov*, pp. 841-51.

30. M. M. Bakhtin, *Problems of Dostoevsky's Poetics*, ed. and tr. Caryl Emerson, with an Introduction by Wayne C. Booth, Theory and History of Literature, vol. 8 (Minneapolis: University of Minnesota Press, 1984), p. 6.

31. A. Boyce Gibson, *The Religion of Dostoevsky* (London: SCM Press, 1973; reprint, Philadelphia: Westminster Press, 1974), p. 170.

32. Janine Langan, "Icon vs. Myth: Dostoevsky, Feminism and Pornography," *Religion and Literature* 18/1 (Spring 1986): 71-2.

33. George A. Panichas, "Fyodor Dostoevsky and Roman Catholicism," *Greek Orthodox Theological Review* 4 (Summer 1958): 22.

34. See the synopsis of this phenomenon in Colin Crowder, "The Appropriation of Dostoevsky in the Early Twentieth Century: Cult, Counter-cult and Incarnation," in ed. David Jasper and Colin Crowder, *European Literature and*

Theology in the Twentieth Century, (London: Macmillan; New York: St. Martin's Press, 1990), pp. 15-33.

35. Panichas, 31.

36. Georges Florovsky, "Three Masters: Gogol, Dostoevsky, Tolstoy," *Epiphany: A Journal of Faith and Insight* 10 (Summer 1990): 51.

37. N. A. Zabolotski, "Fyodor Mikhailovich Dostoevsky Today," *Scottish Journal of Theology* 37/1 (1984): 46-7.

38. Zabolotski, "Fyodor Mikhailovich Dostoevsky Today": 47.

39. Gibson, *Religion of Dostoevsky*, p. 175.

40. Langan, "Icon vs. Myth": 72.

"IS THERE NO BALM IN GILEAD?"

Biblical Intertext in Margaret Atwood's *The Handmaid's Tale*

Dorota Filipczak

"Tu crois que cést l'oiseau qui est libre. Tu te trompes; cést la fleur . . ."[1] says Jacques Derrida in one of his essays. Freedom is asserted in the cycle of defying and accepting one's roots. *The Handmaid's Tale* is haunted by the echo of cultural origins, as manifest via the insidious presence of biblical images in the text. Rooted in the English language legacy of the "Great Code," Atwood's book attempts to destroy these roots via the demonic misrepresentation of Judaic-Christian religion. In the dystopic world conjured up in *The Handmaid's Tale*, the author uses the possibilities of distortion to the full, thereby pointing to the dangers lurking in the process of institutionalization of the sacred text.

The role of the Bible in the state depicted in *The Handmaid's Tale* is ambiguous. Locked in a special wooden box, it becomes a totem of the totalitarian system in every house. At the same time, it is "an incendiary device," available only to the initiated; others are forbidden to read it. Offred, the main character comments on this situation in a revealing way: "who knows what we'd make of it, if we ever got our hands on it?"[2] The Bible is a trapped text turned into a lethal instrument because the régime makes it generate oppressive laws. Everyday life in the state is based on principles whose authors claim that they follow the biblical model. The society fosters male domination and female object status, which is sanctioned by the patriarchal history of Jacob/Israel and by Paul's First Letter to Timothy. "Let the woman learn her subjection" marks the crucial moment in the wedding ceremony. The long list of injunctions is rounded off with: "she shall be saved by child-bearing," which points to the only acceptable vocation of women in Atwood's Gilead.

The institution of surrogate motherhood is the state's main concern because of the plummeting birth rate in the families of the èlite. The relationships within apparent triangles are to imitate the Jacob, Rachel, Bilhah arrangement, triggered off by Rachel's infertility crisis. In fact, this model is often displaced by the Sarah/Hagar conflict, when a handmaid happens to incur her mistress's displeasure. She may be sent off to the colonies, the equivalent of inhospitable wilderness with no merciful Yahvist God to watch over her plight. Handmaids who defect from their vocation rarely evade the intrusive power of the "God of seeing,"[3] as Hagar, their predecessor, calls him. The régime of Gilead owes its omniscience to ubiquitous spies, called "Eyes," who exercise strict control over individuals' activities. "The Eyes of God run all over the earth"[4] says the official slogan, which seems to parody its biblical source, possibly from 2 Chronicles: "For the eyes of the Lord run to and fro throughout the whole earth, to show himself strong in the behalf of them whose heart is perfect toward him."[5]

The impact of the Bible on the reality described in *The Handmaid's Tale* raises the question about the meaning and implications of the biblical code in Atwood's vision. Does the book tell the story of a literalizing misreading,[6] that is to say, a fundamentalist interpretation of the Bible which results in disastrous ideological consequences?[7] In the light of this approach the text that is in itself a guarantee of freedom would be used to enforce the subjection of its victims. The purpose of ideologically conditioned misreading is to break down the text into clearly interpretable, manageable fragments. Hence, the misreading would consist in suppressing the unbounded potential of the text.

Another interpretation that is generally accepted by Atwood critics might be that the author sees the Bible as the text that constitutes a closure for interpretative possibilities. Frank Davey argues that Margaret Atwood seeks to break out of the traditional pattern of quest for paradise, and pursues an "unnamed" and elusive garden, other than Eden which stemmed from the male ideology of patriarchal culture.[8] Rosemary Sullivan and Catherine Sheldrick Ross analyze Atwood's preoccupation with shamanic rites in *Surfacing*, so as to suggest that her narrator achieves fusion with a primordial unity outside the Christian code which the author regards as fake and superfluous.[9]

The answer resolving the tension between the two hypotheses can be found in a closer look at the manifestations of the biblical world in the book. The name of the state in *The Handmaid's Tale*, that is, Gilead, is firmly anchored in patriarchal history. Originally, it may have referred to a range of hills. Later, it was used to denote a strip of land east of the river Jordan. The territory was comprised of the plateau lined with valleys which contained prime grazing areas.[10] The Old Testament mentions Gilead as a backdrop for quite a few important events from patriarchal history. Accordingly, the name triggers off a host of associations which are inscribed in the deep structure of Atwood's book as a powerful intertext. What I would like to do in this article is unravel the fabric of associations related to biblical Gilead, and use their meaning in the comments on Atwood's Gilead. I will try to see whether *The Handmaid's Tale* is a shocking caricature of biblical reality or a logical consequence of imposing the biblical world on a different kind of reality.

The author uses the term Gilead with particular emphasis in two cases. One of them is connected with Offred's training in the doctrinaire center for surrogate mothers. Among the beliefs that are inculcated in students of motherly vocation is: "Gilead . . . knows no bounds. Gilead is within you."[11] Clothed in an aphoristic character, the statement possesses a remarkable rhetorical power. Its binary structure, with the second sentence enhancing the meaning of the first one, contains the pronouncement of total ideology that is not only present in the state's mechanisms, that is, outside individual, but also inside him or her, embedded in the unconscious. There is no escape from Gilead no matter whether one is outward or inward bound, for Gilead is an integral part of the self.

The second reference to Gilead occurs in the hymn which says: "There is a balm in Gilead."[12] The statement is a distorted version of Jeremiah's question: "Is there no balm in Gilead?"[13] An ostensibly slight change in phrasing is fraught with consequences. Jeremiah deplores the corruption of Jewish state which seems past the chance of being healed. According to Robert P. Carroll, balm from Gilead may have been used either to heal wounds or to conceal their festering smell.[14] Thus, on the literal level, the prophet's question seems to urge the Jews to apply Gileadite medicine on the diseased organism of the country. The wry irony that undermines such an assumption is that not even the balm of Gilead could possibly set things right.[15] The fabled medicine is ineffective in the face of widespread destruction. In the official hymn of Atwood's Gilead, Jeremiah's rhetorical question is turned into an unequivocal affirmative. It resounds with propaganda which eliminates any thought-provoking ambiguity.[16] "There is a balm in Gilead" claims that the state possesses some supreme moral value that is a remedy for the corruption of the former permissive culture.

Since both references to Gilead transform the term into an indicator of ideological meaning, it might be useful to comment on the events that take place in biblical Gilead, in order to see whether they have their ideological echo in Atwood's book. The list of fragments that allude to Gilead in different books of the Bible is quite rich. However, I will base my insights on the contexts that are particularly relevant for *The Handmaid's Tale*.

In Genesis, Gilead becomes a symbol of transition, as a setting for Jacob's flight from Laban. Having received God's explicit order to leave the territory of his father-in-law, Jacob takes his family, slaves and flocks; he flees the household which was the place of his toil and humiliation. He breaks loose from the bonds of his previous lifestyle but some reminders of the past are smuggled into his camp by Rachel, who steals the teraphim from her father's place. In the light of the text, these household idols[17] seem to have functioned as the guarantee of the owner's right to his inheritance.[18] Rachel may have wanted to protect her husband's position by an additional trick. Angered at the disappearance of his family and teraphim, Laban pursues the fugitives and catches up with them in the mountainous land of Gilead. He reproaches Jacob for the flight and then rummages through the tents in search of the idols. Rachel hides them within her dress, and thus she avoids the punishment of death which was to be dealt out to the thief on Jacob's order.

The passage across Gilead marks a turning-point in Jacob's spiritual life. After the peaceful parting with Laban, Jacob embarks on the quest for the sacred. He encounters God's Angels in the place that he calls Manahaim, that is, God's camp; he fights a stranger at Penuel, which indicates that the growing intimacy with the sacred involves a risk of death. "Outside . . . with Laban, his life lacked such appearances almost completely."[19]

The undiscovered teraphim provide a link between the two stages in Jacob's life. They represent the insidious influence of the past that crept into the household imperceptibly. Jacob jettisons all the idols on the way to Bethel, the place of divine revelation. The text suppresses the fact of whether Jacob found out about Laban's teraphim later, and connived with their presence in the camp. It can be inferred that his family and servants were secretive about the idols they had. Since the closeness to God was too dangerous to run a further risk, Jacob ordered people to give up all the teraphim which were buried under the terebinth. The camp was thus cleansed of the dubious past, and people started to rely on Jacob's God.

The Gileadite state in *The Handmaid's Tale* is haunted by the numerous teraphim of the past. Some members of the ruling caste, that is to say, "Jacob's sons," are notorious hoarders of things connected with the previous epoch. When Offred is about to turn up for an assignation with her commander, she wonders "what male totems" may be behind his door in the forbidden zone. The room is a typical library containing everything that has been legislated out of existence by the leaders. "What's dangerous in the hands of the multitudes . . . is safe enough for those whose motives are . . . Beyond reproach."[20]

Such is the explanation of this quasi-antiquarian interest. The gifts for Offred are often the objects with the status of cultural detritus, that is, fashion magazines, old cosmetics, a garish night-club costume. All these things avoided burning, and trashy as they are, they arouse Offred's excitement because they are a link with the happy past.

The fact that the Commander is so fond of the cultural teraphim constitutes a shift of emphasis in comparison with Genesis, where it is Rachel that represents a carnivalesque choice. Jacob's reputation is untainted by her theft. In fact, Rachel's deed is set within the frame of femininity that was originally associated with Eve.[21] Irrational and weak, Rachel fits into a typical portrait of a woman who has to look up to the patriarch for care and decision. The system of Atwood's Gilead safeguards Rachel's trespasses. The intrusiveness of the intelligence service and the female collaboration against women of a lower position are meant to prevent the outbursts of carnivalesque.

The storing of teraphim can only be possible for people of a higher position. Offred cherishes memories only; she would not be able to keep anything material in her room because of strict surveillance. The Commander's wife listens to old records when she is by herself, but this is a slight trespass in comparison with the Commander's fondness for subversive literature of the past. The sons of Jacob take care to stamp out such idiosyncrasies. If Offred's Commander is to be identified with

Frederick F. Waterford as mentioned by Piexoto, his death in the purge is the death of an idol-worshipper whose unorthodox interests must be punished. The incident described by Piexoto proves that the leaders of Gilead can be consistent in enforcing ideological tenets. The Commander meets that fate of the thief of teraphim from Jacob's order, which was not executed in Genesis.

The obvious affinities between the reality of Atwood's Gilead and some motifs in Genesis do not expose the Bible as a source of Gileadite constraints. Jacob's story in Genesis has a primarily etiological character.[22]

It does not hold up a model of behavior for imitation. The differences in the attitude of biblical writers can obviously be seen. While the Elohist is at pains to exonerate Jacob,[23] the Book of Hosea is very far from such attempts. The twelfth chapter of the Book of Hosea mentions the crucial events from Jacob's life, but the author's attitude towards the protagonist is marked by reserve, if not suspicion. The chapter opens with a telling verse: "And Yahve has a contention with Israel to visit it upon Jacob according to his ways, according to his deeds he shall return it to him."[24]

The reason for contention is the evil latent in Jacob's nature, and passed on to his sons who yielded to its power. The chapter identifies Gilead with "might" and "delusion." According to Dwight Roger Daniels "delusion" alludes to the idolatrous worship that displaced Yahve's cult among Jacob's descendants.[25] Some scholars are liable to detect such inclination in Jacob, whose uxorious commitment is seen as a euphemism for sexual rites. Thus, one interpretation explains Hosea's dis-pleasure with Jacob's passion as "a sideswipe at the fertility cult."[26] Commenting on Israel's apostasy, the Book of Hosea alludes to the fall to Baal, known as the Baal Peor event in Gilead. It took place in the city of Shittim, where Israelite men defiled themselves by idol worship, which involved sacrilegious intercourse with Moabite women. Described in the Book of Numbers, the offense became an umbrella term for Israel's idolatrous tendencies,[27] which persisted in spite of the prophets' admonitions.

The motif of the fertility cult appears in *The Handmaid's Tale* in the guise of surrogate motherhood whose ideological, pseudo-religious aspects are strongly reminiscent of Lebensborn in Nazi Germany.[28] The pagan fertility overtones in the book are conspicuous even in the image of handmaids' habits: "the color of blood . . . defines us,"[29] says Offred, pointing to redness as the color that is to ensure fertility and continuity of life.[30] Some aspects of Gileadite life reflect the Baal Peor rite. Intercourse ceremonies for Commanders and handmaids can be termed ritualistic because they are sanctioned by the state, and are normally preceded by a kind of religious service.

The link between Gileadite life and fertility ritual manifests itself via the ceremony of human sacrifice called Particicution. During this particular execution, handmaids dismember a man, an alleged rapist, with their bare hands. Professor Piexoto mentions the association with the fertility rituals of an early Earth-goddess cult. The dismembering is also a surrogate for a gratifying contact with the other's body. As Robert Detweiler claims, tortures enforce intimacy with the victim's body.[31]

The significance of fertility rites enacted in ritualistic intercourse and Particicution can be summed up by the meaning of the Baal Peor ceremony. The event at Shittim coincided with the Israelite conquest of the Promised Land. Hence, the goal of the pagan ceremony was to ensure the fertility of the newly gained land by resorting to Baal.[32]

When Hosea dwells on the consequences of Israel's apostasy, epitomized by Baal Peor, he pronounces God's curse on the unfaithful nation: "no birth, no pregnancy, no conception. . . . I shall make them childless among men."[33] As James L. Mays puts it: "through the end of human fertility, Ephraim will face a convincing rebuttal of their devotion to Baal."[34] Atwood's world seems to suffer from the curse in the Book of Hosea. In spite of the state's emphasis on procreation, polygamous families are never successful through legal intercourse. Most men from the èlite are sterile, and conception can only occur due to normally punishable liaisons. The ideology holds that only women can barren. Handmaids who want to avoid deportation to the colonies as unwomen use their doctors. Sometimes wives arrange assignations between handmaids and young men, and then watch for the happy outcome.

In the Book of Hosea, childlessness is framed in the description of the universal annihilation. "Though he be fruitful among his brethren, an east wind shall come up from the wilderness, and his springs shall become dry, and his fountain shall be dried up."[35] The decreation starts with the general barrenness of nature, which signifies the withdrawal of divine Grace.[36] Prophetic visions abound in images of decreation. "I beheld the earth and, lo, it was without form, and void."[37] Such is the condition of

Gilead in *The Handmaid's Tale*, where sterility and general shortage of food result from the changes in an environment contaminated by nuclear fall-out, the world sliding into slow decreation.

The Book of Hosea alludes to Gilead not only in the context of fertility cult and its consequences. On one occasion the place is described as "tracked with blood" because of "evil-doers." The incident that the author alludes to is connected with a murder committed by priests on the road to Shechem. According to James L. Mays, Shechem was a cultic center associated with the Mosaic covenant. The biblical scholar assumes that after the establishment of the state cult by Jeroboam, Shechem continued to be a threatening competitor to the official shrines at Bethel and Dan, a center of dissent against the state cultic programme. Mays implies that priests of the state cult may have gone "to the length of plotting for pilgrims to Shechem to be waylaid."[38] Atwood's Gilead is based on the state religion whose "priests" supervise the mechanisms of terror. Their rule perpetuates a system of gratuitous violence inflicted on potential enemies. Among the groups that become the targets of Gileadite hostility are the clergy and believers of other creeds. Catholic priests are hanged for the neglect of reproductive duties. Nuns are either deported or converted to serve as handmaids. The rite of Particicution and other legalized murders that put an end to otherness mark out Gilead's way towards perfect uniformity.[39]

As every totalitarian régime, Gilead has its own ideology that is a corrupted version of the biblical way towards a better reality. Jacob's quest for the divine closeness is amplified in the fate of his descendants, that is, Israelite tribes walking out of Egypt towards the Promised Land. Here, Gilead surfaces as a zone of transition before the achievement of the actual goal. Chapter 32 of the Book of Numbers shows the Israelites in the moment when the time of wandering in the wilderness is over, and it is only the expanse along the river Jordan that separates the tribes from the Promised Land. The tribes of Reuben and Gad are quick to notice that the land east of the Jordan is fertile and good for cattle-breeding. They approach Moses and request that they should be given the territory. First Moses interprets their words as a sign of cowardice. He tells them a spy-story about their ancestors who shunned exploring the country indicated to them by God. Having thus undermined the courage of others, they incurred God's wrath, and the whole people had to roam in the wilderness for a much longer time, as a result of the divine curse. The tribes counter the implicit charge by saying that they will join others and help them to conquer the land west of the Jordan. Before they set out, they want to build strongholds for wives, children and livestock to ensure their safety while the men are away, taking part in the battle. Moses and the elders fulfill their wish and allocate Gilead to the tribes of Reuben and Gad, warning them against the breach of divine order. The curse would catch up with them in case of defection.[40]

The preparedness for the battle voiced by the tribes of Reuben and Gad is reflected in Atwood's dystopic reality. Gilead spreads an ideology that is geared to the idea of military conquest. The state resembles a war-camp. Its heart, that is, the Red Center and homes of the èlite, are continuously guarded by armed soldiers, protected by barbed wire and searchlights. Handmaids are guardians of biological survival, and their task is, in this sense, similar to that of soldiers. The similarity is enhanced by imagery, for example, they sleep in military cots, covered with US army blankets. Part of the indoctrination in the Red Center is presented in a crude military phrasing: "you are the shock troops, you will march out in advance into dangerous territory. The greater the risk the greater the glory"[41] says Aunt Lydia. Her words could be called a manifesto of Gileadite ideology which entails risk and personal sacrifice. They also point to the liminal quality of the state as a temporary reality which is to prepare the fully reborn civilization.

The military imagery is counterbalanced by the images of future life, for example: "women will live in harmony together."[42] The slogan that should sugar renunciation is: "we are working towards the goal of a little garden for each one."[43] This allusion to the paradisiac image ties in with the biblical urge to return to paradise. The conquest of the Promised Land by the Israelite tribes is one of the mutations of that desire. The passage in Numbers makes it quite plain that the tribes of Reuben and Gad have to walk into the territory west of the Jordan, which turns the reality of the Promised Land into an unavoidable goal. Handmaids and other citizens of Gilead are forced to contribute to the future idyll. Otherwise, they might meet the fate of the offenders from the spy-story in Numbers. The verdict of destruction passed on individuals by the régime is the equivalent of the curse with its possible consequences in Numbers. Films about the colonies or sexual abuse are shown to handmaids to prevent their defection. They perform a similar function as Moses's allusion to the punishment for disobedience. "Consider the alternatives"[44] might be read as Aunt Lydia's rephrasing of Moses' threat.

The possession of land was a crucial element of the Jewish longing in the times of exile or foreign supremacy. The Messianic idea in Judaic tradition was connected with the final reconquest of the Promised Land as the consummation of history. Within this trend, the day of Yahweh was not located in another aeon but it came as the culmination of God's activity in the national history.[45] Here the land was associated with the sense of identity as well as survival. Accordingly, the prophets mention various parts of Israelite possessions that will be restored to the nation through Yahweh's intervention. The name Gilead appears in the Book of Obadiah, when future Israelite territories are enumerated. "Benjamin shall possess Gilead."[46] As a fabled grazing area, Gilead was often coveted and occupied by hostile nations.[47] Thus, the statements express people's desire to enjoy the qualities of fertile land, for example, "Let them feed in . . . Gilead, as in the days of old."[48]

In prophetic writings judgement is envisaged as a final reckoning of Yahweh with the nations, to use W. Eichrodt's phrase.[49] The Day of Yahweh is the day of his revenge on Israel's enemies. God is seen amidst the chosen ones, and through his power the tribes crush their enemies. In this context, Gilead is sometimes mentioned as a part of the Promised Land after its restoration to the Jewish nation. Deutero-Zechariah unfolds a vision of expansion in which God brings his nation to Gilead.[50]

Atwood's Gilead may be compared to biblical Israel in the time of her apostasy when the worship of God was displaced by a fertility cult. On the other hand, it is a caricature of the biblical Messianic state. Political and military events that cause the annihilation of the previous country with its permissive culture parody the day of Yahweh. The Congress is machine-gunned, the power seized, circumstances of history radically changed. New ideology revolves round the gains and blessings of the present time contrasted with a nightmarish past. The régime stamps out different forms of sexual harassment or abuse. Partners are supplied for the nubile girls from the èlite so that they can perform their biological destinies "in peace."

The duplicity of Gilead is unmasked via a comparison of its pseudo-Messianic achievements with Jewish Messianism in its two major versions, that is, prophetic national Messianism and apocalyptic Messianism. The former presupposed the re-establishment of the Davidic Kingdom on earth after God's intervention in history; the latter went beyond the idea of fulfillment in this world and located the new Kingdom in another aeon, which would follow the perishing of history and worldly wickedness.[51] Both, however, emphasize God's authorship in the plan. As Gershom Scholem has it: "The redemption is not the product of immanent developments. . . . It is rather transcendence breaking in upon history, an intrusion in which history itself perishes, transformed in its ruin because it is struck by a beam of light shining into it from an outside source."[52] The Gileadite revolution subverts the basic meaning of the Messianic idea, where it is God's action that heals past evil and founds the new kingdom. Beliefs and actions enforced by the èlite spring from the lethal drive to change human nature by means of imposed constraints. The leaders usurp the divine position, "God is a national resource,"[53] as one of the slogans says, stressing the manipulative function of pseudo-religion.

Atwood's Gilead is permeated with the total absence of God, which exposes its Messianic claims as deceit. The Old Testament prophets see the absence of God as an expression of his wrath.[54] In the Book of Hosea, God withdraws himself from the people who turned to Baal with request for survival in the newly gained land. James L. Mays comments on it in the following way: "He will abdicate his place as their God and their ultimate extremity shall be silent vacant emptiness above and around them."[55] In *The Handmaid's Tale*, a spiritual vacuum is represented by the image of the printing office. The place produces sheets of conventional prayers for different occasions. The members of the èlite are supposed to order such prayers, to conform to the general rule. During one of the walks, Offred and Ofglen stop in front of the office for a subversive conversation under the guise of prayer. The noise of machinery is similar to the voice of the Congregation praying. "Do you think God listens to these machines?"[56] Ofglen asks. Offred answers "No," risking her life. The absurd situation proves that the sacred is completely withdrawn from life in Gilead. The dehumanized temple brings to mind the images of abuse in the Israelite temple of the Lord. The Book of Jeremiah warns people not to be taken in by the staff of the Temple who stand at its gates, repeating monotonously: "The Temple of the Lord, the Temple of the Lord, the Temple of the Lord."[57]

There is one more Messianic element that is completely missing in *The Handmaid's Tale*. The Old Testament prophets who unfold visions of Messianic times usually speak about exceptional abundance in nature as a sign of Yahweh's love and care. The community whose survival was endangered by famine, drought and pestilence is now seen as enjoying the fruit of the earth in profusion. Prophetic descriptions abound in hyperboles reflecting such fullness or even an overspilling of gifts,[58] for example, "the mountains shall drop sweet wine. . . ."[59] As I have tried to prove, analyzing the images from the Book of Hosea, the barrenness of people and the decay of nature are reflected in Atwood's Gilead. Thus, there is no external sign of divine blessing in the spurious paradise.

According to Walther Eichrodt, Jewish Messianism shows a tendency to bridge the gap between the Messianic epoch and old-time paradise.[60] Atwood's text unmasks the sinister outcomes of human urge to make the Messianic/paradisiac ideal the actual reality. The Yahwist passage about Creation seems to have been absorbed in *The Handmaid's Tale* in the way that exposes the ideal garden as a fake or distortion. Reality in Atwood's book mirrors the limitations of the patriarchal mentality that generated the Yahwist myth. Alluding to the generosity of Yahweh, who creates the first woman as a suitable help for man, the author presents the feminine half of Gileadite community in the role of objects that are ready for use on the horizon of male existence and provide it with biological continuum. Women are restricted by their sexual roles of wives or handmaids. Financial dependence on men stresses their property status. Women are defined by men in the same way as Eve is defined by Adam when he gives her the name "iszsza" derived from Hebrew "isz." Handmaids' names, such as Offred, Ofglen, Ofwarren result from a similar linguistic transaction.

Offred is actually coaxed into adopting the role of Eve, who commits the sin that results in banishment. Enticed to cross the boundary between the role of a passive partner in the copulation ceremony and the role of actual mistress in the nightclub, she commits a transgression against the sexual dictates in Gilead. The Commander ushers Offred into the forbidden zone of state secrets, which is reflected in the change of their intimate relationship. The outward sign of the change is Commander's gift for Offred, that is, the nightclub costume. She slips it on, stepping into an unequivocal role. When Serena Joy finds out about this offense, she meets Offred in the doorway as if banning her re-entry into the house, in the usual role which is no longer true. Reproving Offred, she produces the night-club costume. "The purple sequins fall, slithering down over the step like snakeskin, glittering in the sunlight." The tempter, that is the Commander, is absent in the scene of female confrontation. Imprisoned in the ideological paradise from the start and forced to accept its deceit, Offred goes into her room after the encounter with Serena. Shut off from the rest of the world as if in the prison cell, she listens for the rustle of the police van on the gravel, like a sinner who hides herself when the steps of supreme authority start reverberating in the garden. The Cherub with a flaming sword is replaced by spies who literally drive Offred out of paradise, that is, bring her the freedom which gives rise to the story.

The book subverts the claim of Michael Edwards's essay: his opinion is that each story is told out of the inner compulsion to return to the paradisiac point of departure before reality became intolerable.[61] Contrary to his interpretation, Atwood exposes the very paradisiac drive as lethal in its ideological consequences.

At this point, the feminist critique of the male garden is revealed as the critique of the interpretative habits of the community in general. Atwood is on the run from Eden because this biblical image seems to have been generated by the urge to control and channel experience into a meaningful pattern. The Gilead that is in people's hearts can thus be seen as a set of religious stereotypes which turn reality into nightmare. The total claim of such stereotypes and their insidious presence in the unconscious, change the idyllic garden into a masked prison. The accusation implicit in the feminist critique of male garden and in Atwood's dystopia would thus point to the rejection of the Bible as the source of a most pervasive and sinister myth.

The message of *The Handmaid's Tale* can be compared with the ideas in Mieke Bal's texts on women in the Book of Judges.[62] The critic sees the Bible as an accomplice in the patriarchal strategy of marginalizing and victimizing women. Bal states that Jephthah's daughter and the Levite's concubine are sacrificed to ensure the safety of the army, in the first case, and of and individual, in the other.[63] The expendability of women in the Book of Judges has its equivalent in *The Handmaid's Tale*. Gilead functions by the enforced renunciation of subject status by the female half of the community. Mieke Bal's vision of the nameless and subjectless daughter of Jephthah reminds me of the daughters in Gilead. Like victims in the Book of Judges, they are repressed by the narrative.[64] Offred often thinks of her daughter who is probably being brought up in one of the caste families, to serve as a juvenile wife and reproductor. Her photograph in a long white dress brings to mind the scene of the wedding ceremony in Gilead. During the Prayvaganza service, girls veiled in white are given away to husbands appointed by the state. The image of silent passive girls is strongly reminiscent of the filial obedience of Jephthah's daughter. In Gilead silence means obliteration, which is true for most situations involving women. Photographs from the family albums never show handmaids who may be actual mothers of the photographed children. "From the point of view of future history . . . we will be invisible," Offred concludes.[65]

The role of the Bible in generating obliteration strategies need not be seen as unequivocal. Patriarchal interpretation does not always result from the biblical texts. It may arise from the sexist assumptions of the interpreter. Here I would like to refer to a fragment of the first epistle of Paul to Timothy. The fragment concerns the role and conduct of women in church. It is quoted in the Prayvaganza scene towards the end of *The Handmaid's Tale*. Gloria Neufeld Redekop sets out to prove that the traditional reading of verses I Timothy 2:8-15 by church institutions is in fact a misinterpretation.[66] She does it by analyzing the syntactic and lexical aspects of the original. Her conclusions are particularly relevant in contemporary times because some denominations still tend to see this part of the letter as a biblical answer to the pleas for female priesthood.[67] The comparison of Atwood's context for the letter with Redekop's analysis of relevant verses leads to interesting conclusions.

The context of I Tim. 2,8-15 in *The Handmaid's Tale* seems to reflect the circumstances that "skewed" the exegesis of the verses according to Redekop. The Prayvaganza ceremony is based on the paradigm of the church as the patriarchal household of God patterned after the patriarchal household in society.[68] The verse that still causes misunderstanding in exegesis is given particular prominence. The Commander reads out the passage: "Let the woman learn in silence with all subjection." Here he looks us over. "All," he repeats.[69]

Since the text does not specify the object of subjection, submission of women to either husbands or male leaders in the church has been assumed. To counter the patriarchal reading, Redekop argues that what is at stake is in fact submission to the true teachers of the Gospel, as distinguished from the false ones.[70] The Prayvaganza episode in *The Handmaid's Tale* illustrates the situation in which the congregation have been constrained into obedience by a false teacher acting on behalf of an ideology that has distorted the text.

Atwood's vision of the Bible-centered society addresses the patriarchal abuse embedded in the biblical texts. At the same time it sees the patriarchal abuse as prevalent in response to the text that may be void of patriarchal intention, and yet it is violated into complicity with the governing interpretation. My conclusion seems to be corroborated by the closing notes in *The Handmaid's Tale*. The ironic commentary of Professor Piexoto does not really bear up the ideological roots of Gileadite violence. Its detached tone glosses over suffering and death without much compassion. According to Piexoto the Bible is just one of the sources that the Gileadite leaders reached back to. It seems that the unpredictable aspects of the "incendiary device" remain locked up safely throughout Atwood's book. The Bible that is used to perpetuate the male garden is never allowed to subvert it. The fact that the biblical texts talk to each other and sometimes deconstruct each other is not really noticeable in *The Handmaid's Tale*. Consequently the struggle against interpretative closure enforces the stereotype of a monolithic text destroying its victims.

How does this impact post-and pre-Christian viewers?

NOTES

1. Jacques Derrida, *Edmond Jabés et la question du livre in l'ériture et la différence* (Paris: Editions du Seuil, 1967), p. 101.

2. Margaret Atwood, *The Handmaid's Tale* (London: Virago Press, 1987), p. 98.

3. For the importance of the "seeing"-motif see: Gerhard von Rad, *Genesis. A Commentary*, tr. John H. Marks (London: SCM Press, 1979), pp. 191-3.

4. Atwood, *The Handmaid's Tale*, p. 203.

5. Chronicles 16:9. Except where noted all biblical quotations in this paper are from the King James Version.

6. The context and meaning of the term here diverge from the concept of revisionary misreading in Harold Bloom, *The Anxiety of Influence: A Theory of Poetry* (New York: Oxford University Press, 1973), pp. 7-31.

7. See Amin Malak, "Margaret Atwood's *The Handmaid's Tale* and the Dystopian Tradition," *Canadian Literature* (Spring 1987): 9-16.

8. Frank Davey, "Alternate Stories: The Short Fiction of Audry Thomas and Margaret Atwood," *Canadian Literature* (Summer 1986): 5-14.

9. Rosemary Sullivan, "*Surfacing* and *Deliverance*," *Canadian Literature* (Winter 1976): 14-15. Catherine Sheldrick Ross, "Atwood's *Surfacing*," *Canadian Literature* (Spring 1980): 14. Both authors use Mircea Eliade's Shamanism to explain the mystical experience of the female protagonist.

10. John L. McKenzie, *Directory of the Bible* (London: Chapman, 1982f), pp. 310-11.

11. Atwood, *The Handmaid's Tale*, p. 33.

12. Atwood, *The Handmaid's Tale*, p. 230. My thanks are due to Professor Alistair Hunter, who kindly pointed out that the song "There is a Balm in Gilead" is a negro spiritual and can be found in the following sources: ed. H. Dann, *Spiritual for Choral Use*, 58 (1924); ed. R. N. Delt, *Religious Folk Songs of the Negro* (Hampton, Virginia: Normal & Agricultural Institute, 1927).

13. Jeremiah 8:22.

14. Robert P. Carroll, *Jeremiah: A Commentary* (Philadelphia: The Westminster Press, 1986), p. 237.

15. See Carroll, p. 237.

16. Julia Kristeva, *Desire in Language: A Semiotic Approach to Literature and Art* (New York: Columbia University Press, 1980), p. 55.

17. On household idols see: Gerhard von Rad, pp. 308-9.

18. G. von Rad believes that the episode preserves the traces of the possible legal situation involving a contract, p. 310. My comment on the fragment paraphrases the editor's footnote to Genesis 31:19 in: *Biblia Tysiaclecia*, ed. A. Jankowski, L. Stachowiak, K. Romaniuk (Poznán: Warszawa Pallottinum, 1990), p. 50.

19. Gerhard von Rad, *Genesis*, p. 314.

20. Atwood, *The Handmaid's Tale*, p. 166.

21. According to G. von Rad, the Yahwist sees the woman as more vulnerable to allurements of magic, astrology etc., p. 90, or "The woman as a negative figure of contrast was a favourite dramatic device," p. 208.

22. von Rad, p. 312.

23. von Rad, p. 307

24. Translation from: Dwight Roger Daniels, *Hosea and Salvation History* (Hamburg: Dissertation der Universität Hamburg, 1987), Hosea 12:3.

25. Daniels, pp. 79-80.

26. See Daniels's comment on the conclusions of W. Rudolf and H. W. Wolff in: Daniels, pp. 80-1.

27. Daniels, p. 99-100.

28. Richard Grunberger, *Historia spoleczna Trzeciej Rzeszy (A Social History of the Third Reich)* tr. Witold Kalinowski (Warszawa: PIW, 1987) pp. 85-89. Lebensborn was Himmler's foundation of homes where racially pure women underwent medical tests and were "served," that is, inseminated by men, also selected on the grounds of racial purity. The nurses were recruited from Nazi doctrinaires, so called brown sisters. "True German Women" were supposed to spurn the use of anaesthetics during childbirth. Lebensborn gained many followers due to slogans like: "Every woman should give a baby to the Führer". At the end of the war Himmler conceived the idea of patriarchal, polygamous families clustered around the distinguished veterans. The aim was to boost the birth-rate and ensure cohesiveness in the society where the sex balance had been seriously shaken by the ravages of war.

29. Atwood, *The Handmaid's Tale*, p. 18.

30. Dorothea Forstner OSB, *Swiat symboliki chrzesoijanskiej (Die Welt der christlichen Symbole 5. verbesserte und ergänzte Auflage)* tr. W. Zakrzewska, P. Pachciarek, R. Turzynski (Warszawa: Pax, 1990), pp. 117-20.

31. Robert Detweiler, *Breaking the Fall: Religious Readings of Contemporary Fiction* (London: Macmillan Press, 1989), p. 49.

32. James Luther Mays, *Hosea: A Commentary* (Philadelphia: Westminster Press, 1986), p. 133.

33. Translation from Daniels, p. 90.

34. Mays, p. 134.

35. Hosea 13:15.

36. Daniels, p. 100-1.

37. Jeremiah 4:23.

38. Mays, p. 101.

39. Lorraine M. York, "The Habits of Language. Uniformity Transgression and Margaret Atwood," *Canadian Literature* (Autumn 1990): 6-19.

40. Martin Noth, *Numbers: A Commentary*. tr. James D. Martin (London: SCM Press, 1980), pp. 235-9.

41. Atwood, *The Handmaid's Tale*, p. 122.

42. Atwood, *The Handmaid's Tale*, p. 171.

43. Atwood, *The Handmaid's Tale*, p. 172.

44. Atwood, *The Handmaid's Tale*, p. 128.

45. Walter Eichrodt, *Theology of the Old Testament*, vol. 2., tr. J. A. Baker. (Philadelphia: Westminster Press, 1986), pp. 458-61.

46. Obadiah 19.

47. Mays, *Amos: A Commentary* (Philadelphia: Westminster Press, 1986), p. 36.

48. Micah 7:14.

49. Eichrodt, *Theology of the Old Testament*, p. 459.

50. Zechariah 10:10.

51. Gershom Scholem, *The Messianic Idea in Judaism* (New York: Schocken Books 1988), pp. 4-13.

52. Scholem, *The Messianic Idea in Judaism*, p. 10.

53. Atwood, *The Handmaid's Tale*, p. 225.

54. Mays, *Amos,* p. 150.

55. Mays, *Hosea,* p. 134.

56. Atwood, *The Handmaid's Tale,* pp. 176-7.

57. Jeremiah 7:4.

58. Eichrodt, pp. 473, 477.

59. Amos 9:13.

60. Eichrodt, vol. 2, pp. 479- 481.

61. Michael Edwards, "Story: Towards a Christian Theory of Narrative" in ed., David Jasper, *Images of Belief in Literature*(London: Macmillan, 1984), pp. 179-190.

62. Mieke Bal, "Dealing with Women: Daughters in the Book of Judges" in ed., Regina Schwartz *The Book and the Text: The Bible and Literary Theory* (Cambridge Mass: Blackwell, 1990), pp. 16-38.

63. Bal, "Dealing with Women," p. 21.

64. On the question of name and narrative power see Bal, "Dealing with Women," pp. 18, 19.

65. Atwood, *The Handmaid's Tale,* p. 240.

66. Gloria Neufeld Redekop, "Let the Women Learn: I Timothy 2:8-15 Reconsidered," *Studies in Religion/Sciences Religieuses* 19/2 (1990): 235-45.

67. Redekop, "Let the Women Learn": 235.

68. Redekop, "Let the Women Learn": p. 236.

69. Atwood, *The Handmaid's Tale,* p. 233. Gloria Neufeld Redekop renders I Timothy 8:11 as: Let a woman learn, in /an atmosphere of/ peace, harmony and reverence with all submission, p. 240.

70. Redekop, pp. 241-2.

AUSTRALIA 2000

Christ, Ned Kelly, and Religious Culture

John Strugnell

The visitor to Old Melbourne Gaol will find a cell towards the rear of this gloomy building in which is preserved one of the suits of armor worn by the Australian outlaw and bushranger Ned Kelly, although ironically the metal plates were not enough to protect Kelly from the full force of the law. In 1880 he was captured after being shot in the legs in an encounter with police at Glenrowan, Victoria, proving that this hero of Australian folklore had legs of flesh if not feet of clay. One would hesitate to suggest that Kelly's armor invites the devotion inspired by the shroud of Turin, but Kelly's sister did exhibit his personal possessions after his death, and Kelly is remembered in Australia, not for his criminal activities but for his independence and his resistance to law and order.

Kelly is not the first person in history whose execution at the hands of the authorities forms the basis for later idolization. Indeed, in Robert Drewe's recent novel *Our Sunshine*, Kelly has all the right credentials for an Australian Messiah.[1] He is constantly aware that he travels a lonely, difficult and dangerous road. He knows that his gang depends on his leadership. He is betrayed by someone close to him. Ordinary people are well disposed toward him, but the authorities track him down, wound and then execute him. At one point in the novel Kelly remembers how his father, a shadowy figure, called him "Sunshine." Now, Drewe's title implies, Kelly is *"our* Sunshine." However, there is no suggestion here that Kelly can perform the Messianic trick of changing our lives. He is merely a reflection of what we already are. Indeed Kelly illustrates that peculiarly Australian cultural mix, the ordinary man, asserting his value as a human being, who is also the "tall poppy" waiting to be cut down by those who are suspicious of his individuality. The Australian concern for underdogs is paradoxically linked to the Australian demand for conformity. As Donald Horne says in *The Lucky Country*, "Australians like people to be ordinary."[2]

235

Drewe's Kelly likes to remind us that he and the rest of the gang are a bunch of Catholic boys. While the Anglican church was the denomination that represented the British establishment, the Catholic church provided marginalized Irish like the Kellys with a sense of identity, doubly important in a new continent which, as we shall see, challenged the identities of all the European settlers. The Irish, as Edmund Campion points out in *Australian Catholics*, made a major contribution to the idea that Australia was something other than an extension of Britain. Campion refers to Cardinal Moran's response to Empire Day.

> Asked his opinion of Empire Day in 1908, Cardinal Moran replied, "I quite agree that every banner should be unfurled on that day—but let it be the Australian banner." Moran went on to stress the need to promote Australian interests and develop Australian resources. So Empire Day, as such, was not celebrated in Catholic schools.[3]

The Irish after-dinner toast was, "The land, boys, we live in"(59)!

In Drewe's *Our Sunshine*, a crucifix hangs on the wall of his mother's house. It would be possible to view this crucified figure as another of society's victims but, for Kelly, the Christ figure is as much a symbol of the law that condemns him as Queen Victoria herself. Thinking of the Queen's portrait, he imagines the Queen "looking down her nose at them, those puffy little cod eyes following them around the tiny room like Jesus' moist spaniel ones did from the wall above Mother's bed."[4] In the history of modern Australia, in a state established in the first place as a British convict settlement, the church clearly represents law and the requirement to conform to accepted practices, and the Catholic church provides the most obvious example among the churches of a system designed to control the lives of its members. This can be seen in the strong reaction against Catholic institutions which we find in television series like *Brides of Christ*, in plays like Peter Kenna's *A Hard God*, and in novels like Thomas Keneally's *Three Cheers for the Paraclete*.[5]

In Keneally's novel this reaction against the law of the church is seen in the doubts and misgivings of the central character, the Catholic priest Father Maitland, particularly in his feelings that "certainty's only a front-end of a beast whose backside is bigotry"(123). Maitland is ill at ease with the legal certainties of his fellow priests. "Their legalism transformed them momentarily into ciphers"(110), he feels. In any of the discussions that take place between Maitland and his fellow priests, Maitland himself appears more concerned with present survival than with heavenly destiny. Other priests like to bait him about this. "You're the humanist of the group"(111), one of them says to him when a controversial topic is raised.

However unorthodox Maitland may seem to his fellow clergy, humanism is, in many respects, the Australian religion. Donald Horne's comment on Australian life in the sixties remains largely true for the nineties: "Civilization in Australia is now largely secular . . . . Belief in the dignity of man, in the human potential of human life is almost universal. The official beliefs that fit this are retained"(53).

From the beginning of white settlement, survival was the order of the day for the convict in the penal settlement or the free settler battling it out in the bush. Reliance on the human resources of one's fellow creatures was more important than reliance on the spiritual resources offered by the Creator. The struggle for survival gave rise, as everyone acquainted with Australian mythology knows, to that peculiar form of male bonding known as "mateship." While it would be foolish to suggest that Australian culture could be defined by such a simple term, especially since it leaves out the role of the pioneer women, nevertheless Australian visions of humanity's future at the time of the federation of the states were secular rather than religious. In the debates leading up to federation, from 1891 onwards, religion was seen as potentially divisive and dangerous.[6] This secular outlook was essentially an egalitarian one and, as part of the attempt to define the character of the new nation, Australia was presented as a paradise for the workers, not for the saved. There are no Puritan Compacts for Australian shores. The Australian historian Manning Clark included in his collection of Australian historical documents a 1901 extract that celebrated a new nation "free of most of the superstitions, traditions, class distinctions, and sanctified fables and fallacies of the older nations."[7] The future was in the hands of the people who, according to *The Worker*, "were practically of one class." The nation's destiny was a truly democratic nation.

In such new world democracies as the Australian, the earliest religious institutions are inevitably imported from the old country and, as we have already noted, symbolize law and order in the new land. The first thing that strikes the modern visitor to the old convict settlement of Port Arthur, in Tasmania, is the stone Anglican church among the trees. Though only the outer walls now remain, as one looks at its traditional form one can for a moment imagine oneself back in the heart of England.

It would be surprising if the churches had not, at some stage, realized that the Australian landscape was not that of rural England. As an example of the church's acceptance that Australia was a different place, Ian Breward notes the publication in the nineteen-eighties of Bruce Peward's *Australian Psalms* and *Australian Prayers*.(212) A little earlier, in 1978, the Anglican Church in Australia adventurously brought out *An Australian Prayer Book*. However, despite the green and gold cover and the black and white pictures of wattles, bottlebrushes and silky oaks, the book remained essentially what it was, a product of other times, other places. It may be that Australian language, reflecting Australian attitudes, betrays too much skepticism of authority to be used as a liturgical language. This is certainly the opinion of the Queensland poet Bruce Dawe. Like Drewe's Ned Kelly, Dawe is a Catholic and, like Drewe's Kelly, Dawe is skeptical of authority. Dawe was well known for making comparisons in his verse between Hitler and a recent Queensland state premier. Dawe, at my request, once tried his hand at a eucharistic prayer, though he felt Australian speech was too ironic in tone to be easily adapted to eulogizing. In Dawe's prayer to be said over the bread and wine, Christ was not the one who obeyed the will of God but the one who "gave friendship a new dimension." It might be worth adding that a more uniquely Australian form of prayer than is to be found in the Anglican prayer book appears in *A Common Prayer*, written and illustrated by the Melbourne cartoonist Michael Leunig. His prayer in praise of birds contains these lines:

> Especially we praise their disregard for the human hierarchy and the ease with which they leave their droppings on the heads of commoners or kings regardless.[8]

The illustrations of plant life in the Anglican Prayer Book suggest a harmonious relationship between religion, humanity and nature, but Australian writers were quick to show their characters reacting against the alien nature of the continent. Henry Handel Richardson's Richard

Mahoney is, one would think, the most obvious example of this reaction. "Fresh from foreign travel," writes Richardson, "he felt doubly alien; . . . he could see less beauty than ever in [the country's] dun and arid landscape."[9] It is true that he has a number of reasons for his depression, but his feelings about the aridity of the landscape is widely echoed in Australian literature. The interior of the continent is a vast region of desert, rock and bush. Most Australians therefore live in the cities that cling to the continent's edge, and those, like Ned Kelly, who venture into the interior, are drawn into seeing it as a violent country. As the clergyman Gribble puts it in Douglas Stewart's play, *Ned Kelly*,

> Australia's the violent country, the earth itself
> Suffers, cries out in anger against the sunlight
> From the cracked lips of the plains; and with the land,
> With the snake that strikes from the dust,
> The people suffer and cry their anger and kill.
> . . . . I understand the Kellys.[10]

In his turn, Robert Drewe's Ned Kelly, dizzy from the glare of the sun, his eyes full of grit, watches with fascination as a wedge-tail eagle rips to pieces a dingo pup. The Kellys, both in Stewart's play and Drewe's novel, are trapped between the hostility of the land and the hostility of the law.

The seemingly alien quality of the Australian landscape, its sense of otherness as far as the white settlers were concerned, is brought out in a passage near the beginning of David Malouf's recent novel, *Babylon Revisited*, which deals with a north Queensland community's encounter with a white boy who has spent some time with a local Aboriginal tribe. The whites have no experience in dealing with their new environment.

> Out here the very ground under their feet was strange. It
> had never been ploughed. You had to learn all over again
> how to deal with weather; drenching downpours when in
> moments all the topsoil you had exposed went liquid and
> all the dry little creek-beds in the vicinity ran wild;
> cyclones that could wrench whole trees up by their roots
> and send a shed too lightly anchored sailing clear through
> the air with all its corrugated iron sheets collapsing
> inward and slicing and singing in the wind.[11]

Although the Lands Office in Brisbane has mapped the country and numbered its sections, the isolated community is conscious that this means nothing to the native inhabitants. The local myalls challenge the whites' assumptions that they possess the land. The myalls

> were forever encroaching on boundaries that could be insisted on by daylight—a good shotgun saw to that—but in the dark hours, when you no longer stood there as a living marker with all the glow of the white man's authority about you, reverted to being a creek-bed or ridge of granite like any other, and gave no indication that six hundred miles away, in the Lands Office in Brisbane, this bit of country had a name set against it on a numbered document, and a line drawn that was empowered with all the authority of the Law.(9)

There was no conception among the whites that "there might be doors here . . . into some lighter world"(11). Even for the more sensitive settlers in Malouf's novel "the openness . . . was a frightening thing"(110).

Looking for a more positive value in the Australian landscape, some Australian writers have used this emptiness to portray those who penetrate the interior of the continent—always male it should be emphasized—as modern desert fathers seeking a ritual purification not available in urban living. Malouf writes that the qualities of individuals are revealed "when the fabric of pageant and the illusion of noble sentiments had been ripped away"(180). Randolph Stow's missionary Heriot, in Stow's novel *To the Islands*,[12] and Patrick White's explorer Voss discover their human limitations in the desert.[13] Heriot cries out that he is being "torn apart" and, as Voss lies dying, he fears "some final torment of the spirit that he might not have the strength to endure." The Australian desert becomes an equivalent to the desert places set aside in the past for nurturing biblical prophets, and critical works, with titles like *From Deserts the Prophets Come*, have celebrated this "desert"experience as a significant theme in Australian writing.

The deserts appear lonely places to the white characters, but the Aboriginal people saw the deserts as crowded with life. This is a point made in a recent column of *The Australian* in which the writer Ted Snell reviews some exhibitions of Aboriginal art:

> White Australian images of the desert are often devoid of human beings . . . . When it is peopled it is usually by a

> solitary figure to enhance the loneliness . . . . Two
> exhibitions of art from the desert made by Aboriginal
> people, currently on show in Perth, highlight the
> difference between white Australian images of the desert
> and that of the indigenous inhabitants. They show a
> landscape that is full of life, crowded with incident and
> alive with the stories of the people.[14]

The Christian religion of redemption, brought by the Europeans, meant little to a people whose culture made them feel at one with their environment. They were only confused by catechisms like the one recorded in Drewe's *The Savage Crows*.[15] The Aboriginals in this instance have been called Neptune, Nelson and Bonaparte by the whites. "'What will God do to this world by and by, Neptune?' 'Burn it, Father Clark.' 'What did God make us for, Nelson?' 'His own purpose, Father Clark.' 'Who are in heaven, Bonaparte?' 'God, angels, good men and Jesus Christ, Father Clark.'"(12)

It is only comparatively recently that there has been any real attempt to understand the culture and, in particular, the spiritual viewpoint of the Aboriginal people. Violence against the Aboriginal people forms a sad chapter in Australian history. The only hope for those who survived lay, whites assumed, in removing all traces of Aboriginal culture.

> Aboriginal religion remained a closed book. Where there
> were traces of dialogue, the missionaries were adamant
> that their own understanding of Christianity should be
> accepted . . . . There were some, like William Ridley and
> Archbishop Polding, who preached and wrote about the
> equality of Aboriginal people before God, but such
> emphases struck no cultural or emotional chords . . . .
> Missionary and government policies shared paternalistic
> assumptions. One of the most tragic attempts at solving
> the "problem" was the 1844 Protection of Children Act in
> New South Wales, which authorized the removal of
> children from their parents in an attempt to socialize and
> civilize them—a policy which lasted until the 1960s.[16]

For the Aboriginal people, this world is not a "fallen" one. Life is a continual rediscovery of "that timeless moment known as the Dreaming."[17] This had inevitable implications for the way the land could be interpreted.

> Thus what to the early European settlers of the country
> was little more than a pristine landscape, was for the
> Aborigines a complex and luminous spiritual edifice
> reminiscent of an open-air cathedral. They were not
> living in a lonely and desolate place, but in an
> environment conducive to well being and happiness
> provided that the land be respected for the icon that it was.
> (25)

Although novels like *Remembering Babylon* and *Voss* show whites experiencing the Australian wilderness as equivalent to purgatory, this is not to say that the colonizers made no attempt to appreciate the new landscape, even if that appreciation only bore a limited resemblance to Aboriginal attitudes to the continent. The first generation of European writers and artists in the colonies, bringing with it tastes created by European Romanticism, struggled desperately to reshape the landscape so that it could become a source for human renewal. Even official representatives of the mainstream churches sometimes feel nature is the missing element in people's lives. At the beginning of *Three Cheers for the Paraclete*, Father Maitland suspects that his hearers "had never felt, as he did, that they and he had been separated from their origins in the earth"(2). Maitland is a fictional character, but we can find an even more pertinent example of the valuing of nature in the autobiography of E. H. Burgmann, Bishop of Goulburn. Burgmann's *The Education of an Australian*, is an interesting admission that Australian religion is less dependent on institutional sources.[18] Guidance for the individual will come not from law but from Australia's unique environment. Burgmann's autobiography is a celebration of the God of Nature. It is essential, Burgmann tells his readers, "to keep a close relation to the soil, to keep our roots well down in good earth"(55). Robert Drewe's Ned Kelly knows the value of the open air life. As he says to Lord Normanby, "How about a little man-to-man hard drinking in the ranges? Do you good to ride rough and shoot to eat, roll up in a blanket on the ground, wake up with frost silvering your muttonchops. You can have a hearty bushman's breakfast— a spit, a piss and a good look round"(76).

Kelly's speech to Lord Normanby brings together some diverse elements in Australian culture. Here is the defiance of the law, the companionship of people in adversity, linked to a feeling for the land itself.

One of the most vigorous presentations of the Kelly view of life occurs in Kylie Tennant's *The Battlers*, a novel about the unemployed who travel the roads during the Great Depression.[19] The central character is a man called Snow, self-reliant and contemptuous of authority, the typical "Aussie battler" as the novel's title suggests. Despite the toughness of his life and the harshness of the land he travels, he feels the real menace comes from the fences, wires and railway lines "cobwebbing the country"(198). With the menace of civilization in mind, Tennant goes so far as to give Snow a speech in which he compares himself and his mates to the Aboriginal inhabitants of the country, "the wandering tribes who cannot upset the balance of nature"(221).

Nevertheless, whatever images writers perceive out there in the desert places, Australians live in cities like Melbourne, Sydney, and Brisbane. Like Stephen Crisp, the central character in Robert Drewe's *The Savage Crows*, people find their pictures of life framed by corner delicatessens, liver-colored brick buildings and plastic detergent bottles floating in the harbor (7). Urban religion is only interested in outback visions as aids for urban survival. In Brisbane, which one might take as an example of the Australian city, we find the usual range of urban forms of religion: at one end of the spectrum, evangelical Christian Outreach Centers and, at the other, a New Age bookshop next to the fashionable eating places, and a new Anglican Spirituality Center in the western suburbs where one can expect talks on Matthew Fox and Aboriginal spirituality. These places indicate the range of religious products available to the consumer society. In the Australian cities the institutional churches are somewhat cautious about stressing spiritual matters and prefer to concentrate on social questions. In Brisbane the Catholic diocesan magazine fills its pages with articles on social justice; the new archbishop of the Anglican church comes from a background in welfare work, and his views on social matters are frequently headlined in the media. Commenting on the Australian religious scene, Patrick O'Farrell argues that Australians have never felt at ease with religion: "An Australian style of religion has never evolved nor been built by churches that bear all the worst marks of migrants . . . . The ordinary Australian dons a religious garb when necessary (for rites of passage) but with a sense of wearing someone else's suit . . ."[20] It may be that, for Australians, the true religious festivals are those that celebrate themselves (Anzac Day) or their sporting achievements (Melbourne Cup day) and that holding the Olympic Games in Sydney in the year 2000 will supply a sufficient glimpse of heaven.

The Australian continent, through its location on the globe and through its original inhabitants, has challenged Western perspectives, particularly religious perspectives. However, Australian society has been exposed to further influences. Australia is also close to Asia, and its population includes a large number of Asians. Indeed, in the future, Australia may well possess a Eurasian society. In referring to Asia, I am not now thinking of the Australian prime minister's recent comments on the Australian flag nor of his comments on the need for Australia to trade with Asia rather than Europe. I am thinking of the increasing number of novels like Christopher Koch's *The Year of Living Dangerously*, in which Australian writers have turned their attention to Asia.

One of the most significant novels in this respect is Randolph Stow's *Tourmaline*, set in Stow's home state of Western Australia.[21] Tourmaline is a rundown mining town out in the desert. Its inhabitants cannot remember when they last had rain. A travelling water-diviner named Michael offers to do something about the water shortage, but all he succeeds in discovering is gold, which involves the community in a considerable amount of hard work. This gold-mining operation is taken over by Kestrel, who owns the local pub and he brings in tools and machines to do the job properly.

Part way through the novel the reader might be tempted to see Michael as a spiritual force in the community and Kestrel as a material one, but it is clear in the eyes of the narrator that these men are two of a kind. They like to lay down the law, they like to dominate and they like to reshape things to suit themselves. The narrator I mention is a shadowy figure, himself referred to as the Law, though he has nothing in common with the law with which Ned Kelly had to contend. This narrator draws our attention to another local character, Tom Spring (whose name only too obviously indicates his significance). Tom Spring's philosophy provides a way of accepting the world as it is. From the narrator's viewpoint, Spring's philosophy provides a better foundation on which to base the law. From Spring's conversation, as recorded by the narrator, it does not take long for the reader to discover that Tom Spring is a Taoist philosopher in disguise. Indeed, if there are any doubts, we can direct our attention to Stow's poem, "The Testament of Tourmaline," which contains such statements as, "In the love of the land, I worship the manifest Tao."[22] This Taoist reflection reveals that men like Kestrel and Michael possess a typical Western attitude: they impose their values on the world without regard for what is actually there.

This remains the problem for Western religion in Australia. Traditionally, religion has been maintained in Australian society to preserve group identity. However, the actual experience of living on the continent, at least as far as some Australian writers are concerned, raises major questions about the forms Australian religion may take in the next century. I do not mean the image of Christ and the image of Ned Kelly will need to merge, but we might expect Australian religion in the future, again if we use the writers as evidence, to be related more closely to the experiences of the Australian community and to the experience of the continent itself. The delight that can be taken in the resistance and vitality to be found in ordinary people, accepting life for what it is, is demonstrated in two recent Australian novels that have received wide attention, Peter Carey's *The Tax Inspector* and Tim Winton's *Cloudstreet*. Winton's chief characters "are lighting up the morning like a dream . . . . It's a sight to behold. It warms the living and stirs the dead"(423).

Ned Kelly, as Robert Drewe pictures him, reflects two Australian reactions to life. Both are likely to survive the year 2000. On the one hand, life makes us feel that everything depends on us. We can expect no help from outside. It is often a case of us against the law. "Regina versus Us"(155), is how Kelly puts it. On the other hand, at the end of Drewe's novel, as Kelly watches the storm coming down from the Woolshed Hills and the Broken River brimming from the storm, he says, "Everything was—is—on our side"(180). The world itself provides some kind of encouragement and support.

NOTES

1. Robert Drewe, *Our Sunshine* (Sydney: Picador, 1991).

2. Donald Horne, *The Lucky Country: Australia in the Sixties* (Ringwood, Vic: Penguin Books, 1964), p. 28.

3. Edmund Campion, *Australian Catholics* (Ringwood, Vic: Viking, 1987), p. 70

4. Drewes, *Our Sunshine*, p. 99. Henceforth, numbers in parentheses following quotations indicate pages in the respective texts in which the quotations are to be found.

5. Thomas Keneally, *Three Cheers for the Paraclete* (Ringwood, Vic.: Penguin, 1988).

6. See Ian Breward, *A History of the Australian Churches* (St. Leonards, NSW: Allen & Unwin, 1993), p. 98.

7. Ed., Manning Clark, *Sources of Australian History* (London: Oxford University Press, 1957), p. 467. The extract is from the Brisbane *Worker* (January 5, 1901).

8. Michael Leunig, *A Common Prayer* (North Blackburn, Vic: Collins Dove, 1992), n. p.

9. Henry Handel Richardson, *The Fortunes of Richard Mahoney* (London: Heinemann, 1930), p. 701.

10. Douglas Stewart, *Ned Kelly in Four Plays* (Sydney: Angus & Robertson, 1958), p. 141.

11. David Malouf, *Remembering Babylon* (Sydney: Random House, 1993), p. 11.

12. Randolph Stow, *To the Islands* (London: Macmillan, 1958), p. 129.

13. Patrick White, *Voss: A Novel* (London: Eyre & Spottiswoode, 1958), p. 416.

14. Ted Snell, "Art," *The Australian*, No. 9109 (December 3, 1993): 14.

15. Robert Drewe, *The Savage Crows* (Sydney: Picador, 1987), p. 12.

16. Breward, *A History of the Australian Churches*, p. 46.

17. James Cowan, *Mysteries of the Dream-Time: The Spiritual Life of Australian Aborigines* (Bridport, Dorset: Prism Press, 1989), p. 49.

18. E. H. Burgmann, *The Education of an Australian* (Sydney: Angus & Robertson, 1944).

19. Kyle Tennant, *The Battlers* (London: Macmillan, 1954).

20. Patrick O'Farrell, "The Cultural Ambivalence of Australian Religion," in ed. S. L. Goldberg & F. B. Smith, *Australian Cultural History* (Cambridge: Cambridge University Press, 1989), pp. 8-14.

21. Randolph Stow, *Tourmaline* (London: Macmillan, 1963).

22. Randolph Stow, *The Counterfeit Silence: Selected Poems of Randolph Stow* (Sydney: Angus & Robertson, 1969), p. 71.

23. Tim Winton, *Cloudstreet* (Ringwood, Vic: Penguin Books, 1992).

WHERE IS FEMINIST CRITICISM TAKING US IN OUR READING OF TRADITIONAL RELIGIOUS LITERATURE?

Helen Wilcox

As my title question indicates, this paper is an audacious, and no doubt therefore doomed, attempt to explore an enormous issue in a very limited space. I am perhaps also engaged in a fruitless struggle to push a theological camel through the eye of a critical needle. But I will persevere, nonetheless. In the tradition of little excursions into large matters, this paper will raise many more questions than the initial one taken as its title, and certainly more than it can hope to answer. But my plan is to express first some brief, general thoughts on feminist criticism and the difference it can make to our reading of literature; then I will consider a sentence from the Bible and, in greater detail, two seventeenth-century English devotional poems which would seem to stem from that text. The poems have been chosen from the period and kind of literature on which I do most of my research work, but I trust that the issues raised in the analysis of these religious lyrics—by George Herbert (1633) and "Eliza" (1652)—will be applicable in general to the relationship between feminist readings and devotional literature.

First, then, what is feminist literary criticism up to? It is important to point out immediately that there is really no such thing as "feminist criticism" in the singular, but a series of related feminist criticisms which use a variety of strategies and foci, from textual or historical to cultural or psychoanalytical, in the study of women and literature. The new priorities emerging from these studies have had (and continue to have) a significant impact in each of the three main fields tended by traditional criticism: author, text, and reader—the secular trinity of literary criticism.

Feminist critics, through determined and diligent critical archaeology, have first and foremost brought to the attention of the reading public enormous numbers of neglected texts by women authors from almost all periods of literary history. The consequences of these discoveries cannot be ignored. Not only do we hear new and exciting female voices in our literature, but we must also rewrite our literary histories to include "herstories," and learn to read in a different way the texts we already knew. For example, take the case of the early seventeenth-century English writer, Aemilia Lanyer, author of *Salve Deus Rex Judaeorum*, published in London in 1611. Here we have a fascinating text in its own right, written by a woman who previously only warranted a footnote in literary history as the possible inspiration for the "dark lady" of Shakespeare's sonnets. From being considered a "muse" or created image in a male-authored text, Lanyer has become recognized instead as a creator of images herself, and powerful ones at that; the nature and arguments of her texts make it essential that we now re-consider classic seventeenth-century male-authored works, including Jonson's "To Penshurst" and Milton's *Paradise Lost*.[1]

When it comes to already familiar texts such as these, feminist critics have been busy alerting us to the new investigations and interpretations which a gender-conscious criticism can evoke. What are the cultural and historical stereotypes of female roles, for example, upon which so many literary characters are (often unconsciously) modelled? What difference does it make to interpret Hamlet's problems from the point of view of Ophelia or, perhaps more controversially, of Gertrude his mother? How far can language itself, in its structures and metaphoric patterns, be said to be gendered? And to what extent are our traditions of "greatness" in literature—our hierarchies of styles or genres, for example—based upon implicit assumptions of the superiority of all that is deemed masculine? Questions like these can stimulate refreshing readings of texts by both men and women and make us newly sensitive to the underlying links between society, texts, and history.

The third partner in the literary trio of author, text, and reader is of particular interest to feminist critics. Much feminist critical work begins with a focus on the role of the reader, being acutely conscious of the often overlooked difference that it makes to read as a woman. Feminist criticism of all kinds consistently prioritizes the experience of individual readers, seeing criticism as a sort of autobiography, an account and analysis of the relationship between reader(s) and text(s). This radical attention to that which is both within and beyond the text is of particular significance for the interpretation of religious literature, in which the relativity of reading and being, of word and action, is especially acute.

In this brief sketch of the three-pronged activity of feminist literary criticisms, their closeness to the work of feminist theologians begins to be apparent. Following the same trinity of concerns, feminist theology has first brought to light the presence of female textual voices—such as the excluded narratives of Lilith in the Old Testament and Mary Magdalen in the New—and consequently has raised questions, as have feminist literary critics, concerning the original formation of the canon of approved or sacred texts. The re-interpretation of such texts, from Genesis onwards, and the attempt to construct and understand women's devotional responses to them, again run in parallel to the second and third strategies of feminist literary critics. Together, these new approaches in the world of literature and theology give rise to major implications for the reading of religious literature. Whose word is the Word? What sort of language do we employ when talking about or to God? How do written texts define our sense of the human relationship with God?

Let us look at a biblical sentence on the nature of the love of God, and two seventeenth-century English devotional poems addressed to and in response to that love, in order to consider more closely some of the questions raised by a feminist critical reading of traditional religious texts. The biblical statement comes from St. John's Gospel (15:13): "greater love hath no man than this, that a man lay down his life for his friends." There are interesting hints of complexity already in this apparently simple biblical vocabulary of the English Authorized Version (1611). The terms "love" and "friend" seem to co-exist easily in the sentence, as they do also in the language of the Song of Songs, but they can represent two quite different and often rival vocabularies, those of a sexual relationship and a Platonic friendship. "Love" and "friend" are, on the other hand, similar in both being ungendered terms in English, whereas "man" and "his" introduce a gender-specific awareness of the maleness of this love, and of Christ to whom the statement refers. A further complexity is contained in the notion of "laying down" a life, which is an emblem here of a great and active love, and yet suggests a passivity more often associated with the feminine. So we have all the ingredients in this sentence for the difficult tangle of language, gender, and emotions to be found in love poems written about, or to, God.

"Most love poetry is talking only to itself," we are reminded by a character in A.S. Byatt's recent novel, *Possession*.2 This may be particularly true of religious poetry, which talks to itself as a means of reflecting the unknown divine object of love, making an image of God in our own image, as it were. In most periods of literary history, and especially in the seventeenth century in England, the words and generic mode of the secular love lyric are found appropriate for giving form and expression to the inexpressible formlessness of God: the object of belief is both encountered, and created, through this worldly language of love. So it is that the complexities of love, friend, man, and laying down a life, implicit in the passage from St. John's Gospel, all resurface with a physical immediacy a devotional love lyric by George Herbert. It is the final poem of his sequence of over 150 lyrics in *The Temple* (1633) and is entitled "Love"(III). This is indeed a powerful and moving lyric, in its combination of a courtly host with the Eucharistic "host" and the earthly communion with an image of the heavenly banquet. It balances Christian generalization—the fact that Christ "bore the blame" for human "dust and sinne"—with personal intimacy, in the speaker's recognition of this divine generosity in the immediate personification of a "Love" which/who "takes" his "hand." It is a subtle mixture of dialogue and lyric, of vivid richness vying with the plainness of the closing line. But for all this, what exactly is the model used for this ordinary Christian's relationship with "Love"?

Herbert's poems operate for the most part with two distinctive metaphors for the speaker's bond with Christ: they are best "friends," recalling the language of St. John, or God is the "Lord" and the speaker is a child, as in the famously rebellious poem "The Collar." There are echoes of both these kinds of relationship in the dialogue of "Love"(III), but as it is also written in the tradition of love lyrics sung by a man to a woman, we must ask ourselves further about this love poem to the "man" who "lays down his life for his friend." This is a profoundly spiritual poem, but it is expressed in terms of physicality: contact, hesitation, and final consumption (containing within it the possibility of consummation). A gender-conscious reading would initially seem to suggest that the poem implies a homosexual encounter, since the speaker is consciously male throughout *The Temple*, and Christ is traditionally recognized as the specifically male expression and offspring of a patriarchal God. However, we should not stop there, since this reading is complicated by the heterosexuality of background texts such as the Song of Songs; and the love convention, whether homosexual or male/female, generally leads to the relative feminizing of one of the parties.

There is plenty of evidence here for the feminizing of Christ. He is described as "quick-ey'd," for example; in the love poetry of this period it was conventional for the male poet/lover to feel the powerful and sometimes piercingly destructive influence of the beloved's bright or dart-like eyes.[4] Christ is also welcoming, "sweet," "smiling," all of which were traditional female traits. Perhaps we should not be surprised at this womanly Christ; Milton, later in the same century, depicted Christ in *Paradise Lost* as the gentle, compassionate son who "lays down his life," a feminized hero in contrast to the aggressively masculine heroism of Satan. More recently, feminist theology has laid great stress on Christ's humanity rather than his specific gendering. Read from this perspective, the more masculine partner in Herbert's "Love"(III) would therefore seem to be the speaker, whose "slackness" signifies physical as well as spiritual impotence and whose withdrawal recalls the action of the male lover in the Song of Songs (5:6).

However, it is just as true to say that in devotional writing the speaker is often feminized, traditionally identified as the bride of Christ and reduced metonymically to a feminine soul. Though the poet here is male and the speaker is addressed as "he," the focus of the poem is indeed his more female "soul." This uncertain devotional being who draws back out of guilt displays many culturally engendered "feminine" traits, such as a crippling sense of unworthiness and "shame," the need to be invited to look up from the humble "dust," and an obligation to "serve." Viewed from this angle, the speaker's attitudes are gendered as female, while Christ, in contrast, remains the more masculine figure: taking the initiative, correcting (however gently), taking the speaker by the hand and finally commanding him to "sit" and "taste my meat."

In this complex web of possibilities, one over-riding conclusion seems possible: that devotional voices and relationships are ungendered. Or, is devotion at least genderless in the sense of rendering conventional gender distinctions irrelevant? Literature, particularly concerning love, and religious experience are alike in that both take us outside of ourselves, into a transcendental otherness, a kind of silence.[5] Is there perhaps a devotional silence which is outside or beyond gender?

Tempting though this idea may be, I am not sure that such a gender-free space is actually possible, even allowing for the fact that religious poetry could be said to use the language of gendered human love only in order to transform and transcend its imperfections. At the very least, male and female writers will be likely to inhabit that traditional love convention differently. After all, gender is a vital part of our materiality, and therefore will inevitably color even our attempts to transcend that materiality.

It would be appropriate at this point to look at the example of another seventeenth-century love lyric, this time one written by a woman. It is important to point out before we do so that this poem is not meant in any way as a rival to Herbert's lyric; the significance of feminist critical rediscoveries is much more profound than merely to offer an alternative gallery of the greats. Our vastly enlarged awareness of writing by women has undoubtedly called into question the formerly accepted, predominantly male, "canon" of great literary works; indeed, feminist criticism has contributed in a major way to the current recognition that any notion of "canonical" works must remain problematic. However, the greater presence of women's texts in literary studies and critical discussions is at its most stimulating when it leads to a re-ordering of our fundamental sense of how writing functions and what its conventions take for granted. In this case, the placing of a near-contemporary female-authored devotional poem alongside that of Herbert should enable a sharpening of our perception of the gendered elements in traditional religious literature, and of the role they play in the interaction of author, text and reader.

This second poem, then, comes from *Eliza's Babes: or The Virgins-Offering* (1652), a collection whose title ensured its author the relative anonymity of "Eliza" but clearly indicated her gender—a common practice (at once self-protective and defiant) when the act of writing, even of devotional verse, was considered unfeminine. The book's double title, offering the poems as the "babes" of a "virgin," fascinatingly combines motherhood and maidenly purity; presumably the maternity represents her writerly creativity and the virginity her spiritual state. But in her motherly chastity she obviously recalls the Virgin Mary, and if her poem is her "babe" then it is Christlike, the Logos given (male) poetic flesh. Thus in her own relationship to her text, this anonymous female writer is already undoing our hypothesis of a genderless state for the devotional writer; she claims the femininity of the act of writing and produces the text as her linguistic male other. But what indeed happens in her poem, "The Lover"? We should begin by observing the slight but significant difference between the titles of the two poems—"Love" and "The Lover"—and the shift of attitude implied in this change. Eliza personalizes her sense of "love" into a "lover," a less abstract and more defiantly sexual presence. Her "lovely Lord" is not only the "delight" of her "soule" but also a physical being who is "desir'd" by her and who alone is able to "gaine" her "heart." She is thus more specific than Herbert in visually depicting the person about whom she speaks; in "Love"(III) it is not so much the appearance of "Love," but rather his "sweetly questioning" voice, which dominates. Eliza's poem also addresses a more specific reader (or listener) than is the case with Herbert's poetic narrative. "The Lover" is evidently a conversation with someone else who is earthly and human, namely another woman who may ultimately "discover" (show forth or confess) the identity of her lover, too. *Eliza's Babes* as a whole, it is important to note, is dedicated "to her Sisters," whereas the only reader mentioned by Herbert—apart, that is, from God—is one whose "sweet youth" identifies him as male.[7] Taking her cue from the Song of Songs (5:9), Eliza begins the poem with an animated comparing of notes about the respective lovers of her "sister" and herself. The sentence from St. John's Gospel considered earlier would almost seem to be parodied here: greater love (in the sense of receiving it) hath no woman than this. The terms "friend" and "love[r]" from St. John appear to be set in opposition to one another at first (in line 2), but by the end of the poem they are merged; the "loved friend" who lays down his life to save her from "eternall pain" is everything to her. She will not allow the sister's lover any chance of rivalling her perfect lord, and the poem's firm closure on the word "end," asserting in ironic contrast a love that "will not end," establishes the eternal superiority of her "true, and constant friend."

This enthusiastic, even triumphant, celebration by a female speaker of a male friend and lover would be utterly startling if it were to be found in a secular context in the seventeenth century. Lady Mary Wroth, for example, was vilified a few years earlier for writing a sequence of love sonnets, *Pamphilia and Amphilanthus*, in which the expressively sighing lover was not the conventional male but a woman. The reversal of lovers' roles in Wroth's sonnets—thereby implying active desire on the part of the woman—and the stir that this caused, revealed the asymmetry of gender stereotypes in text and society. Wroth was firmly advised to abandon the writing of such "amorous toys" and to turn instead to "a volume of heavenly lays and holy love."[8] But devotional poetry itself could, ironically, be a form of sanctioned liberation for a woman writer; the depiction of "holy love" could create a "heavenly" space in which to explore radically earthly modes of thinking and feeling. Eliza found, we might suggest, in the depiction of devotional love in "The Lover" a language for the expression of female heterosexual desire.

Once again, however, things are not quite so clear cut. In the tradition of the Song of Songs, Eliza's lover is shown to be "lovely," but this loveliness of Christ, the "Prince of Peace," is a feminine beauty. He is likened in the third stanza to the "purest red and white," a phrase not only recalling the "white and ruddy" lover in the Song of Songs (5:10) but also traditionally associated with the red lips and white skin of poetry's pastoral shepherdess and other icons of natural female loveliness such as the red "Rose" and the white "Lilly" also invoked by Eliza. His "pleasant haire," which is described in stanza 4 as hanging "with seemly grace," may be punningly linked to the divine "grace" of the redeeming Christ but is at the same time an emblem of female attractiveness, and even of feminine temptation, in this period.[9] His eyes are typical of a Petrarchan mistress with their "arrows" which "pierce" the speaker's heart. There is no questioning the female voice of the poem or the collection of *Eliza's Babes* as a whole; so instead of the potentially male homosexual world of Herbert's "Love"(III), perhaps here we have a potentially lesbian love celebration. Is Christ envisaged here as the greatest of all Sisters?

This question returns us interestingly to the idea of love poems speaking to themselves, or addressing a kind of linguistic mirror, envisaging their God (in the case of religious literature) as a version of themselves. We might also extend this self-reflexive theory to include the human readers envisaged by the two poets—Herbert's "sweet youth" and Eliza's "sisters"—in each case intensifying the predominantly single (same-sex) gendered nature of the devotional writing. However, the question of exclusive femininity in "The Lover" also raises once again the possibility of the femininity of the devotional experience in general. After all, Herbert's "Love"(III), like Eliza's poem, gave us a strong impression of the likeness of the soul and Christ in feminine terms; the soul is humble, dependent, and passive, while Christ is gentle and sacrificial, asserting power only by negating it, gaining authority by surrendering his life. Is femininity, perhaps, the common ground in this "great(est) love"? There would certainly seem to be liturgical and biblical support for the idea of the believer, individually and collectively, as feminized; the soul and the church are frequently imaged as "bride," and the believer is de-masculinized as a "eunuch" for the sake of the kingdom of heaven.[10]

To stress the femininity of devotional experience and language is to identify the self in worship as "other," always taking on in relationship to God the position of woman with relation to man. More radically, to stress the mutual femininity of the worshipper and Christ is also perhaps to suggest the "otherness" of Christ in relation to God the father. Christ's act of "laying down his life," uncreating in order to re-create, is paralleled by the soul's prostration in devotion, abandoning the self in order to gain an eternal selfhood. Both these attitudes assert brokenness as a pre-requisite for wholeness, a paradox of Christianity found in the Eucharistic overtones of Herbert's "Love"(III). This cluster of ideas can crucially be linked to cultural and psychoanalytical theories of femininity as divided and multiple, and as present through absence or negation.[11] There is a clear overlap here between the fundamentals of Christian devotional attitudes based on the life of Christ, and feminist critical assumptions about female experience and the construction of femininity.

I should like to suggest that these ideas find useful and genuine expression in the theory of *ecriture feminine,* the much-discussed (and frequently misunderstood) model of writing and gender put forward by some French feminists. The essential point about this phenomenon, especially as established by Helene Cixous, is that *ecriture feminine* is not a term used only about the work of women writers. It encapsulates a kind of writing which emerges metaphorically from the nature of the female body—it overflows, it is expansive, it breaks down binary oppositions— but it can be written by authors who are physically of either sex. It is not, however, a genderless language, but uses gendered language and experience to break down difference.[12]

Perhaps, then, devotional writing is the ultimate *ecriture feminine*. Its origins, after all, lie in experiences with relation to God which are paralleled in traditionally constructed femininity: the enforced recognition of weakness, constant awareness of dependency, and a sense of otherness. In the case of devotional attitudes, these traits identify human nature rather than specify femaleness; the human soul of a male or female believer is always perceived as the imperfect "other" to God's divinity. In the binary mode of religious thinking, what is human (and not divine), earthly (and not heavenly) or mortal (and not eternal) may be identified with what in the gender system is female (and not male). But the experience and expression of devotion, though tied to the language of such oppositions, has as its aim the breaking down of the boundaries between earth and heaven, the subsuming of the individual in the whole, the merging of self and other. Thus the phenomenon of devotional writing (and devotional attitudes in general) has in its radical humility many of the features of *ecriture feminine*, using the expression of otherness in order to undermine that very category.

Herbert's lyric "Clasping of hands" exemplifies and explores the riddle of self and other which underlies religious devotion. This teasing but passionate poem, exploring the implications of two possessive personal pronouns, turns upon the closeness and yet the difference of "thine" and "mine." They form one of only two rhyming pairs used throughout the lyric, the other being "restore" and "more," a recurrent vocabulary of health, increase and redemption. "Thine" and "mine," on the other hand, recall the language of secular love poems, celebrating mutual possession and reflection, as in Donne's "The Good-morrow": "My face in thine eye, thine in mine appears."[14] Rhyme, however, though revelling in a harmony and reciprocity of sounds, also depends upon some element of distinction between them. The point of Herbert's use of this lovers' vocabulary is both to stress the reality of the distance between his existence and Christ's, "mine" and "thine," and also to invoke the power of Christ's love to minimize that distance, even to melt the rhyming pair into one word—or rather, one Word. This is a poem, then, written in the vocabulary of personal (and sexual) difference, the language of the secular love lyric with its unequal gender perspective; at the same time, it explores the boundaries of difference with a view to transgressing them or, ultimately, rendering them meaningless. Here we find a hint of a devotional expression which is not only beyond the "thine" and "mine" of particular gender—an idea raised earlier in connection with "Love"(III)—but also beyond the differences imposed by language itself: the last line implores Christ to "make no Thine and Mine!" This daring conclusion, imagining the end of individualism as well as the dissolution of linguistic systems, mirrors the fluidity, the challenge, and the transforming power epitomized by *ecriture feminine*. To parallel the femininity of spiritual experience and the radical implications of devotional writing with the comparable processes of *ecriture feminine* may well offer a way towards further understanding of the intersection of gender, literature, and religion.

These brief enquiries into feminist criticism and the reading of seventeenth-century English devotional poems should have shown one thing, if nothing else—that feminist criticisms will take us towards and into the new century with a healthily questioning attitude to writing and theology and their inter-relations. Feminist critical strategies can surprise—they can (of course!) annoy—but they will, importantly, take us by new routes to the central questions, such as those concerning our understanding of the nature of God and the limitations, and the possibilities, of human language. Feminist criticisms can alert us not only to the newly appreciated contribution of women writers and thinkers in the realm of religious experience; they can also highlight the significance of gender in our interpretation of, and responses to, written devotion. In this way, we as readers are helped, as Eliza put it, in the fullest sense to re-"discover, / Who is our friend, and who our Lover."

NOTES

1. Lanyer's small book contains a topographical poem of praise, "The Description of Cook-ham," which probably predates Jonson's "To Penshurst" as the earliest known English example of the genre known as the "country house poem"; her long poem on "The Passion of Christ" contains material, particularly in "Eve's Apologie," which raises the question of Adam and Eve's relative responsibility for the fall, thus challenging the treatment of this issue in the work of Milton and other seventeenth-century male writers.

2. A.S. Byatt, *Possession: A Romance* (London: Chatto and Windus, 1990), p. 290.

3. Ed. C. A. Patrides, *The English Poems of George Herbert* (London: Dent, 1974), p. 192.

4. Compare, for example, the description of Stella's eyes in Sir Philip Sidney's sonnet sequence, *Astrophil and Stella*, sonnet 42.

5. David Atkinson presented a paper at the Sixth Annual Conference of Literature and Theology in Glasgow, Scotland that discusses the parallels between religious experience and literature in terms of their use of silence.

6. *Eliza's Babes* (London, 1652), pp. 24-5; also available in ed., Germaine Greer et al, *Kissing the Rod: An Anthology of 17th Century Women's Verse* (London: Virago, 1988), pp. 146-7.

7. See the opening of "The Church-porch" in Herbert, p. 33.

8. See ed., Josephine A. Roberts, *The Poems of Lady Mary Wroth* (Baton Rouge: Louisiana State University Press, 1983), p. 34; the words are those of Lord Denny.

9. Compare the description of Eve's hair in Milton's *Paradise Lost* Book IV lines 304-311, and the attention paid to Mary Magdelen's hair in sixteenth and seventeenth-century paintings of this prominent New Testament female.

10. See, for example, Jeremiah 2:32, Revelation 21:9, Matthew 19:12.

11. In social and historical terms, it is argued that women are denied a single identity but are always perceived as dependent and multiple (a man's daughter, a man's wife, the children's mother, a homemaker as well as worker, etc.) In psychoanalytical terms, woman is seen as "a sex that is not one" (in Luce Irigaray's phrase), defined by multiplicity, decenteredness, lack or otherness. For an excellent summary of these views and their embodiment in literary texts, see Patricia Parker, "Coming Second: Woman's Place," in *Literary Fat Ladies: Rhetoric, Gender, Property* (London: Methuen, 1987), pp. 178-233; see also ed. Elaine Marks and Isabelle de Courtivron, *New French Feminisms: An Anthology* (Hemel Hempstead: Harvester Press, 1981), pp. 57-113.

12. For useful explorations of Cixous' ideas concerning *ecriture feminine*, see ed. Susan Sellers, *Writing Differences: Readings from the Seminar of Helene Cixous* (Milton Keynes: Open University Press, 1988) and ed. Helen Wilcox et al., *The Body and the Text: Helene Cixous, Reading and Teaching* (Hemel Hempstead: Harvester Press, 1990).

13. Herbert, pp. 164-5.

14. Ed. Theodore Redpath, *The Songs and Sonets of John Donne* (2nd edition, London: Methuen, 1983), p. 227.

FROM MYTH TO PLOT
or

The Gospels as Historical Novels

Douglas A. Templeton

SUMMARY

1. As in all the humanities (or divinities), the study of the New Testament involves three disciplines: philosophy, history, and literature.

2. The New Testament overlaps, no, co-incides with literature, rather than with philosophy or history.

3. The Gospels are historical novels, not histories. In so far as they are *historical* novels, they do permit the historian to do history. In so far as they are historical *novels*, they do not permit the historian to do the job very well: "You can use a table-cloth as a bath-towel, but it won't do the job very well, because that is not what it is designed for."[1] The Gospels contain also a more or less significant "scifi" component.

4. The Gospels however are more Barbara Cartland than Proust. They are, if highly sophisticated,[2] folk-literature. Can one speak of the "folk-novel"?

5. As historical novels they are based on history. As novels they are fiction.

6. Fiction makes truth-claims. To deny this is not only to dismiss Aristotle's claim that "poetry is more philosophical than history"[3] and *Hamlet* and *Oedipus*, but also the author of the Good Samaritan and the Prodigal Daughter (as Feminists would need to call it).

7. But these truth-claims are made in the medium of story and image, which, in Spinoza's view, are the lowest form of knowledge or "confused cognition." I think Spinoza is too dismissive here, for the analysis of ambition, for example, is, to my mind, as well done by the "ten thousand" words of *Macbeth* as by the five-word definition Spinoza gives it (*ambitio est immodica gloriae Cupiditas*).[4]

8. In order to state *what* truth-claims are being made, you can either turn, as Strauss and Bultmann did, to philosophy, or, as more daily are doing, to literary criticism.

9. But why was *that* fiction *then* the one that *that* author wanted *there*? This question I do not discuss.

10. The mind or imagination of the New Testament novelists is, in my submission, best approached by Austin Farrer, who is himself asymptotically approached by John Ashton and Burton Mack.

11. Mark, operating rather under the constraints of literature than of history, writes his *Waverley*, but earlier. Unlike Scott, he get his hero right. Unlike Scott, he gets his history wrong.

12. God or Nature belongs here, as here belongs to God or Nature: *Hilaritas excessum habere nequit* (Spinoza IV, XLII).

"In general," says Aristotle (1461b 9ff.), "the impossible must be justified by reference to artistic requirements." This stuff, the Gospels, is impossible, impossible in Aristotle's sense and in many others. How can grown men deal with it? Fairy tales, merely.

But there is a world, or at least what Joyce calls a "chaosmos." Or there is a *deus sive natura*, what Spinoza would call a "substance" (*Ethica* I, *def*. III: *substantia*). There is a substance, with the attributes of thought and extension. And there are finite modes of infinite substance.

In this area of inquiry, it may be suggested that three disciplines are mainly involved: philosophy, history, and literature, with literary criticism parasitic on the latter. History has *had* a run for its money, from Hermann Samuel Reimarus to Ed Parrish Sanders, and literature is *having* a run for its money.

If we need philosophy, there is the question of *what* philosophy we need. But, leaving out Rudolf Bultmann's "right philosophy"[5] and "right" philosopher, Martin Heidegger, let us take Spinoza. Let us suppose, or let Spinoza prove, *more geometrico*, that we and Jesus of Nazareth are finite modes of infinite substance, extended for a while and thinking a little. And free a little, if also in some servitude to the bestialities of ourselves and our governments. If Spinoza is right to say that "a free man thinks of nothing less than of death" (*Ethica* IV, *prop*. LXVII), it follows, as the day the night, or as the sum of the square on the hypotenuse to the sum of the squares on the other two sides, that the wise man does not think about death, but only of the death of his passions and his politicians. "Hilarity" (*hilaritas*) names the game, the game of *homo ludens* or *animal risibilis* (*Ethica* II, *prop*. XL, *schol*. I), the sporting, or laughing animal.

History has had its day and its say and found only little bits of Jesus and those little bits of not much interest.[6] And it has shown that in interpreting the New Testament, "one is in the same position as a person who tries to understand the histories of Denmark and Scotland by reading *Hamlet* and *Macbeth*."[7] But not only, nevertheless, does a remarkable character obtrude sufficiently for the historian to mark it, but also an idea of incarnation, that while it appears only once *expressis verbis* (*verbum caro*, John 1:14) appears there with such force and clarity as to shed light on many like instances, which it assembles and collects, as a Secretary assembles a Senate, or a Stentor an army of Argives. For God is extended in his modes. God is extended in his christs: "who, being in the form of God, thought it not robbery to become equal with God." This famous, Philippian song (2:5-11) is one such like instance. And another is like it, if the reader may infer what Paul must imply, when, in declaring that God has "anointed" (the active verb: *kai chrisas hemas theos*, 2 Cor. 1:21), he is declaring his reader "anointed" (the passive adjective, i.e., christ/*christos*).

History has had its day and such little bits of history as there are come wrapped in the integument, trapped in the net of myth, through the "interstitial vacuities"[8] of which all little fish fall. And the Jesus of history slips through this net, texture, text, this net that is cast for the redeeming fish, the brontoichthyan form, the ΙΞΘΥΣ (ichthus) that demands an "ichtheology,"[9] that storied acrostic (I(esous) Ch(ristos) Th(eou) U(ios) S(oter), "Jesus Christ, Son of God, Savior"), not beast of abyss (or 666), but man from the height (or 888, so "Iesous" by gematria).

And why should we not go for the "brontoichthyan form," the "thunder-fish"? Why should we not go, not for the historical, but for the mythical Jesus? And, if "myth" is plot and plot is story and story is literature, why should we not go for the literary Jesus, the Jesus of narrative fiction? Art can catch fish that escape the net of history.

Oh, yes, you can do history with this stuff, if you want. As Ashton vulgarly puts it in *Understanding the Fourth Gospel*, "You can use a

table-cloth as a bath-towel, but it won't do the job very well, because that
is not what it is designed for" (430). Oh, yes, you can do history all right, if
you are really convinced that a table-cloth is as good as a bath-towel. But
Jesus of Nazareth is more successfully concealed than revealed by the New
Testament myth, by the plot of the New Testament story. But what do we
have on our hands, when we do not have history on our hands? We have
literature. Folk-literature for the most part, but literature all the same.
The New Testament is a table-cloth on which a literary banquet is spread,
but not a bath-towel with which the historian can dry himself.

We have fairy tales, fairy tales about feeding five thousand, fairy tales
about butcher meat in Corinth, or the Sunday joint of the Christian
housewife. But Paul's Sunday joint is something of a red herring, so it is
better to take Paul's trumpetology, the *tuba mirum spargens sonum*. For
Paul's butcher meat is, at the plain historical level, plain butcher meat, but
the meat comes wrapped in pagan and Christian story—there are tables of
Demeter and Asclepius, or tables of demons, on the one hand, and tables,
on the other, proleptic of the end of the story. But Paul's Christian story
surfaces more obviously with his trumpet. Even the most obviously, plainly
historical material, not only in the Gospels, but in the Epistles, in the New
Testament as a whole, occurs in the context of myth, of story, of story-
world and plot. Even where there are facts, the problem of fiction arises,
the problem of fiction *and its truth*.

But Ashton's term "fairy tales"—or rather my use of it, for Ashton,
more strictly, speaks of "the fairy-tale atmosphere of the resurrection
stories"—deserves an apology. Somewhat extravagantly, the phrase is
being used here to cover loosely all that in the New Testament is not
historical, an "all" that includes a scale, a gamut of writing, that runs from
Jesus saying soberly what he did not say in the Fourth Gospel to the
fantastic geology of Jerusalem New Town in the Book of Revelation. The
term, "literature," is wider and will do as a covering concept, that covers
also fairy tales, but not fairy tales only.

In the fifties and sixties, in New Testament study, the word we
wanted was "myth" (and if it was not the word we wanted, it was the
word we got"!). What we want now is "plot" and Aristotle shows us the
way. The story of Jesus, Aristotle would say, and say perspicaciously, has
"a beginning, a middle and an end," followed by what, in Greek, he would

call a *peripeteia* ("peripety") and, in German, *das happy end*. Then to that story (the story of Jesus) add first the story of the early church, then Paul's correspondence about both stories and add finally the chrysoprase, jacinth, and jasper "scifi" of St. John the Divine; and set those three stories within an overarching story, or story-world, that runs from Eden to the Heavenly City, that begins in a garden susceptible to thistles and ends in a garden, where the only thistle is the spiritual body of John Knox.

This literature can be used for historical purposes, can be used to answer the question, what actually happened? But to do this is to use it for a purpose for which it was not written. And literature anyway (Aristotle again, 1451b 5) is "more philosophical than history," *in part*, at least, because it offers the reader possibilities: the story of Jesus is the reader's autobiography. But if the story is to be used for the purpose for which it *was* written, to provide, namely, a folk-novel for folk, a number, not a finite, but an indeterminate number of questions arises.

But before touching on one or two of these, something may be said about John. For nobody nowadays needs to be persuaded that what Jesus said in John is what Jesus did not say. And that what Jesus did, he did not. The omniscience of Jesus slides into and is swallowed up (much as death by victory) by the omniscience of the author. Jesus of Nazareth is omniscient in the Fourth Gospel, because the author of the Gospel is an omniscient author. Nor does the picture substantially alter when the necessary qualifications are made, such as that, for example, Jesus really, historically, was put under arrest. For that fact, too, is encapsulated within John's fiction, that makes the arrestors the "arrestees," the biters bit ("they went backward, and fell to the ground" (18:6). The *Grundkonzeption*, moreover, the central motif of the work, is the notion of Jesus as the alien from outer space,[10] a space into which the reader too is shoe-horned, or transposed, or made to rise: in the café, at the corner of the universe, the father sends the son on a mission to go, with fortitude, to earth, to get the synagogue off the back of the infant church in Ephesus (to assume this provenance for the work). What is *not* an assumption, but plainly demonstrable, is that, while *formally* the Gospel of John is the history, or "history," of Jesus, it is, as far as *content* is concerned, a history, or "history" of the church life of its author.[11] Put all this together and what we have is as near as dammit (the *mot juste*, perhaps) a historical novel in a fantastic framework of pre-, or proto-gothic, or gothicizing "scifi," though the epithet, "astringent," would be juster, as John's apocalyptic crotchets are "reduced" (in comparison, or contrast, with the Book of Revelation). The son is sent, but little is said on the geology, or uranology, of where he starts from. On jasper and jacinth, chrysoprase and amethyst, we have aposiopesis.

What is the logic of evangelical propositions? What is the logic of *these* evangelical propositions? John's propositions are literary propositions and relate to reality as fiction does, relate to what is the case and to what the case could be, relate to reality "more philosophically than history."

If we are going to have commerce with the New Testament, it is with literature, rather than either philosophy or history, with which we have to do. Nor need such an approach hinder anyone who wishes to use a table-cloth for his bath-towel, should the wish, the desiderating wish, be to fill in the back of a picture post-card with cautious assertions about the historical consumption of historical wine by the historical Jesus.[12] You *can* ask historical questions of the Gospels. It is more promising to ask literary ones. And the discipline that puts these questions is literary criticism.

For parasitic on the body of literature is literary criticism, which occupies the no-man's land between philosophy on the one hand and history on the other, a discipline that overlaps with both. With philosophy literary criticism overlaps in two ways, the one in tension with the other: first, literature is bad philosophy, but, second, literature provides the philosopher with accurate evidence, evidence which he can obtain more accurately nowhere else.

In the hierarchy of knowledge, according to Spinoza, the imaginative knowledge, that finds expression in literature, occupies the lowest rank, below both scientific (or rational) and intuitive knowledge. In the hierarchy of knowledge—imagination, reason, and intuition—imagination is the lowest form of animal. The New Testament (so Spinoza) is confused cognition (*confusa cognitio*).

Take Mark's voice at the baptism. A voice from the sky does not cohere with what we otherwise know of voices, unless we are bound to think of Winnie the Pooh at the end of a balloon. And why a dove, or dove-like descent? Mark does not tell us—though we may not be doing wrong to tell him that he is drawing an ornithological inference from a Hebrew participle in the feminine ("brooding over," "moving over": Gen.1:2), an inference to which Luke in his turn makes his own substantial contribution: the dove is "in bodily form" (Luke 3:22). It is true that (according to Spinoza) God's infinite thought is accessible to the finite thought of human beings. But Mark's story is a mess of anthropomorphism, jejune chronology, and spatial location. The father opens his mouth in the sky and speaks to his son on the ground. "We find," writes Hampshire on Spinoza,[13] "that (the old Jewish prophets) . . . were ignorant men brilliantly gifted to instill faith and obedience in an ignorant society by myth and story." This is, I think, as true of Mark as of "the old Jewish prophets." They belong in one bag.

And yet, and yet . . . . For not only did Mark (to take only him) produce something that was more philosophical than history, but also something that was, or may be claimed to be, more philosophical than philosophy. For does not the literary imagination that produces "myth and story" produce better what the philosopher produces worse? Take Spinoza's definition of ambition: "Ambition," he says, "is the immoderate desire of glory or honor" (*Ethica* III, *def. XLIV: ambitio est immodica gloriae cupiditas*). But the question arises whether *Macbeth* does not define ambition as well as, or better than, Spinoza. For is not our idea of ambition clearer and distincter after five acts of *Macbeth* than after five words of Spinoza? Or is Spinoza speaking five words with his mind against Shakespeare's ten thousand in a tongue? Spinoza has ground a lens, Shakespeare painted a picture. What is clear is that Mark had read neither Heidegger nor Spinoza. Mark "with his many miracle stories shows the secret epiphany of the one who achieves his full glory at Easter."[14] Mark, telling stories within an overarching story, depicts the free and finite mode of infinite substance, which cannot be grasped by those who are in servitude to their passions, for Mark, or the kingdom of God, is a mystery to outsiders (Kermode 1979). Secrecy has here a genesis. Mark produces in his Gospel a secret epiphany, not in the philosophical, but in the literary mode, a mode (why not?) more philosophical than philosophy.

"Whatever is is in God," says Spinoza (*Ethica* I, XV: *quicquid est, inDeo est*). To be "in God," says Mark, is to be sitting *in* a nest and *under* a pigeon, if and only if the pigeon is broody. Which is to be preferred, the artist or the philosopher?

The problem is to begin where Strauss, in his *Leben*, leaves off. As he puts it (or Ms. Eliot), "The boundless store of truth and life which for eighteen centuries has been the aliment of humanity, seems irretrievably dissipated; the most sublime levelled with the dust, God divested of his grace, man of his dignity and the tie between heaven and earth broken."[15] The problem is to begin where Bultmann's negative program of *de-*mythologizing leaves off and to move forward, not into, or not straight into philosophy, but into the *Zwielicht*, chiaroscuro, or clear-obscurities of literary criticism.

It makes much more sense to say that these authors did what they did than to say that they knew what they were doing when they did it, though again it is probable that they were here much wiser than we often think them. John, certainly, has at least the rudiments of overt reflection and many of our more flat-footed fundamentalisms, what Northrop Frye might have called "imaginative illiteracy," they would all regard with a wild surmise. Folk-literature may be folk-literature, but folk are not all that dumb. Folk-literature can be little less Proustian than Proust. Farrer's *Mark* is no Boeotian pig, or, if Boeotian, then still no pig.

The Fourth Gospel can be compared with the historical novel, for instance *Waverley*: "There are mists too," thinks our hero, Waverley, as he looks back on Flora and Glennaquoich,[16] "in the mental as well as the natural horizon . . . and there are happy lights to stream in full glory upon those points which can profit by brilliant illumination." As the sun of John's imagination rises, the early-born Jesus is shadowed by the light of John's rosy-fingered pen. But, moreover, the Fourth Gospel can also be compared with "scifi," with, for instance, *A Hitch-Hiker's Guide to the Galaxy*.[17] Both of these comparisons say something, I believe, about the Fourth Gospel. But if the Fourth Gospel is really a work of genius, it is not likely that *Waverley* and the *Hitch-Hiker's Guide* will exhaust the possibilities of comparison and evaluation. For the Fourth Gospel is also a symbolist work, in which the writer spins a diaphanous web of such symbols as bread and water—and other prison fare devised by one of the more creative indwellers in "the prison-house of language." In a lapidary style "that is distinctive to the point of monotony" (Ashton, *Interpretation*

16), these symbols are also themes around which the writer revolves, in a retreating and returning dialectic: vine, wine, light and life: abide in these.

But apart from telling us that Judaism is a watery religion and not the real McKay, or Daniels, a drink for no real man; from telling us that Jesus is the best thing before sliced bread, who sheds light on God the gardener, as he grafts or prunes with a will, John does something even more important, something already adumbrated in the adjective of "historical novel" and in the name, "Jesus." For his book, or booklet, takes the form of a biography, even if that biography is constructed out of only loosely concatenated—and indeed *non*-biographical—scenes.

Since Ashton, Martyn, Strauss, and others, we have learned, it is true, to read the Fourth Gospel as a thinly disguised history of the church in Ephesus, with its insiders, outsiders and boundary Nicodemuses, the prudential visitors under the cover of the dark. But it is plain fact that the writer has disguised his history of the church as the history of Jesus, his history of Ephesus and Asia Minor as the history of Palestine. And John can do this, because there is a similarity between the history of his own time and the history of Jesus (*that* is at least *part* of what is meant by calling his work classical). Both Jesus and John's church had problems with the Jews. Why Jesus, why the historical Jesus was at odds with the authorities John's fiction does not tell us, but *that* he was he strongly implies. That skeletal plot of Jesus's life, of opposition and defeat, successful defeat (for the way up and the way down are one and the same), is a myth, is a plot that eternally returns, that must "ever anew" (*je und je*, Bultmann) be recapitulated in the life of human beings: *tua res, nostra res agitur*. The pattern of opposition, defeat, and victory is a myth, a pattern, a structure that recurs, eternally returns. John is "more philosophical than history." In this novel, in other words, two histories, two sociologies, two biographies, constitute a structural component.

To concede this much to the historian is to concede to him *only* so much. For by and large these writers are not operating under the constraints of history, but under the constraints of literature. Jesus is being measured not by historical, but by literary criteria. Anything, Mark tells us, Moses or Elijah could do, Jesus could do better. Anything, John tells us, Moses or Elijah could do, *I* could do better. Jesus, that is, is beyond measure, beyond *that* measure. He out-Moseses Moses and out-Elijahs

Elijah. Jesus in the Gospels is dressed in borrowed plumes. It is not John's text that is the problem, but his intertextuality. Jesus is a stick dipped into the stream of Old Testament thought and only seen as refracted.

Strauss and Bultmann have said it all. But our task is not to turn with them from their *muthos* (Bultmann) or *mythi* (Strauss) to philosophy, be it sub-Hegelian or super-Heideggerian and transposed; not to turn from the discomforts of myth to the rationality of philosophy, not to turn *from*, but to turn *to*, or *remain with* the enjoyment of literature. For "there can never be too much merriment" (*Ethica* IV, *prop*.XLII). The task is thus to assume uninhibitedly the critical vocabulary not of evidence, fact, eye-witness testimony, authority, and the like, but of imagery, metaphor, style, characterization, plot, narrative-world, and the like, spiced, if you must, with words like "foregrounding," "sub-text," and (but not too often) "hetero-," "homo-," "hyper-," or "hypo-diegetic analepsis."[18]

Not one but two responses are possible to the enjoyment of the text: 1) writing literary criticism, and 2) writing literature. For a movement of man that is not writing words about the Word is as little a movement as one that is not singing *Lieder*, hymns, or songs. There are movements and there are "stopments," the "rush of the sap in spring"[19] and sheer petrefaction. But *however* we write, we cannot write like them. For one thing, it has been done before. And for another, it cannot be done again. Take James Joyce and Nikos Kazantzakis: however hard they tried, what came out was not the *Odyssey*, but *Ulysses* or *The Odyssey: A Modern Sequel*. The best tribute we can pay to the New Testament is by writing something else, much as John did something else with the synoptic gospels. What John does with Jesus is what *Ulysses* does to the *Odyssey*.

The energy with which Strauss seeks to demolish the New Testament as history (with such cautious *caveats* as that phrase deserves) serves no purpose so well as to establish the New Testament as literature. History dispelled with Strauss's pitchfork returns as literature. But what is it to return as literature, to establish as literature? Strauss establishes, of course, that the astonishing brevity, lithic lapidarity (to be, for a moment, perhaps properly tautologous) of the evangelical style is dependent on literary models from the Old Testament. But what is the relation between style and truth? What is the truth of fiction? What is the truth of *this* fiction? Not what relation is borne by Dickens's London to London, but what relation is borne by the portrait of Jesus to Jesus?

In losing, or prescinding from, history we gain literature. But, in gaining literature, do we lose the truth? No, we gain *literary* truth. And what is literary truth? Take Mark. What is Mark's literary truth? Would it be right to say that Mark, the poet, makes the historical claim, "Jesus was like that," but supports that claim, not by, or, on the whole, history, but by story? But his stories are not there so much to support his claim, as to explain what his claim was, namely, that Jesus was like the Moses that we find in Exodus and the Elijah that we find in Kings.

Mark makes a claim, then, but does not provide us with the evidence that would allow us to make up our minds whether his claim is true. Intertextuality, as it is called, here raises its ugly head: the Jesus of popular fancy Mark creates on the model of the popular fancy that created Moses and Elijah. Jesus of Nazareth provides food for thought, for thousands, for nine thousand (for five and four are nine), and is anxious to relax some of the legal restrictions to which extended substance is prone where an Antipas or a Pilate extends his sway. And, as the ravens "forget their natural voracity"[20] and feed Elijah, so the angels forget their supernatural voracity and feed the Messiah in the wilderness, as he journeys through a new wilderness on a new exodus without the *goggusmos*, or grumbling, of the first. Texts here are redolent of texts. The imagery occurs and recurs in a hall of mirrors.

The critics agree that the historical novel begins with Scott, with *Waverley*. But need we agree with the critics? May we not, with pleasure and instruction, antedate the emergence of the genre to the Gospels, and antedate, in turn, that antedating to the Court Narrative of King David (2 Sam. 9-20, 1 Kings 1 ff.). For is Dan Jacobson, with his *Rape of Tamar* (1970), doing something so very different by writing a novel from the novel on the basis of which he writes it, or, advancing to the Gospels again, by writing *Her Story*, and not *His*?[21] Is there an analog between Waverley's backward look at heathery Glennaquoich and clarsach-clutching Flora and the backward look, the ideological retrospection, as Lukacs might call it, of Mark and the early Christians at the metaphysically laundered Jesus, in "raiment . . . shining, exceeding white as snow; so as no fuller on earth can white them" (Mark 9:3), the one who out-glowed at once both Moses and

Elijah? For "All that was common-place—all that belonged to the every-day world—was melted away and obliterated in those dreams of imagination, which only remembered with advantage the points of grace and dignity that distinguished" (Scott 226). That distinguished whom? "Flora from the generality of her sex"? That is Scott on Waverley. It might as well have been either Mark or John on Jesus. "What must the truth have been and be if that is how it looked to men who thought and wrote like that?" (Hodgson 1968: x).[22] Hodgson's question stands, but any answer to it, that in its remit seriously includes "thought and wrote like that," must transcend (must it not?) the bounds of historiography. Any answer must be more novel.

As the year 2000 approaches, it may be that the question of the presence and extent, the meaning and the truth, of the fiction in the New Testament will return and keep returning. That meaning, it may be, will lie not far either from Shelley's assertion, that he falls "upon the thorns of life and bleeds," or from Paul's ontologically vehement fiction[23] that he has been "crucified with Christ," as a letter-writer patently cannot be, for you cannot write letters with your hands spread out to a rebellious people, even if, at the same time, you cannot nail creativity down.

We may broadly agree with Strauss and Bultmann, with the *mythi* of the former and the latter's myth. We may broadly agree that it is legitimate to turn to philosophy for the rational expression of the content of the Gospels. But it is also legitimate to turn to literary criticism, to Kermode (for example) from outside theology and Farrer (for example) within it. The peculiar blend of history and fiction in the gospels makes it reasonable to turn away from the gospels to history, but also reasonable to stay with, to perdure with their peculiar blend of history and fiction and regard them as what we would nowadays call "historical novels," of the kind of Tamar and *Her Story*'s heroine, a heroine who does not appear in the gospels, but whose existence may reasonably be implied there. Particular stress here has been laid on the Moses-Elijah typology in Mark, and John may not be altogether dissimilar. But to take the gospels in this way, as narrative fiction, raises with some urgency the question of the truth of fiction, a matter on which R. W. Hepburn makes pertinent comments: To what extent, one wonders, is the "optative" a feature of Mark's amalgam? To what extent do the evangelical assertions, or quasi-assertions exhibit "the power of art both to modify our grasp of the real and even partly to *constitute* it?"[24] If we do not read, or watch, Shakespeare for nothing, it follows that it is not for nothing that we read the gospels.

Mark's hero is not *Waverley*, but a *Firmley*, who makes us firm. *Tua res, nostra res agitur*: the reader is in question here.[25]

NOTES

1. John Ashton, *The Interpretation of John* (Philadelphia: Fortress, 1986), p. 430. Hereafter cited parenthetically as *Interpretation*.

2. See John Ashton, *Understanding the Fourth Gospel* (Oxford: Oxford University Press, 1991); Austin Farrer, *A Study in St. Mark* (London: Dacre, 1951), hereafter cited parenthetically; and Burton Mack, *A Myth of Innocence* (Philadelphia: Fortress, 1988).

3. Aristotle, *The Poetics*, ed. Samuel Henry Butcher (London: Macmillan, 1925), 1451b 5. Hereafter cited parenthetically.

4. Benedictus de Spinoza, *Opera*, 3 vols., ed. Carolus H. Bruder (Leipzig: Tauchnitz, 1843-6), III, *def.* XLIV. Hereafter cited parenthetically.

5. Rudolph Bultmann, *Glauben und Verstehen*, IV, (Tübingen: Mohr [Paul Siebeck], 1965), p. 169.

6. Étienne Trocmé, "Un Christianisme sans Jésus-Christ?," *New Testament Studies* 38 (1992): 321 ff.

7. So Alfred North Whitehead, according to Allison H. Johnson, *Whitehead's Philosophy of Civilisation* (New York: Dover, 1962) p. 59. Compare Robert Alter, *The Art of Biblical Narrative* (London: Allen & Unwin, 1981), p. 35 and Stephen Prickett, *Words and the Word* (Cambridge: Cambridge University Press, 1986), p. 204.

8. Samuel Johnson, "Net," *A Dictionary of the English Language* (London: Jarvis, 1786).

9. William Tindall, *A Reader's Guide to James Joyce* (New York: Farrar, Straus & Giroux, 1959), p. 156.

10. Wayne A. Meeks, "The Man from Heaven in Johannine Sectarianism," in Ashton, *Interpretation*.

11. See James Louis Martyn, *History and Theology in the Fourth Gospel*, 2nd. ed. (Nashville: Abingdon, 1979) and Ashton, *Understanding*.

12. Rudolph Bultmann, *Exegetica* (Tübingen: Mohr [Paul Siebeck], 1967), pp. 451 ff.

13. Stuart Hampshire, *Spinoza* (London: Penguin, 1988), p. 154.

14. Ernst Käsemann, "The Canon of the New Testament and the Unity of the Church," in *Essays on New Testament Themes* (London: SCM, 1964), p. 96.

15. David Friedrich Strauss, *The Life of Jesus*, 2 vols., tr. George Eliot (St. Clair Shores, Michigan: Scholarly Press, 1970) p. 867.

16. Sir Walter Scott, *Waverley* (Harmondsworth: Penguin, 1972), p. 226. Hereafter cited parenthetically.

17. Douglas Adams, *A Hitch-Hiker's Guide to the Galaxy* (London: Barker, 1979).

18. Robert W. Funk, *The Poetics of Biblical Narrative* (Sonoma, CA: Polebridge, 1988), p. 304.

19. D. H. Lawrence, *The Rainbow* (Harmondsworth: Penguin, 1949), p. 8.

20. William E. Addis, "Elijah," *Encyclopaedia Biblica,* ed. Thomas K. Cheyne and John S. Black (London: Adam & Charles Black, 1914).

21. Dan Jacobson, *The Rape of Tamar* (London: Weidenfeld &Nicholson, 1987) and *Her Story* (London: Deutsch, 1987).

22. Leonard Hodgson, *For Faith and Freedom* (London: SCM, 1968), x.

23. Paul Ricoeur, *The Rule of Metaphor* tr. R. Czerny, K. McLaughlin, and J. Costello, (London: Routledge & Kegan Paul, 1978).

24. Ronald W. Hepburn, "Art, Truth, and the Education of Subjectivity," *Journal of Philosophy of Education* 24:2 (1990): 188-9. See also *Wonder and Other Essays* (Edinburgh: Edinburgh University Press, 1984).

25. The bibliographical assistance of Dr. Simpson, Librarian of New College, *in extremis* was invaluable to the author *in extremis*.

ENGENDERING CONFLICT

Reading the Future of Gender in the Texts of the Hebrew Bible[1]

Jan Tarlin

As we move towards the year of 2000, the issue of gender is taking on profound importance in Western scholarly discourse. In many disciplines, gender is coming to be viewed as a social construct rather than a biological fact, and analyses of the political, ideological, and symbolic processes by which gender is constructed are acquiring greater theoretical sophistication and are being put forward with increasing moral urgency. The result of these analyses has been the beginning of a complete re-thinking of the Western gender system, a rethinking whose implications are just now becoming clear to us and whose end results lie far beyond our present field of vision.

This re-thinking aims to articulate and explore alternatives to the absolute male-female dualism on which gender identity is based in the West. That the study of literature and religion has much to contribute to this re-thinking is self-evident. The question of what my own particular discipline, the study of the Hebrew Bible, has to offer this project is, however, a difficult one.

Certainly the Hebrew Bible offers rich material for the study of the origins, history, and structure of the present Western gender system; but does it have anything helpful to offer to the attempt to *remake* that system? There is an excellent case to be made that the answer to this question is an emphatic "No!" Should not any Western attempt to reconfigure gender into more liveable forms simply refuse any intercourse with a text so deeply implicated in the constitution of the very male-female opposition that stands in need of dismantling? Such a refusal would be well-advised were it possible, but the evidence suggests that it is not.

Whenever the West speaks of gender, even to reimagine it, the Hebrew Bible enters the conversation whether it is invited or not. Consider the way the rhetoric of Genesis 2-3 with its specific interweaving of gender imagery and fantasies of primal paradise keeps turning up in

277

every corner of Western culture. Though myths of a golden age have been produced in many, if not all, cultures, it is the West's very own biblical Eden that haunts its popular media, its art, and its intellectual life.

Three examples, briefly discussed, must serve here to illustrate the breadth of reach that the rhetoric of Eden exercises over the West. These examples are taken from the fields of advertising, fiction, and philosophical reflection. They represent, respectively: a conservative discourse that simultaneously reinforces and draws its power from the existing Western gender system, a liberal attempt to expand that system in the direction of greater freedom, and a radical move to restructure Western gender relations completely.

My example from the realm of advertising is not a specific text but rather a genre: the televised beer commercial aimed at adolescent males. These ads invite their target audience into Eden-like settings well-supplied with tempting, even slightly sinister, helpmates fit for them. From the seductive fantasy of "wouldn't it be great if. . ." to the assertion that for those who drink the proferred elixir of life "the world is a very cool place," the discourse of these commercials both draws upon and gives new life to the rhetoric of Genesis 2-3.

My second example of the persistence of Eden in the Western language of gender is John Fowles's novel *Daniel Martin*.[2] This love story is peopled by characters most of whom are explicitly and resolutely creatures of a post-religious culture, a culture which the narrator seems quite definitely to share. Yet even as these characters attempt to find their way to identity and relationship without the guideposts of religious tradition, their existential freedom takes much of its depth and poignancy from the fact that their story cannot resist shaping itself as a return to Eden. The hero recovers the lost true love of his youth and returns with her to the lost rural paradise of his childhood. The life of Fowles's title character, an atheist writer of plays and film scripts, thus structures itself according to patterns that would have been entirely familiar to the biblical apocalyptic seer after whom he was named by his clergyman father. Fowles's work reminds us that the Hebrew Bible is a presence in any act of Western story-telling whatever the religious or philosophical convictions that dominate the surface of its discourse.

The Hebrew Bible can also be found lurking in the unconscious of a recent attempt to create a radical feminist philosophy that would break with the Western gender system altogether. In *Gyn/ecology: The Metaethics of Radical Feminism*,[3] Mary Daly articulates a vision of a women's separatist utopia, free not only of patriarchy but also of men. According to Daly, women naturally belong to this sacred eschatological order just as men are by nature excluded from it.

The Christian feminist-ethicist Beverly Harrison has convincingly argued that Daly's thinking is unconsciously structured by a biblically-based Thomist vision that opposes the biological sexes to each other on the basis of their differing natures in the same way that it opposes the world in which we live to a supernatural paradisial otherworld. Harrison contends that this unconscious dependence leads Daly simply to invert rather than actually to break with the dualism of the Western gender system.[4] Thus, following Harrison, I would suggest that because Daly's philosophy is founded on oppositions rooted in Genesis 2-3, it preserves the basic *form* of Western gender relations even as it tries radically to separate itself from the content of those relations.

If the influence of the Hebrew Bible reaches across the entire spectrum of the Western discourse of gender—from sexist beer commercials, through liberal humanist romance, to radical feminist philosophy—we are unlikely to be able to keep it out of the process of rethinking our gender system. Rather than let this crucial Western text sneak up on us from behind as we move towards the year 2000, we will have to confront it directly. The considerable energies of the Hebrew Bible that currently support the Western gender system will have to be seized and appropriated for the effort to construct alternatives to that system.

The power of the Hebrew Bible in Western culture and the necessity for those of us rethinking gender in the West to confront that power arise from the privileged role this text plays in the ideological life of our communities. The conception of ideology on which I rely in making this assertion is taken from the French Marxist philosopher Louis Althusser. In Althusser's words, "All ideology has the function (which defines it) of constituting concrete individuals as subjects."[5] Ideology is thus the set processes by which individuals within a particular social order are pressured to adopt subjectivities, structures of identity, accommodated to the smooth functioning of that order.

That the Hebrew Bible has been and still is a primary source of such normative identity structures in Western and Western dominated societies is readily apparent to any student of the West's cultural, political, or religious history; the three examples with which I began the essay demonstrate, I hope, the degree to which this text continues to exercise its structuring power specifically over gender identity in contemporary Western communities. To explain how a written text can exercise such power over identity formation, and to ascertain what options are available for challenging, resisting, and redirecting that power will require some detailed theoretical elaboration. I shall argue, following the film theorist and semiotician Kaja Silverman,[6] that texts act as ideological mirrors in which normative subjectivities are encountered, submitted to, elaborated upon, contested, or remade. I shall move from theory to practice, offering a close reading that contests and reworks the dominant images of gender identity in a specific text from the Hebrew Bible.

Ideological forces are at work both within the texts we read and within our activity as readers. Within a text, ideological forces operate on behalf of the social order from which the text emerged, manifesting themselves as socially sanctioned subjectivities (structures of identity) in the form of main characters, narrating voices, authorial voices, and other similar linguistic constructions. When we, as readers, seek to orient ourselves within the world of the text, we are pressured to identify with these approved subjectivities. Similarly, ideological forces representing the social order in which we have been taught to read shape the intellectual and emotional needs we bring to the text as well as our strategies for satisfying those needs. Our educations have prepared us to read ourselves into forms that our societies can live with.

Texts act as verbal mirrors in which readers perceive a subjectivity formed and promoted by the ideological processes of a specific society. That ideology operates so as to persuade the reader that identity, acceptability, and, indeed, existence as a self are dependent upon identifying with the image in the mirror. The conventions which we have been taught to read with tell us what to look for in the mirror and how to respond to what we see there; they tell us what features of subjectivity are most important, which qualities of those features should be accentuated and which should be disguised or altered.

The ideological processes that have structured the image presented by a textual mirror and the ideological processes that have taught a given reader how to look at or respond to that image may be either in harmony or in conflict with one another. Even when the two ideologies are nearly identical, or at least form a harmonious system, the identity or harmony, like all human artifacts, contains some degree of internal contradiction. As I shall argue in more detail later, how much we pursue or resist identification with the images we encounter in textual mirrors depends upon what we make of the ideological conflicts and contradictions we experience as we read. What the textual mirror can make of us—the reconstitution of our subjectivity in the process of reading—is thus bound up with what we make of the cracks that emerge as we contemplate its surface.

Since all sign systems, whether verbal or non-verbal, can be regarded as texts upon which the subject reflects, the interpretation of written documents must be understood as simply a special case of the textual mirroring through which culture and subject produce, reproduce, and restructure each other. Consequently, Silverman's theory of textual mirroring begins at the pre-verbal level of human existence. The fact that this theory encompasses the development of individual subjectivity from infancy forward renders it particularly useful for examining the role textual mirrors play in producing gender identity.

Silverman's argument for the mirroring function of texts is based on the late French psychoanalyst Jacques Lacan's theory of the mirror stage in infant development. Silverman writes: "Lacan tells us that somewhere between the ages of six months and eighteen months the subject arrives at an apprehension of both itself and the other—indeed of itself *as other*. This discovery is assisted by the child seeing, for the first time, its own reflection in a mirror. That reflection enjoys a coherence which the subject itself lacks—it is an *ideal* image."[7] In Lacan's own words: "This jubilant assumption of his specular image by the child . . . still sunk in his motor incapacity and nursling dependence, would seem to exhibit in an exemplary situation the symbolic matrix in which the I is precipitated in a primordial form . . . . This form would have to be called the ideal I. . . [it]

situates the agency of the ego, before its social determination, in a fictional direction, which will always remain irreducible for the individual alone . . . ."[8]

Silverman, however, argues that there is no pre-social determination of identity. Following Althusser, Silverman asserts that "identifications [never] occur spontaneously" because "the subject is from the very outset within culture."[9] Lacan's mirror, therefore, is a vehicle for socially constructed images of identity: a non-verbal text that acquires meaning in relation to other texts among which it is placed. Even in the pre-linguistic mirror stage, the process of identity formation is socially mediated. "That mediation may be as simple and direct as the mother's interpretation of the mirror image for the child, or as complex and diffuse as the introduction into the child's environment of various representations (dolls, picture books, trains, or toy guns) which determine the way in which it will eventually regard itself . . . . [W]e cannot interpret the reflection within which the child finds its identity too literally; it must be understood to some degree as a cultural construct."[10]

Neither, according to Silverman, is the sense of incoherence that the child tries to relieve by identifying with that reflection pre-cultural. A sense of incoherence is not a natural consequence of the child's "motor incapacity and nursling dependence." The experience of these physical realities as constituting incoherence is as much the result of cultural processes as is the experience of the reflection as constituting coherence.

From the moment a child is born, cultural sign systems such as those that constitute socially acceptable modes of feeding, clothing, and physical contact mediate between the infant and its direct experience of internal and external reality.[11] This mediation simultaneously produces a cultural identity for the infant and estranges it from both its own biological existence and the material reality of its environment. As a result of these estrangements, the infant experiences gaps both within the self and between self and other.[12]

Non-verbal texts, such as mirrors, offer the infant culturally approved and meaningful images with which to close or articulate the estranging gaps that culture itself has created in his or her experience of self and world. The infant is surrounded by messages suggesting that it can attain the grasp it craves of its identity and environment by identifying with the imaginary subjectivities reflected in texts. Yet the promised coherence remains forever elusive because identification presupposes an "irreducible distance" between the self and the reflected imaginary object with which it is to identify.[13] The mirror stage is the encounter with "the self *as other*."

The situation becomes even worse once the child acquires (or, more accurately, is acquired by) language. Once the child's cognitive capacities are sufficiently developed, language replaces non-verbal signs as the means by which cultural forces shape his or her subjectivity. This change is traumatic for the child because, while non-verbal signs *mediate between* the subject and the real, language *seals off* the subject *from* reality completely and permanently. The child's experience of incoherence becomes a sense of irremediable lack.[14]

This transition occurs because of the arbitrary nature of linguistic signs. Although the non-verbal signs that structure the pre-linguistic infant's subjectivity are cultural artifacts, their meaning is still "motivated" by an "existential bond" with the reality they mediate.[15] Language, on the other hand, is an abstract, arbitrary, non-representational sign system whose meaning derives from an internal play of difference between its signifying components rather than from any relation between linguistic signifiers and extralinguistic reality.[16] Once it has assumed a linguistic form, the subject exists only insofar as it lacks any relationship with external or internal reality.[17]

Yet the linguistically structured subject continues passionately to desire what it lacks: an impossible direct experience of its own material reality and an equally impossible direct contact with the material world around it.[18] Once again, cultural forces are brought to bear to soothe the estrangement that is inseparable from subjectivity, to heal the wound that has been culturally inflicted. Linguistic texts are now held up as mirrors reflecting unalienated, natural selves with which the subject is urged to identify. Silverman's theory of the spoken subject will be useful in clarifying how language can function as a mirror.[19]

Silverman arrives at the concept of the spoken subject by building on the work of the linguist Emile Benveniste. According to Benveniste, every act of speech takes place at the intersection of two subjects: the speaking subject and the subject of speech. The speaking subject is the real biological individual who utters the sounds that constitute speech. The subject of speech is the linguistic structure of identity that is generated in the course of the speech act.[20] To this schema Silverman adds the spoken subject: the subject that comes into being when an individual identifies with the subject of speech. Thus, the spoken subject may be realized either through the identification of the speaking subject with its own discourse or by the identification of another individual with that discourse.[21]

Written texts function as mirrors because they offer readers subjects of speech (characters, narrator's voice, authorial voice, etc.) with which to identify. The reader who accepts such an invitation to identification becomes the spoken subject of the text, just as the child becomes a cultural subject by identifying with the image in the mirror. Mirrors are rudimentary texts, and linguistic texts are highly developed mirrors.

It should be clear by now, though, that neither the infant before the looking glass nor the reader before the text is entirely at the mercy of the ideological processes that operate to structure their subjectivity. There is always some flaw in the mirror that leaves the gazing self room for creative manipulation of the reflected image. Such manipulation may range from minor embellishment or deletion to complete restructuring from playful cooperation to full-scale resistance.

I have already alluded to the factors that combine to produce flaws in textual mirrors; three of these factors affect linguistic and non-linguistic texts. alike. First, the process of identification is based upon a perceived absolute distinction between the self and the object with which it identifies. The very perceptions that make identification possible ensure that the process is never complete. Second, the gaps or lacks that the self tries to make good by identifying with textually proffered subjectivities are the results of the self's incorporation into culture. Texts are cultural constructions and therefore cannot offer real healing for the wounds of enculturation. Third, texts are always encountered in the context of other texts. The more texts encountered, the greater the chance of contradictions between them that will limit the degree of the self's identification with any single text.

Two additional factors put extra curbs on the power of linguistic texts to compel identification. To begin with, the fact that language is a system of abstract, non-representational, arbitrary signs ensures that linguistic texts will ultimately frustrate the quest for material reality that the self pursues through the process of identification. Further, since language generates meaning by establishing systems of differences rather than by constructing positive representations, simple shifts of emphasis in reception can produce multiple, or even contradictory, meanings from a single text.

Thus, although texts are structured, they are neither stable nor univocal. Subject formation is not simply an imposition by the text on the reader but an interaction between the text and the reader. The cultural repertoire of possible subjectivities is not just perpetuated in the reading process; it is recreated. The human subject is never static, finished, and unified; it is constantly in process, gapped, and contradictory. But the fluidity, gaps, and contradictions that produce human freedom also provoke fear in the subject, and Silverman argues that precisely this fear produces the Western gender system.

Reminding us that "lack of being is the irreducible condition of [human] subjectivity," and that "in acceding to language, the subject forfeits all existential reality, and forgoes any future possibility of 'wholeness,'" Silverman concludes that "if we were in possession of an instrument that would permit us to penetrate deep into the innermost recesses of the human psyche, we would find not identity, but a void."[22]

Gender, Silverman argues, is not a biological endowment but an effect of discursive positioning in relation to the void at the heart of human subjectivity. Silverman defines "male" discourse as a strategy for denying the central lack around which human subjectivity is built by claiming for the "male" subject a delusionary wholeness, coherence, power, and solidity. This delusion is shored up by projecting lack, inconsistency, vulnerability, and instability on to an "other" constructed by that process of projection: the "female."[23]

I have placed the words "male" and "female" in quotation marks to emphasize their status as constructs of discourse rather than biological realities. Silverman argues that although Western culture encourages the identification of "male" discourse with biological masculinity and privileges individuals in whom that identification is embodied, both the link between discursive gender and biological sex and the privileging of "male" gendered masculine individuals over all others are ideological formations that are highly unstable and can be radically restructured. I shall now offer a reading of a text from the Hebrew Bible in which I undertake precisely such a restructuring.

That text is 1 Kings 19:9-18: Elijah's encounter with Yahweh on Horeb. Here gender plays a covert, complicated, and extremely powerful role. Viewed from one angle, the entire corpus of Elijah texts in the Books of Kings (I Kings 17-19, 21 and 2 Kings 1-2:18) can quite correctly be read as a manifesto of patriarchal Yahwism, with the theophany at Horeb constituting a highpoint of "male" bonding between the prophet and his God. Yet reflected on from another angle, the very center of this textual mirror—the speech of Yahweh—suggests a way of contesting the patriarchal subjectivity that shapes the dominant readings of this text.

In the texts leading up to 1 Kings 19:9-18, Elijah speaks an unbending "male" claim to authority and potency. Elijah's word is the penetrating fire which can dry up the rain and the dew (1 Kings 17:1), the disempowering blow which can bring low his royal or religious rivals (1 Kings 18:36), the sword which can kill those whom the prophet regards as Yahweh's enemies and his own (1 Kings 18:40). Precisely because Elijah's word can drain fertility, power, and life from others, it seems to absorb those qualities into itself, thereby becoming the embodiment of that which its victims lack. The word of Elijah signifies both the price that must be paid to establish the covenant of Yahweh as the prophet understands it and the power which enables and feeds off the exaction of that price. When Elijah speaks he is attempting to establish power relations in which he and his God occupy positions of patriarchal dominance.

At first, the word of Yahweh seems to constitute a "female" discourse of gratuitous inconsistency. Yahweh does not initially speak as a patriarch, rewarding those who have paid the price of submission to him and punishing those who have not. Yahweh lets the spring which nourishes the zealous Yahwist Elijah dry up (1 Kings 17:7), but performs life-giving miracles for people totally outside the Yahwistic covenant: the widow of Zarephath and her son (1 Kings 17:10-24). The rain returns to the northern kingdom not because Ahab, Jezebel, and their subjects have become obedient to Yahweh but simply because Yahweh has decided that it is time to send rain—even on a nation that is still in a state of rebellion against the covenant (1 Kings 18:1).

Appearances are deceptive, however, for although the word of Yahweh is more than "male," it is not "female." From the first of the Elijah texts on, there is an unspoken complicity between the discourse of Yahweh and the discourse of Elijah. Yahweh sustains the man who has spoken drought on the northern kingdom. Yahweh maintains an ambiguous silence as Elijah's word instigates the extermination of the prophets of Baal. During the encounter at Horeb, Yahweh's unspoken complicity in "male" discourse is spoken for the first time.

Elijah arrives at Horeb having recently suffered two deeply unsettling challenges to the power and potency of his discourse. First, Jezebel, the Baal-worshipping Phoenician queen of Ahab, King of Israel, vows in the name of her gods to kill Elijah in revenge for his massacre of her prophets of Baal (1Kings 19:2); the oath is similar in kind to the oath in the name of Yahweh by which Elijah brought drought on Israel. Women are not supposed to wield "male" discourse in this way! Elijah flees in fear before this uncanny phenomenon.[24]

As a fugitive, alone in the desert, Elijah tries to reassert the power of his word. In a display of suicidal bravado, Elijah prays to Yahweh for his own death (1 Kings 19:47). Yahweh thwarts Elijah's word by sending an angel to force the prophet to eat and drink, thereby renewing his life. It is at this point that Elijah decides to go to Mount Horeb, better known as Sinai.

Elijah's reasons for coming to Yahweh's most sacred ground are unclear at first. He certainly does not state his business like a supplicant. In response to Yahweh's *mah l^{e}ka poh* (What is here that concerns you?), Elijah adopts a tone which, though self-pitying, is basically boastful (19:9-10). Elijah says that he "has surely been zealous for Yahweh," behind which may be read a not so veiled suggestion that he has, indeed, been more zealous *than* Yahweh. After all, Yahweh's word of life looks like pretty weak stuff next to the prophet's word of destruction. Elijah further declares (by implication, of course) that he is a very important person. Elijah is the only zealous spokesperson for Yahweh left in Israel; yet his activities are so important that the Israelites (*en masse* it would seem) seek his life. The prophet begins to sound rather as if he has come to challenge Yahweh on the deity's home turf. Having had his word turned against him by Jezebel and thwarted by the angel, Elijah seems to have come to Horeb to undertake the final test of his word against the ultimate antagonist.

Yahweh's response to Elijah in 19:11 suggests that the deity has indeed understood the prophet's words as a challenge. The deity adopts a rhetoric of abrupt command and orders Elijah out of the cave in which he has taken refuge. "If you really wish to test your strength with me," Yahweh says in effect, "come and stand upright before me in the open where my home ground really is."

At this point the discourse of the text's narrator merges with the "female" facet of Yahweh's discourse. A passage of exposition constructed around a series of participial verb forms suspends any attempt on the part of the narrator at wholeness, completion, consistency, or clarity. The voices of Yahweh and the narrator seem to have united to speak against the "male" discourse of Elijah. I shall risk a rough translation of the lines in question, structured to convey something of the effect which this speech has in Hebrew. My translation begins in the middle of 19:11 and ends in the middle of 19:12: "Yahweh passing by. And a great and strong wind breaking the mountains and shattering the cliffs before Yahweh—not in the wind is Yahweh. And after the wind, an earthquake—not in the earthquake is Yahweh. And after the earthquake, a fire—not in the fire is Yahweh." This passage culminates in what is perhaps the most powerful expression of "female" discourse in any of the Elijah texts. The self-disclosure of Yahweh is described as follows: "and after the fire—*qôl d^emamah daqah*" (19:12). The phrase I have left in the Hebrew is untranslatable because it has no fixed meaning in its original language. The first word *qôl* is a noun used in the construct: it can mean either sound or voice. The second word, *d^emamah,* is a substantive which might be derived from any one of the three meanings of the verbal root *dmm*: to speak softly/ to grow silent, to moan or wail, to abuse. The substantive *d^emamah,* then, may mean soft speech, silence, moaning, wailing, or abuse. The last word, *daqah,* is a verbal adjective derived from the verb *daqaq*: to crush, pulverize, thresh, or be fine. Thus, the adjective *daqah* may mean thin, scarce, fine, or crushing.[25]

The phrase *qôl d^emamah daqah* may, then, be plausibly translated in ways as various as the RSV's "still small voice," "roaring thunderous voice,"[26] "a sound of thin silence,"[27] "the sound of utmost silence,"[28] "the voice of slender silence,"[29] "a thin petrifying sound,"[30] and "a thin silent sound."[31] Of these translations, the last seems most true to the radical indeterminacy of the original. Perhaps, though, more radical combinations might be even more on target: "a roaring silence" or "a still silent thunder," for example.

Elijah covers his face before this manifestation of Yahweh's presence, but he does not abandon his challenge. He will test his word against the *qôl*. When the *qôl* asks him once again what there is at Horeb which concerns him, Elijah repeats his arrogant, self-pitying challenge from 19:10 verbatim (19:14). Elijah and Yahweh stand word to word in a stalemate!

The stalemate is broken from the side of the deity: as Yahweh speaks the word of Elijah! Yahweh pronounces a death sentence against all Baal worshippers in Israel. In order to beat Elijah at his own game, Yahweh has swallowed and incorporated the "male" word with which the deity had previously maintained a silent, critical, distanced complicity. From here on there is no question of Yahweh's word being "female."

But if Yahweh's discourse is not "female," neither is it "male." From here on in the Elijah texts, the divine word becomes an unsteady mix of doom and salvation, consistency and inconsistency, strength and weakness, "male" and "female." What 1 Kings 19:9-18 reveals when read in this way is the impossibility of maintaining a purely "male" or purely "female" discourse—even, or especially, for God. Further, that impossibility points to the fundamental untenability of the entire Western gender system.

Rather than presenting a seamless communion of the divine ground of patriarchy with its human representative, the text embodies a struggle between Elijah's unbendingly "male" discourse and Yahweh's ambiguous mix of conflicting "male" and "female" discourses. Gender is revealed as disputed territory, both between Elijah and Yahweh and within the deity itself. Judged by the norms of the Western gender system, God, in this reading of the text, has a gender identity conflict.

I suggest that the gender conflict at the core of Yahweh's self-revelation in 1 Kings 19:9-18 is played out in various ways throughout the Hebrew Bible. (Compare Genesis 1:27: "So God created man in his own image, in the image of God he created him; male and female he created them.") Rereading the Hebrew Bible with this conflict in view will enable the West not only to reimagine both Yahweh and the other biblical characters, but most importantly to reimagine itself. If the God in whose image we Westerners understand ourselves to be made is a site of conflicting gender discourses, who, then, are we? Answers to this question will be of crucial importance in rethinking gender toward the year 2000.

NOTES

1. Portions of the material used in this essay also appear in "Toward a 'Female' Reading of the Elijah Cycle: Ideology and Gender in the Interpretation of 1 Kings 17-19, 21 and 2 Kings 1-2:18" forthcoming in ed. Athalya Brenner, *The Feminist Companion to the Bible: Samuel, Kings, Chronicles*, Sheffield Academic Press. I wish to take this opportunity to thank the Unitarian Universalist Scholars Program for several grants that gave me the summer leisure to pursue the research on which these publications are based.

2. John Fowles, *Daniel Martin* (Boston: Little Brown, 1977).

3. Mary Daly, *Gyn/ecology: The Metaethics of Radical Feminism* (Boston: Beacon Press, 1978).

4. Beverly W. Harrison, *Making the Connections: Essays in Feminist Social Ethics* (Boston: Beacon Press, 1985), pp. 3-7, 20-21 and 272 n. 31.

5. Louis Althusser, *Lenin and Philosophy* (London: Monthly Review Press, 1971), p. 171.

6. Kaja Silverman, *The Subject of Semiotics* (New York: Oxford University Press, 1983) and *The Acoustic Mirror: The Female Voice in Psychoanalysis and Cinema* (Bloomington, IN: Indiana University Press, 1988).

7. Silverman, *Subject*, p. 157.

8. Quoted in Silverman, *Subject*, pp. 157-8.

9. Silverman, *Subject*, pp. 216-7.

10. Silverman, *Subject*, p. 160.

11. Silverman, *Subject*, p. 155.

12. Silverman, *Subject*, pp. 155-6.

13. Silverman, *Subject*, p. 158.

14. Silverman, *Subject*, p. 166.

15. Silverman, *Subject*, pp. 19, 25, 165.

16. Silverman, *Subject*, p. 163.

17. Silverman, *Subject*, pp. 171-4.

18. Silverman, *Subject*, pp. 176-8.

19. Silverman, *Subject*, pp. 43-53 and pp. 195-9.

20. Silverman, *Subject*, pp. 43-7 and pp. 195-8.

21. Silverman, *Subject*, pp. 48-53 and pp. 198-9.

22. Kaja Silverman, *Male Subjectivity at the Margins* (New York: Routledge, 1992), p. 4.

23. Silverman, *Mirror*, pp. 1-41.

24. I am indebted to Cynthia Blakeley of the Emory University Graduate Institute of the Liberal Arts for a conversation that greatly clarified my understanding of the role played by Jezebel in the Elijah cycle.

25. Johan Lust, "A Gentle Breeze or a Roaring Thunderous Sound?" *Vetus Testementum* 25 (1975), pp. 110-113; and F. Brown, S. R. Driver, C. A. Briggs, *The New Hebrew and English Lexicon* (Peabody: Hendrickson Publishers, 1979), pp. 198-200.

26. Lust, "A Gentle Breeze," p. 113.

27. John Gray, *1 and 2 Kings: A Commentary*, Second Edition, The Old Testament Library (Philadelphia: The Westminster Press, 1970), p. 406.

28. Samuel Terrien, *The Elusive Presence: Toward a New Biblical Theology*, Religious Perspectives, Vol. 26 (New York: Harper & Row, 1978), p. 232.

29. Martin Buber, *The Prophetic Faith* (New York: Macmillan, 1939), p. 77.

30. Dieter de Boer, cited in Burke O. Long, *1 Kings—With an Introduction to Historical Literature*, Forms of Old Testament Literature, Vol. 9 (Grand Rapids: Eerdmans, 1984), p. 199.

31. Robert Coote, "Yahweh Recalls Elijah," in ed. Baruch Halpern and Jon D. Levinson, *Traditions in Transformation* (Winona Lake: Eisenbrauns, 1981), p. 118.

NOTES ON THE CONTRIBUTORS

ROBERT DETWEILER teaches in the Graduate Institute of the Liberal Arts at Emory University, Atlanta, Georgia.

GREGORY SALYER teaches in the Religion and Philosophy Department at Huntingdon College, Montgomery, Alabama.

JAMES CHAMPION teaches in the Lilly Fellow Program at Valparaiso University, Valparaiso, Indiana.

JUDITH LEE teaches in the English Department at Rutgers University, New Brunswick, New Jersey.

WERNER JEANROND teaches in the Department of Biblical Studies at Trinity College, Dublin.

IRENA MAKARUSHKA teaches in the Religion Department at Bowdoin College, Brunswick, Maine.

BERNARD ZELECHOW teaches in the Division of Humanities and the Department of History at York University, Toronto, Ontario.

ROBERT SCHARLEMANN teaches in the Department of Religious Studies at the University of Virginia, Charlottesville, Virginia.

GRAHAM WARD teaches philosophy and modern Christian doctrine at Exeter College, Oxford.

AVRIL HORNER teaches in the Department of English at the University of Salford, Salford, England.

MARK LEDBETTER teaches in the Department of Religion at Millsaps College, Jackson, Mississippi.

DAVID CUNNINGHAM teaches in the Department of Theology at the University of St. Thomas, St. Paul, Minnesota.

DOROTA FILIPCZAK teaches in the English Institute, Lodz.

JOHN STRUGNELL teaches in the Department of English at the University of Queensland, Brisbane.

DOUGLAS A. TEMPLETON teaches in the Department of New Testament at the University of Edinburgh, Edinburgh.

HELEN WILCOX teaches in the Department of English at the University of Groningen, The Netherlands.

JAN TARLIN is a doctoral candidate in the Graduate Division of Religion, Emory University, Atlanta, Georgia.

INDEX

Achebe, Chinua—xi
Adorno, Theodor—5, 22-4, 29-31, 132, 169
Allen, Paula Gunn—48
Althusser, Louis—279, 282
Anselm—143, 149-50
Aquinas, Thomas—138, 150
Aristotle—10, 12, 190, 263, 264, 268-9
Arnold, Matthew—19
Ashton, John—264, 265-6, 271
Attridge, Derek—167
Atwood, Margaret—6, 10, 52-3, 215-33
Augustine—7, 8, 107, 110, 122-4, 126, 127, 138, 202
Austin, J. L.—162, 168, 169

Bakhtin, Mikhail—205
Bal, Mieke—227-8
Barth, Karl—8, 72, 131, 133-9, 143-4, 146, 148-54
Bateson, Mary Catherine—6, 52
Benjamin, Walter—7, 109-10, 114
Blake, William—164
Bloom, Harold—19-20
Bonhoffer, Dietrich—126
Branner, H. C.—56, 60
Brecht, Bertold—81
Breward, Ian—238
Brooks, Cleanth—20
Bultmann, Rudolph—2, 138, 139, 142, 146-8, 264, 270, 271, 272, 274
Burgmann, E. H.—242
Byatt, A. S.—252

Cameron, Anne—6, 48-9
Campion, Edmund—236
Carey, Peter—245
Carroll, Robert P.—217
Carroll, Robert—xi
Cartland, Barbara—12, 263
Christ, Carol P.—43

Cixous, Hélène—257
Clark, Manning—237
Clive, John—105
Coleridge, Samuel Taylor—97, 164, 166
Cone, James—198
Culler, Jonathan—18, 21
Cupitt, Don—169
Césaire, Aimé—xi

Daly, Mary—43, 279
Daniels, Dwight Roger—220
Davey, Frank—216
Dawe, Bruce—238
De Man, Paul—18
Derrida, Jacques—ix, 5, 8, 19-24, 25, 31-2, 33, 115, 137-9, 142-3, 144, 151, 153, 154, 215
Descartes, René—24
Detweiler, Robert—1, 2, 221
Dews, Peter—33
Dilthey, Wilhelm—104, 108
Dinesan, Isak—6, 44, 55-63
Donne, John—258
Doolittle, Hilda (H.D.)—53
Dostoevsky, Fyodor—10, 81, 203-9
Drewe, Robert—235, 239, 241, 242, 243, 245
Durkheim, Emile—92

Eagleton, Terry—191
Eco, Umberto—73, 191
Edwards, Michael—227
Eichrodt, Walter—224, 226
Eliade, Mircea—80
Eliot, T. S.—1, 9, 20, 163, 164
Emerson, Ralph Waldo—7, 89-101
Erdrich, Louise—89

Farrer, Austin—12, 264, 274
Feuerbach, Ludwig—149
Fowles, John—278
Freud, Sigmund—5, 19, 22-5, 30